MY ANCESTC
MORMON

by Ian Waller

SOCIETY OF GENEALOGISTS ENTERPRISES LTD.

Published by
Society of Genealogists Enterprises Limited
14 Charterhouse Buildings
Goswell Road
London EC1M 7BA.

ISBN: 978-1-907199-11-0

British Library Cataloguing in Publication Data.
A CIP Catalogue record for this book is available from the British Library.

The Society of Genealogists Enterprises Limited is a wholly owned subsidiary of
the Society of Genealogists, a registered charity, no. 233701.

About the Author

Ian Waller is a Fellow of the Society of Genealogists and a professional genealogist specialising in English research. He is a council member and currently Vice-chairman of AGRA (The Association of Genealogists and Researchers in Archives). He is a member of the LDS Church. He has taught family history to various U3A groups and at various adult education establishments in Bedfordshire and Hertfordshire as well as lecturing widely at the Society and to interest groups around the Home Counties. He has also written several articles for the family history press.

Cover - A typical hand cart used by the Pioneers (Public Service Broadcasting – Sweetwater Rescue re-enactment at Platte River).

CONTENTS

You will have presumably picked up this book because you have a connection with someone who was a Mormon. Many family historians with British roots will encounter non Anglican religions in their ancestry. They may well have been Mormons. Membership of the Church of Jesus Christ of Latter-day Saints (Mormons and/or LDS) grew both in the United Kingdom and across Europe from its inception on 6 April 1830. However, most people will associate the Church as being, in modern times, very much America based, which indeed it is, but the growth of the church in the early years was in many ways down to the British (and to some extent the Scandinavians) in their new found quest for a 'living' religion.

It was the British church members who emigrated, almost en-masse, that enabled the church to become established in Salt Lake City. Even today the church is still fast growing in a secular world and now has over 13 million members. Most of the early pioneers, who suffered persecution and hardship for the sake of their new religion as they travelled across the USA, were native Britons. Many of the early converts, despite being encouraged to emigrate, never left these shores making sure that the church had, and continues to have, a strong base in the United Kingdom. The content of this book revolves mainly around finding Mormon ancestors originating in the United Kingdom and Europe.

Most of you are fully aware of the contribution the LDS Church makes to family history research and all this exists because of its doctrinal beliefs. As researchers we would have been floundering without the IGI and lately the 'Family Search' finding aid. The establishment of local Family History centres has also enabled us to obtain microfilm of every conceivable type of record from across the world to help us locate our ancestors. Today with the advent of free digitised images we can begin to research in the comfort of our own front rooms.

The church also kept extensive historical records of its own members and has a huge collection, based in Salt Lake City, of journals, diaries, membership and congregation records relating to all its members worldwide both past and present. This book details the history of the church in context with where to find the records which are full of genealogical value on the lives of church members who number amongst our ancestors.

CHAPTER ONE

The beginnings of the LDS church

In order to fully understand the records that are available to locate
information about your ancestors who joined the Church of Jesus Christ
of Latter-day Saints (the Mormons) it is necessary to have an
understanding of how and when the Church was established and to realise
some of the challenges and trends which affected its growth and existence.

The Mormon Church can be viewed as a worldwide Christian religion that
was established in 1830 initially in the midst of American Revivalism
although there was a time early in its history when there were actually more
members in the United Kingdom than anywhere else in the world.

The LDS Church was formally organised in Fayette, New York State,
United States of America on the 6 April 1830. In the first decade following
the Church's organisation, its members experienced persecution and
financial difficulties; the headquarters of the Church moved several times
from New York State to Ohio, then to Missouri, and on to Illinois. Joseph
Smith, the then prophet, leader and facilitator of the Church was
assassinated in 1844, aged 39 years, whilst in Carthage Gaol, on unfounded
charges of riot and treason. Following their prophet's martyrdom church
members faced continued persecution. Under the direction of Brigham
Young, who succeeded Joseph Smith in Church leadership, most of the
Latter-day Saints journeyed across America to settle in the Salt Lake Valley

and other western communities although when they began the journey they were unsure of their final destination. These migrants were predominantly British, Scandinavians and Europeans. Today the church that began with only six members in 1830 now has more than 13 million members worldwide.

The LDS religion included a theology and a standard of morality, an economic philosophy and a gift of community building that inevitably meant political and economic tensions with their neighbours including some of the mainstream Christian churches that existed at the time.

Many church members throughout the world today are literally the heirs of some 65,000 British church members who emigrated to provide the strength needed to initially establish the church in Nauvoo, Illinois and subsequently in the Salt Lake Valley of Utah, USA.

In July 1837 seven missionaries namely Heber C Kimball and Orson Hyde, together with Willard Richards, John Goodson, Joseph Fielding, Isaac Russell and John Snider (known as Elders) arrived at Liverpool on the Dramatic Shipping Line's packet ship 'Garrick', charged with a commission to establish the church in England by teaching and baptising. They were the first church missionaries to set foot on English soil. They moved out from Liverpool and established themselves at Preston which today boasts many historical church sites and was where the first branch of the church in England was organised. Heber C Kimball wrote in his journal the following, dated Saturday 22 July 1837:

'We started for Preston by coach. We got there four in the afternoon. Our things were taken off the coach and Brother Goodson was hunting a boarding house and Elder Hyde and Brother Snider and myself were standing by our trunks. All at once I looked up and there was a large flag standing right before us written on it 'Truth will prevail'.'

This message was the motto on an election banner for the forthcoming Parliamentary elections as used by one of the local candidates but so admirably described the mission of Elders Kimball and Hyde in this country that they adopted the theme for the work they had to do on behalf of the church in the UK. The industrial towns and cities throughout Victorian England yielded plenty of eager converts who were enthusiastic about the new life the Mormon Church promised them. Migration and emigration will be discussed later.

Elders Kimball and Hyde were aided in their missionary efforts by a well established law passed by Parliament in 1812 which provided freedom of worship in the United Kingdom. Interestingly, they began their mission at the time of the accession of

Queen Victoria to the throne whose reign heralded many social and economic changes.

Within nine months of their arrival in this country Elders Kimball and Hyde had converted and baptised thousands of members in areas as far afield as Bedford and Leeds. They even arranged for the Book of Mormon (scriptures which, for the Latter-day Saints, enhance the teachings of the Holy Bible) to be printed in England and in 1841 a copy was presented to Queen Victoria herself and is now kept in the Royal Library at Windsor Castle.

By 1850 the members of the church in the United Kingdom outnumbered all of those in North America (USA & Canada) and the rest of the world. The Church had 30,747 members in England compared with 21,092 elsewhere. The British Isles became a strategic location where the church was easily able to reach other areas of Europe, particularly Scandinavia, France, Germany, Switzerland and Italy to carry on its missionary work, so, not only did the church grow in the United Kingdom but it did so rapidly across the majority of Western Europe.

Growth in Scotland, Wales, the Isle of Man and Ireland was also unprecedented for a non Anglican or Catholic religion. Many ordinary British people played important roles within the LDS church organisation. For example the Mormon Tabernacle Choir, now world famous, can trace its roots to Wales as its first conductor was John Parry from Flintshire. The British Isles also provided many prominent church leaders including the third President (Leader) of the Church John Taylor who was born in Milnthorpe, Westmorland.

Even the novelist and journalist Charles Dickens stood in awe of the church and in his book 'All the Year Round' described the British Saints as the 'pick and flower of England', particularly those who had uprooted and decided to emigrate to strengthen the church in America.

It is highly probable that many of us will have ancestry who joined the Church of Jesus Christ of Latter-day Saints and thus will hopefully find, within the pages of this book, a wealth of information and pointers to the records that will help piece together their trials and experiences as well as providing vital information and facts about their lives.

The effects of industrialisation caused a mass migration of population in this country from the rural areas into urban centres mainly within the north of the country where new industry quickly became established because of the availability of good natural resources. Amazingly the average life expectancy of those in industrial areas was only to be 30-35 years whereas those who remained in the rural areas could be expected to live on average 20 years longer. Many of those families who had subjected themselves to internal migration were disillusioned and were therefore looking for something new having moved, as it were, 'from the frying pan into the fire'. Religion generally offered people new hope hence the rise in religious Revivalism particularly in the industrial centres. Many different nonconformist and 'breakaway religions' came and went. However many families wanted much more than these religions and the established Anglican church could give, so joining the Church of Jesus Christ of Latter-day Saints gave them the new hope that they needed.

The United States of America and the North American British Colonies had, for a long time, held an appeal for those wanting to emigrate and start a new life. Changes in employment conditions, the economy and rapid industrial growth in Britain did not always bring prosperity and security. Thousands of poorer working class families were unable to sustain themselves and desperately wanted a better quality of life. The 1830s saw a large and sustained increase in the number of British emigrating to America. 'The grimmest period of the nineteenth century' including the depression of the late 1830s and early 1840s, and the Irish potato famine encouraged (almost necessitated) such emigration. Many who had previously emigrated also joined the church in America and Canada encouraged by their fellow Brits and relations in this country.

Why the church records are important to family historians

The Church has a doctrinal practice of performing temple ordinance work for deceased family members and as well as its own comprehensive records has, in support of this, gathered and maintained masses of genealogical records from around the world. The Church maintains the largest genealogical library in the world located in Salt Lake City, Utah and this also supports more than 4,600 Family Search Centres around the world all having access to over 2 million rolls of microfilm and a huge amount of modern digital imagery stored in the Granite Mountain Records Vault in Little Cottonwood Canyon located to the south of Salt Lake City. In May 1999, the Church also launched its renowned Family Search website.

All this was made possible by the church when it established, in 1898, the Genealogical Society of Utah (now Family Search) that began preserving records of early church history and membership, later extending its preservation and conservation services to archives worldwide. In 1938 the Genealogical Society of Utah commenced a huge microfilming project which continues to this day, although 21st century technology now involves digital imaging and storage.

There are many specific LDS resources of interest to family historians who have or will discover Mormon ancestry. The Church keeps comprehensive and detailed lifetime records including infant blessings (the naming of a new born child), baptisms (at or after the age of 8 years), confirmations, marriages, and deaths, but tracing an LDS family's history is also effectively accomplished using many other church sources. From its beginnings, the Church encouraged members to keep individual records such as journals, diaries and personal accounts, many of which are deposited with the Church History Library at 15 east North Temple Street, Salt Lake City. Early official church records also include newspapers, periodicals, temple records, and above all membership records. These will be discussed in detail later.

The growth of the church in Britain

Was your ancestor a convert to the church
In the early years between 1841 and the start of the First World War there was significant growth in the membership of the church. Ordinary working people formed the mainstay of that growth and are the most likely social group to be amongst your ancestry.

The landing in Liverpool of two American men with a new religious message was nothing new. As early as 1805 there were others who tried to bring revival movements into England. The Millerites and Campbellites had some success around the same time and in the early 1800s the Primitive Methodists had been thrown into slight turmoil by some of the popular American preachers of the day.

This revivalism was welcomed by the British people particularly in the suppressed areas of west Lancashire as it seemed to bring new hope and provide an 'exciting experience' for many. Industrial growth in that area was massive and the advent of steam to power the mills had a significant effect on the economy of the area. Liverpool itself was becoming a thriving community and supported one of the busiest ports in the country used by the cotton industry to import its raw materials and to export its finished products. However the docks were also used extensively by the iron and coal industries. The growth of Liverpool as a prominent passenger port and gateway to America was also unprecedented.

Elsewhere in the country, mostly towards the south, industrialisation had a much lesser effect, particularly where rural industries still predominated and agriculture remained the largest single employer. Even London was not affected to any great extent even though it had a population explosion nearly doubling its population.

In setting the scene for the growth of the church we need to look at the life of the ordinary people whose lives were rapidly changing. Religion had been very traditional in everyday life as had the social and class patterns of most people. Within the early Victorian period there seemed to be a greater emphasis on class distinction than before which for many meant the changes were hard to adapt to. With the advent of more religious freedom came many new religious groups, some of which thrived and others of which were short-lived.

It is interesting to note that Elders Kimball and Hyde felt prompted to travel a few miles to Preston to begin their evangelical mission. Preston does indeed figure very prominently in early Latter-day Saint church history in this country. It was typical of most industrial towns but only had a population of about 45,000. The cotton mills were the main employer with about a third of the inhabitants so employed. Preston at the time had about 38 cotton mills which were unique in as much as they were amongst the first to put all of the cotton manufacturing processes under one roof. There were also a variety of other industries including iron and brass foundries, breweries and soap manufacturers. However it was 'Cottonopolis' which predominated although not without serious disruption to the main 'cottage industry' in the area - that of the hand loom weavers, who, because of the mills, found themselves being wiped out.

It was not just the tensions in the economy of the cotton industry which affected every inhabitant as the town was also a little volatile in regard to class. The lowly workers had very little say or power as the collaboration between the mill owners and property owners predominated. Maybe it was not much different in other industrial areas but the rapid growth of Preston meant that it was perhaps more accentuated.

Like many other English communities Preston could not really cope with, and suffered from, rapid urbanisation as the end of the industrial revolution approached. For many their accommodation was well below standard as the newly established local authorities seemed to ignore poor sanitation; lack of any sort of town planning; overcrowding and the cramped conditions that working class members of society had to endure.

Most housing was built by the mill or mine owners as 'back to back' slums with outside toilets that were often shared with other households and not connected to any form of sewage system creating a breeding ground for all manner of disease and thus contributing to a high mortality rate amongst the working classes.

The early efforts to establish a church in Preston were hampered because of the acute economic challenges. The situations encountered by many families is poignantly illustrated in the journal of an early church member - Thomas Kirby, the son of a farm worker who, at the age of 7 years, was sent to work in a silk mill at Ditchingham, Norfolk to help support his family.

'Most of those who had charge of us younger children were ignorant and cruel to us and would whip us for the least little mishap. One old man by the name of Smith was an ugly cross old fellow and I shall never forget him nor his ugly features and another tall muscular fellow by the name of Palmer who used to appear to me was always watching to give some poor boys a knock with his big hand.

In winter we worked from 7am to 8pm. We had half an hour for breakfast, used to eat in the breakfast room but the small children could seldom get to the fire. At 1pm dinner for one hour. At 5pm 15 minutes for tea as it was called. Then work till 8pm. Then I used to hunt up my sister Sarah Ann or Charlotte or both to go home with them. As they did not work in the same room as I did we often found it very difficult to find each other amongst the hundreds who flocked out of the gates like so many sheep. My sisters and I had about 2 miles to go home and some part was over Ditchingham Dam. There were no houses or anything to shelter us from the cold winds and storms and sometimes we did not have very warm clothing or shoes and sometimes not very much food as our wages were low'.

Similar conditions were common amongst many factory workers and miners wherever they were located and it was not unusual for people to die of disease and starvation particularly in the winter months.

Elders Kimball and Hyde were concerned by the problems encountered by the working classes as were other Elders who joined them as missionaries from the church in America. They were also concerned by the distinctive class segregation which existed. In spite of the wealth which prevailed in some sections of early Victorian society the early church leaders described the situation as a 'Babylon on the verge of destruction' so much so, that the compassion shown by those church leaders played an important role in the success of converting many within the working classes. Their message was a simple one - flee these evils of society and build Zion in America. Few, if any other religious organisations, were brave enough to condemn the society in which they lived.

At around the same time political reform was under way with the Parliamentary election of 1837 seeing the rise in Chartism and the disturbances associated with its growth. Whether any early church members were involved in the riots and disturbances is not known but some Christian ex-Chartists did join the church.

However for the majority of early members politics did not play an important role in their lives but certainly trade union membership and involvement with the various friendly societies did.

So - were Latter-day Saint converts average working class people? Most certainly were. Of all those who emigrated across the Atlantic only about 10 - 11 % were considered middle class. Some were skilled workers or artisans, often the most prosperous group amongst the working people. Unlike its nearest rival, the Primitive Methodists, the LDS church did not attract as many artisans and the nucleus of its members were from the lower social classes. This situation is well defined by looking at the early records of the Preston Branch. The branch at the time only had just over 30 members, 4 of which were middle class including a doctor, but the remainder were from the working classes whose occupations included weavers, cotton spinners, a policeman, mechanic and corkscrew maker and of course labourers. As this branch grew the number of migrant members from surrounding villages and the rural countryside increased. Not surprisingly membership of the church throughout England grew more in areas where there was already a large concentration of nonconformists. Typically membership conversions happened from most religious organisations particularly where people felt alienated from their former churches of worship. The Anglican Church (Church of England) and the various Methodist, Baptist and Independent Protestant religions provided most converts alongside those who were seeking religion or had Christian inclinations but were not specifically affiliated.

Like many other breakaway religious groups in the country the LDS church was not without its enemies and in 1838 in Preston Richard Livesey, a Methodist preacher, publicly denounced the church in a leaflet entitled 'An Exposure of Mormonism' which essentially consisted of arguments against the origins of the church and discrediting both Joseph Smith the President and the church's key scriptures the Book of Mormon (first published in England in 1840 as a revision of the original 1837 version). Despite this and other opposition the LDS church grew rapidly throughout Britain.

Religious harassment was of course not just confined to the LDS. Primitive Methodists, Bible Christians and several other nonconformist organisations all encountered mobs and serious opposition. Generally it is believed that these harassments were led by the Anglican vicar and the local squire particularly in the more rural areas. They tended to retain their influence over the populous and were certainly very intolerant towards breakaway families. The vicar and squire were often backed up by the power of the local magistrates and justices.

About 600 people joined the church between July and December 1837 but by the end of 1841 there were 6,729 new members in various areas of the country. The LDS church was considered to be the fastest growing religious organisation in Britain during the 1840s. The reasons that most people converted to Mormonism was said to be due to its simplicity, plainness of doctrine and spiritual manifestations. Christianity and the church was more to do with spiritual then temporal matters. The following table taken from early European Mission records shows the stated reason for conversion:

Primitive simplicity, plain doctrine	32%
Spiritual manifestations	17%
Concept of authority	10%
Book of Mormon	8%
'Voice of Warning'	7%
Impressed with missionaries	7%
Other	19%

In the early years of the church many British members undertook prominent roles within the organisation of the church or had a significant influence on church growth. Most of these were from amongst the working class and some examples are given shortly.

William Lang, a young farm labourer, living in the 1840s stated:

'What a contrast! Instead of long robed Gentleman preaching sprinkling of Infants, Hell and damnation etc. I saw a man who looked like a farmer in plain attire quoting from the Holy Scriptures and preaching the Gospel of Christ in its ancient purity.'

William Lee, an ordinary worker of the same time period stated:

'I began to think, deserted my rude companions, forsook whiskey and tobacco entirely and searched among the different religions for something on which to pin my faith' [he was impressed by the Mormon missionaries'] 'simplicity and unassuming manners and the authority and assurance with which they spoke together with the plainness in which they proved their principles from the Bible.'

These are just two of the many recorded examples amongst church member's diaries and journals.

Last known religious affiliation of members before joining the LDS church

Methodist	26%
Minor non-conformist groups	12%
Baptists	11%
Primitive Methodists	11%
Independents	6%
Total non-conformists	**66%**
Church of England	20%
Not affiliated	14%

Onward from Preston

Although the conversion and missionary work began in Preston in July 1837 growth resulted in five branches of the church being formed by October 1837. Nevertheless the church was beginning to feel the effects of persecution so by Christmas 1837 the missionaries decided to widen their proselyting efforts outside of Preston. The prime areas visited next were Alston in Cumberland, close to the Scottish border and because of the connections with Joseph Fielding and his family, they also went to Bedford.

Elders Richards and Goodson arrived in Bedford on 2 August 1837 and established contact with Reverend Timothy Matthews, a brother in law of Joseph Fielding. Timothy Matthews was well known in the area having been the curate of Bolnhurst and Colmworth Anglican Parish Churches and was currently the preacher at Christ Church Bedford which at the time was part of the Primitive Episcopal Church, a breakaway from the Church of England. The chapel at which Matthews preached was opened up for the LDS missionaries to preach and use as a base. That facility was closed when Matthews later ceased to accept the teachings of Mormonism but this did not stop the conversion process and many of his congregation together with friends and relatives were baptised members of the church but alas not Timothy Matthews.

Missionary work flourished in this area which gave rise to the establishment in December 1837 of the Bedford branch with members from the town and also from a wide area including the surrounding villages of Potton, Kempston, Bassingbourne, Morden, and the towns of St Albans, Baldock and Gamlingay. Because of growing numbers a second branch was established in Bedford in March 1838 and this gave rise to the Bedfordshire Conference.

Despite the growth outside of Preston and the Ribble valley convert numbers were initially insignificant compared to the growth which continued in the Preston area. There was however, opposition from clergymen of opposing religious organisations.

The Reverend Robert Aitken, an Independent Protestant minister, (a friend and colleague of the Reverend Timothy Matthews), Reverend Worrell, a Methodist minister and William Giles were the main perpetrators. William Giles, a Baptist minister, was the person who did more harm in promoting opposition to the church than any other person. He delivered what became known as the 'Giles Lectures' and the local newspapers were quick to report details of the proceedings.

The 'Preston Observer' reported 'The Reverend W Giles delivered an able and interesting lecture on the claims of the Book of Mormon to divine authority. The objective of the lecture which was the first in a series was to expose the alleged absurdities contained in the book and pretending to be a new Revelation. He was listened to throughout a long lecture with intense interest and profound attention and unquestionably gave great satisfaction to the large and respectable audience which attended. Mr Giles will resume the subject next Thursday evening.'

The many adverse reports within the local press meant that the converts in the Preston area had to exercise great faith and overcome ridicule in order to continue their course in the church. However, over time it proved from the growth of the church that the 'Giles Lectures' had little effect and greater numbers than ever ultimately joined the church.

Such was the impact of the first missionary messages that the church growth spread across the British Isles resulting in other areas featuring in early church history. This success was helped by other prominent churchmen who came over from America as missionaries. Besides Preston, Alston and Bedford the church grew rapidly in many other areas including South Wales, (especially Merthyr Tydfil, Llanelli and Cardiff), the Malvern area of Worcestershire, Ledbury, Birmingham, the Potteries, elsewhere in Lancashire including Liverpool, Downham and Manchester, the Isle of Man, Carrickfergus, Lisburn and Belfast in Northern Ireland and throughout Scotland as far north as Thurso. So what of the church's impact in these communities?

The West Midlands
Missionary efforts were also well established in the Staffordshire potteries centred on the town of Hanley. William Benbow a grocer, trading and residing in the Market Place, Hanley and his wife Ann were amongst the first to join the church in that area. This family offered lodgings to the missionaries and in so doing talked with them about their connections with Herefordshire.

Prominent locations of the growth of the early church in the West Midlands

Following these discussions it was decided that the missionaries accompanied by William Benbow and his eight year old son would travel to Herefordshire to visit William's brother John Benbow who was a yeoman farmer of some substance. This initial meeting was instrumental in the conversion en-masse of the members of the United Brethren and was also the location of the first British LDS Chapel at Gadfield Elm. Wilford Woodruff was invited to preach at the home of John Benbow and also at the nearby villages of Frommes Hill and Stanley Hill. The first six people to join the church in Herefordshire were John Benbow, his wife Jane and four other preachers from the United Brethren. The conversion work continued in earnest and a few days later two clerks, sent as spies by the local Rector, were converted together with twelve other members of the Benbow family.

Herefordshire

The largest concentration of LDS converts in 1840-1841 in Britain was in the geographical area around Ledbury, primarily in Herefordshire but also extending out towards Worcester and Gloucester. Wilford Woodruff continued with missionary work amongst the United Brethren, a breakaway group who had left the Methodist Church and organised their own religious meetings led by Thomas Kington. From the time Wilford Woodruff arrived at the home of John Benbow on 4 March 1840, the growth of the Church in this area surpassed any previous missionary work in Britain.

There is one source that lists the 600 converts which includes all of the United Brethren and that is Wilford Woodruff's own journal recorded in 1840. The names of the men and women who were converts to the Church at this time are listed in the journals by date and place of their baptism. The original fifteen volumes of his journal are held by the Church History Library in Salt Lake City. A typescript of the journals is available at the Family History Library amounting to nine volumes. Unfortunately an index of the names of those who joined the church has not been produced. The records are not on microfilm but if you suspect that your ancestor was amongst the members of the United Brethren then employing a professional researcher in Salt Lake City is the best option.

Although Wilford Woodruff preached in over fifty different locations in the area and organised branches of the Church in many of them, there are perhaps six areas which are significant to the church growth.

Castle Frome - Hill Farm & Benbow Pond
John and Jane Benbow lived at Hill Farm just outside the village of Castle Frome and it was from here that Wilford Woodruff began a ministry that brought all of the United Brethren into the Church in the ensuing months. Many were baptised in the pond at Hill Farm and regular church services were held in the hall at the farm. The pond remains as an historic church site reached by a small footpath from the farm access road.

Hill Farm (author's photograph)

13

Benbow Pond (author's photograph)

It was to the aforementioned hall that a local constable went with the intention of arresting Elder Woodruff but he liked what he heard and stayed to listen and ultimately joined the church. The conversion of the two clerks previously mentioned, sent by the priest at Castle Frome, prompted the minister to circulate a petition to the Archbishop of Canterbury requesting he obtain a parliamentary sanction for banning the missionaries from England. This of course was not successful!

Close by is Moor End Farm, which was owned in 1840 by Edward Ockey, a friend of John Benbow and also a member of the United Brethren. Ockey auctioned his farm in order to provide financial support to poorer members of the church who wanted to emigrate to America.

Dymock

Thomas Kington, then head of the United Brethren, lived in the village of Dymock at the time of his conversion.

Dymock is also important because it is where a notable healing performed by Brigham Young took place. Brigham Young had arrived in England on a mission in 1839 and visited Wilford Woodruff and the converted United Brethren members. Whilst doing so he met William Pitt and his sister Mary who joined the Church in Dymock. Mary had been an invalid for eleven years and was promised she would be healed. A priesthood blessing was given to Mary by Brigham Young only one day after she had joined the church. The very next day she laid down her crutch and was able to walk through the streets of Dymock unaided proclaiming the truth of the restored gospel. This so infuriated the local minister that he led a mob in stoning the building where members of the Church were assembled. To protect Wilford Woodruff, William Pitt braved the hail of rocks and bricks to get the names of those in the mob.

The parish church in Dymock is also noted as the location of the development of the first 'parish hymnal' in the Church of England. William Pitt had served as choirmaster for the church and after his emigration organised the Nauvoo Brass Band which played a prominent role in early Utah music and theatre.

Ledbury
Ledbury was, in the 1840s, the provincial market town for the area around Castle Frome and Dymock and became a natural base for the Church missionaries. Wilford Woodruff was visiting in Ledbury when he was approached by the minister of the Baptist Church with an invitation to preach in the chapel. After that service he baptised several members of the Baptist congregation in the chapel font. The church still exists to the north of Ledbury town centre.

Gadfield Elm - The oldest Mormon chapel in the world

In their heyday the United Brethren owned forty-five homes which were licensed for preaching as well as their chapel, built in 1836, at Gadfield Elm near the village of Pendock in Worcestershire, the legal title to which was held by John Benbow. As virtually the entire membership of the United Brethren became members of the LDS Church, Benbow gifted the title to the church, making this the first LDS chapel in the British Isles, and the oldest LDS meetinghouse still standing anywhere in the world and which is still in the ownership of the church.

Gadfield Elm Chapel acted as the focal point of Church activity for thousands of Latter-day Saints until the majority emigrated to the USA to fulfil their dream of building a new Zion in the United States of America.

As most of the members from this area emigrated to America, the chapel was sold to assist the poorer Saints who still remained to make their journey. Subsequently the chapel was used as a farm building ultimately becoming derelict. Most of the roof had gone and an external wall had been opened to allow the building to be used as a garage.

The chapel was subsequently bought by a private trust, restored and given back to the Church of Jesus Christ of Latter-day Saints for a second time. It was officially accepted by the then President of the church, Gordon B. Hinckley, in May 2004.

Gadfield Elm chapel, built of local stone and standing in an isolated location in the Worcestershire countryside, is the last surviving memorial to the United Brethren converts and today has a seating capacity of 100 people.

Gadfield Elm Chapel - the oldest LDS Chapel in the world. (author's photograph).

The chapel is located near Eldersfield and is today a visitors' centre where you will be able to discover the stories of the people who once lived in the area before leaving for a new life in America. Gadfield Elm has a unique history.

• March 1836: Land purchased by the United Brethren for £25 on which to build the chapel.

• April 1840: Wilford Woodruff (4th President of the Church) preached and baptised 11 people.

• Three hundred members of the United Brethren were baptised into The Church of Jesus Christ of Latter-day Saints in the pond on John Benbow's farm. Eventually 600 United Brethren were baptised. Many subsequently became prominent pioneering figures in the American West.

- 17 May 1840: Brigham Young, (who after the death of Joseph Smith became the 2nd President of the Church), addressed the membership gathered at the chapel.

- 14 June 1840: The Bran Green and Gadfield Elm conferences of the British Mission were organised by Wilford Woodruff and consisted of twelve branches which were based upon the former congregations of the United Brethren namely Bran Green, Gadfield Elm, Kilcot, Dymock, Twigworth, Ryton, Lime Street, Deerhurst, Apperly, Norton, Leigh and Hawcross.

- 7 September 1840: As the United Brethren no longer existed the chapel was given to The Church of Jesus Christ of Latter-day Saints.

- 14 September 1840: Wilford Woodruff attended a Conference at Gadfield Elm followed by another at Frome Hill. At these two conferences 40 branches of the Church were represented, containing 1,007 members. Five branches were added - Cheltenham, Bristol, Weston, Cranham & Highleadon.

- 14 December 1840: Brigham Young presided over a conference at the chapel.

- 15 March 1841: More Branches of the Church were formed - Forest of Dean, Flyford, Pinwich, Nantom Beachom, Hill Common, Frogmarsh, Walton Hill.

- 1842: Chapel was sold to help finance the emigration of church members to the USA and was used essentially as a farm building / barn until the late 20th century.

- 12 October 1994: The Chapel was bought at Auction by the Gadfield Elm Trust. Restoration of the building and grounds commenced almost immediately.

- 23 April 2000: Gadfield Elm Chapel was re-dedicated by Elder Jeffrey R Holland of The Quorum of the Twelve Apostles as a 'Mormon chapel'.

- 26 May 2004: the Gadfield Elm chapel is handed back into the ownership of the Church, with a presentation to President Gordon B Hinckley by representatives of The Gadfield Elm Trust.

Hawcross
Wilford Woodruff seldom encountered physical abuse during his time in Herefordshire, but one notable exception occurred at Hawcross.

He went there with the purpose of visiting the homes of friends and relatives of some recently converted members. When some of those friends and relatives desired baptism following the meeting, Wilford Woodruff went with them to the local pond.

He walked into the water and baptised five persons while they were being pelted by a mob with stones, one of which hit Woodruff on the head nearly knocking him out. Whilst it is not possible to identify the specific homes and pond in which this experience took place, there is a pond alongside the main road at Hawcross which is believed to be the most likely place.

Herefordshire Beacon
The beacon is a site of an ancient Roman camp and even earlier fortifications, overlooking the Malvern Hills and was a favourite spot of Wilford Woodruff during his time in Herefordshire. He climbed the beacon at least four times to pray and contemplate his work. At the conclusion of the visit of Brigham Young and Willard Richards to Herefordshire, the two men accompanied Wilford Woodruff to the Beacon where they held an important council meeting at which it was decided to publish the Book of Mormon in Britain plus a hymn-book. Immediately following this council meeting, Brigham Young returned to Manchester and set in motion the realisation of their plans. Both John Benbow and Thomas Kington had contributed a total of £300, a substantial amount of money equivalent in today's terms to about £10,500, to enable the two publications to go ahead. In recent times, other prominent leaders of the church have visited the Herefordshire Beacon retracing Woodruff's steps. The climb is rewarded with spectacular views of both the Malvern Hills and looks over the many villages that Wilford Woodruff preached in. On a clear day the three cities of Hereford, Gloucester and Worcester are visible.

The conversion of all of the United Brethren and of approximately 1,800 other members within eight months in the Herefordshire area remains to this day one of the most significant missionary experiences in the history of the LDS Church. Reflecting upon the times Woodruff wrote the following in his journal:

> 'The whole history of this Herefordshire mission shows the importance of listening to the still small voice of the spirit of God, and the Revelations of the Holy Ghost. The people were praying for light and truth, and the Lord sent me to them. I declared the gospel of life and salvation, some eighteen hundred souls received it, and many have been gathered...In all these things we should ever acknowledge the hand of God, and give him the honour, praise, and glory, forever.'

Other areas of Britain significant in Mormon conversion

Besides the areas around Herefordshire there were, throughout the United Kingdom, other areas which played a vital role in the growth of the early church and are likely to be of particular interest to family historians with ancestry from these locations. The early converts from these areas would have been instrumental in establishing the church locally and many would also have emigrated to America. If any of your ancestors were from these localities then it is worth researching LDS church records (described later) to see if there was a family connection with the church.

Alston, Cumberland
One of the earliest Branches was organised here in 1837 by Isaac Russell and John Snider, two Englishmen who had been converted in Canada and then came back to serve as missionaries alongside Heber C. Kimball.

Bedford, Bedfordshire
Bedford was mentioned earlier in the section 'Onward from Preston' but a branch of the Church was established in 1837 through the efforts of Elders Willard Richards and John Goodson.

Belfast, Northern Ireland
John Taylor (see below) went to Belfast in 1840, but a branch of the church was not organised until several years later. Belfast was the headquarters for the Church in Ireland throughout the nineteenth and for much of the twentieth centuries.

Bishopston, Renfrewshire
The first baptisms in Scotland took place on 14 January 1840, but the Scottish story begins in the Scots second homeland of Canada. Samuel Mulliner baptised the first Scottish converts Alexander and Jessie Hay, who were friends of another church member, James Lea. He joined the church in Preston and was working on the railways in Bishopston near Glasgow. The Hays were baptised in the River Clyde. Mulliner was originally from Midlothian but he settled in Canada before returning to Scotland as a church missionary accompanied by Alexander Wright, a fellow Scot. In late 1839 they came to Liverpool on board the Tarolinta and arrived in Glasgow around Christmas of 1839. They made contact with relations, Mulliner concentrating on Edinburgh and Wright working the area around his home town of Marnoch. Yet again there was a connection with the clergy. Wright's sister was employed by a local minister with whom he engaged in discussion about the church. This was the start of 9,000 plus Scottish people becoming church members in the 19th century.

Douglas, Isle of Man
John Taylor had a special reason for visiting the Isle of Man, his in laws. He visited the Isle of Man for the first time in 1840, dedicated the land, and held a celebrated debate with a local minister. He organised a branch of the church in Douglas and preached in other towns on the island to relatives of his wife, Leonora Cannon.

Eccleston, Lancashire
Eccleston was the home of Hannah and Matthias Moon who became church members in 1837 through the efforts of Heber C. Kimball. Their sons all served missions for the Church in Britain, and one of them, John Moon, led the first company of church members across the Atlantic to America in 1840.

Edinburgh, Scotland
Edinburgh was paramount in the establishment of the church in Scotland. Alexander Wright and Samuel Mulliner preached the first LDS sermon in Scotland, on 22 December 1839. Orson Pratt arrived there on 18 May 1840 and the following morning climbed Arthur's Seat and dedicated Scotland for the preaching of the gospel. Edinburgh served for many years as headquarters for the Church in Scotland. The first branch of the Church in Scotland was however established in Paisley in May 1840.

Hillsborough, County Down, Ireland
The first branch of the Church organised in Ireland on 1 October 1840 was established in Hillsborough although the first convert in Ireland was Thomas Tate who joined the church in July 1840 at Lough Brickland also in County Down.

Liverpool Lancashire

The Reverend Timothy Matthews had moved to Liverpool and was a preacher at the Aitkenite Chapel in Hope Street. The first LDS missionaries landed at Liverpool on 19 July 1837. One prominent church member, a native of the city, was George Q. Cannon who was born in Liverpool on 11 January 1827. Between 1873 and 1901, Elder Cannon served as Counsellor to four different Presidents of the Church. Liverpool was the headquarters of the Church in Britain from 1842 to 1929. It was also the chief port of embarkation for America and the place where the *Millennial Star* and other important Church publications were published.

The early church headquarters in Islington, Liverpool.

London

Henry Connor, a watchmaker, was the first person to join the church in London on 31 August 1840. The Headquarters of the church moved from Liverpool to London in 1930.

Manchester, Lancashire

Manchester was the headquarters of the church in Britain from 1840 to 1842, and was where Brigham Young served most of his mission in 1840-1841.

Some early and prominent British Church members

Many early church members from ordinary and often humble backgrounds throughout Britain became prominent leaders within the early church, and indeed still do so today. Brief biographical sketches of some of the more notable members are shown below, all of whom were emigrants from this country. Maybe your ancestors also played an important role within the church.

John Taylor

John Taylor.

John Taylor became the third president of the Church of Jesus Christ of Latter-day Saints. He was a son of James and Agnes Taylor, and was born on 1 November 1808 at Milnthorpe, Westmorland. James Taylor, his father owned a small estate in Hale. The family were staunch members of the Church of England, and John accepted the doctrines of that church until he was about fifteen years old when he joined the Methodists, ultimately becoming a local Methodist preacher.

He left England at the end of 1828. His parents had left two years previously and settled in Toronto, Canada. John ultimately resided in Toronto after visiting New York, Brooklyn and Albany. He married Leonora Cannon, daughter of Captain Cannon, from the Isle of Man, who was a member of the Methodist church in Toronto. John Taylor joined the LDS Church in 1836. On the 8 August 1839 he sailed back to England to begin work as a missionary. He was sick for eleven weeks on the voyage but recovered and arrived in Liverpool on 11 January 1840 in good health. He immediately commenced his missionary work, preaching, baptising, organising branches, and with other missionaries regulated the Church throughout the British Isles. He was instrumental in introducing the church into Ireland, the Isle of Man and later worked in Scotland. He published several tracts, setting out the beliefs of the LDS Church. He also helped to prepare and publish the first edition of the Latter-Day Saints' Hymn Book. After a successful mission in the British Isles he returned to his home in Nauvoo arriving there on 1 July 1841 where he found his wife seriously ill but she soon recovered. He returned to England for a second time as a missionary arriving on 3 October 1846 and returned home in the following spring after which he was in charge of a company of British church members who journeyed to the Salt Lake Valley arriving in the latter months of 1847. He spent two years in Salt Lake and was active in founding and building the city. He built one of the first saw mills in Utah, where he also worked. In October 1880, he became the third President of the Church.

Jospeph Fielding
Joseph Fielding, the second president of the British Mission, was born on 26 March 1797, at Honeydon, Bedfordshire, a village about nine miles north east of Bedford. He was the son of John and Rachel Fielding. He emigrated to Upper Canada in 1832, where on 21 May 1836 he became a member of the church and moved to Kirtland, Ohio in the following May. In June 1837, he was assigned by the then President of the church, Joseph Smith to accompany other missionaries including Heber C. Kimball; Orson Hyde on their first mission to England. They sailed from New York on the ship 'Garrick,' which arrived in Liverpool, England on 20 July 1837. The successful opening for preaching the gospel in Preston, England, was partly due to the fact that Joseph Fielding's brother James was living there. James Fielding was the minister at the Vauxhall Chapel in Preston, loosely Independent Protestants who held no particular affiliations to any other denomination. As an Independent congregation, they received their instruction from their minister rather than having a central doctrinal affiliation. The Reverend James Fielding had formerly been a Methodist but like many had become disillusioned. This was not the first time that James Fielding had heard of the Mormon gospel, as he and Joseph had corresponded regarding the beliefs. James often read the letters to his congregation and as such they wanted also to be taught about Mormonism. James offered the Vauxhall Chapel so that further meetings could be undertaken. Thus, began Joseph's successful mission in his native land. On 30th July 1837, George Darlington Watt, the first British convert was baptised in the River Ribble along with nine others, all members of Reverend James Fielding's congregation. A few thousand people lined the banks of the river to witness the event. Joseph Fielding was in charge of the church organisation in Great Britain in the spring of 1838 and presided over the British Mission until the arrival of Brigham Young and other church leaders from America in April, 1840.

The following year Joseph Fielding left Great Britain to return to America. He sailed from Liverpool 21 September 1841, on board the ship 'Tyrean,' in charge of a company of emigrating saints, who arrived in Nauvoo, Illinois, in November 1841. Joseph Fielding remained in Nauvoo until the migration of the Saints in 1846, when he encountered persecution and hardship having been driven away from Illinois by mob violence. After spending about two years on the frontiers, he arrived in the Salt Lake Valley in the latter part of 1848. He resided in Mill Creek, Salt Lake County, until his death on 19 December1863 aged 66 years.

George Darlington Watt

George was the first member to join the LDS church in England and was born in Manchester on the 12 May 1812. While living in Preston as a young man, Watt was a member of the Reverend James Fielding's congregation. He later led a group of 378 church members as they emigrated from Liverpool on board the 'Ellen Maria' leaving on 2 February 1851 and arriving in New Orleans on 7 April that same year. He was accompanied by his wife Molly and their son George Darlington Watt junior. He is remembered because he competed with another to be the first to be baptised and of course won the race! In 1840 and 1841 Watt worked as a Mormon missionary in Scotland.

George D Watt - first British church member.

George was a skilled Pitman Shorthand writer and used those skills in Utah as a reporter on the local church newspaper called the 'Deseret News'. He was also assigned to record the sermons of church leaders and in 1853 he proposed that they be collated and published in Britain. Whilst working as a journalist he was appointed to a committee that created a phonetic alphabet to help non-English speaking Latter-day Saint immigrants learn English.

In 1869, Watt was dis-fellowshipped (a form of congregational discipline restricting membership rights and privileges) from the LDS Church for following the teachings of and becoming one of the leaders of the 'Godbeites' and was eventually excommunicated from the LDS Church on 3 May 1874.

The Godbeites were members of the Godbeite Church, officially called the Church of Zion, organised in 1870 by William S. Godbe. This offshoot of The Church of Jesus Christ of Latter-day Saints was aimed towards embracing all belief systems. The Godbeite church ceased to exist by the mid 1880s.

In 1868 William S. Godbe and other Mormon merchants began criticising the economic demands and policies of the LDS Church, through the medium of the press, principally in the *'Utah Journal'*, which later became the *'Salt Lake Tribune'*. Godbe, along with others was excommunicated from the church because he wanted to reform the LDS Church and believed that political reform could help spur religious reform.

George died in Kaysville, Utah at the age of 65.

John Rex Winder
John R Winder was born 11 December 1821 to Richard and Sophia Collins Winder in Biddenden, Kent. He served in prominent leadership within the church from 1887 until his death on 27 March 1910. He was well-known for his business abilities and was also active in politics and the local militia in Utah after his emigration. He originally worked as a shoe and leather retailer in London. He married Ellen Walters in London in 1845 after which he was recruited to manage a shoe store in Liverpool. It was whilst working in the shoe shop in Liverpool that he was introduced to the LDS Church and subsequently joined. In February 1853 he left Liverpool for America but suffered from smallpox on the way. On arrival in New Orleans he travelled the Mississippi to St. Louis, Missouri and onward to Keokuk, Iowa, ultimately arriving in Utah on 10 October 1853.

Subsequently he served closely with John Taylor. During this time, the U.S. government began to victimise the church resulting in the Edmunds-Tucker Act in 1887, which necessitated church leaders to go into hiding. Winder's farm on the south of the city served as a sanctuary during these years and also acted as temporary Church headquarters.

John R Winder also managed the interior construction work to the Salt Lake Temple and was successful in completing it ahead of schedule earning him praise from church leaders. After the temple dedication he served in the presidency of the temple, a position he held until his death.

He was responsible for the publishing of a proclamation called *The Origin of Man* in 1909 clarifying the Church's position on human evolution.

George Q Cannon

George Quayle Cannon was born in Liverpool on 11 January 1827, to George Cannon and Ann Quayle. He was the eldest of six children. His aunt, Leonora Cannon, married John Taylor (3rd president of the Church). News of the wedding reached the Cannon family and four years later, when Taylor came to Liverpool, they joined the church. George Q Cannon was 13 years old at the time. Cannon's siblings were Mary Alice, Ann, Angus, David and Leonora. In 1842, the Cannon family emigrated to the USA and joined with the other church members in Nauvoo, Illinois. Ann Cannon, George's mother unfortunately died on the voyage. On arrival in Nauvoo George Sr. married for a second time to Mary Edwards and had another daughter, Elizabeth.

In Nauvoo, George Q. Cannon was sent to live with John & Leonora Taylor. He worked as a printer with *'Times and Seasons'* and the *'Nauvoo Neighbour'* both of which were church publications which John Taylor edited.

In 1846, when John Taylor travelled to England to organise the affairs of the church George Q. Cannon accompanied John Taylor's wife and family to Winter Quarters, Nebraska. He continued to travel with the Taylor family eventually arriving in Salt Lake in October 1847.

George Q Cannon married Elizabeth Hoagland after which he assisted in publishing a newspaper in California. After meeting Orson Pratt in California, Cannon subsequently became a mission president in Oregon and California at the age of 28 years. He served in this capacity until he heard of the Utah War in 1857. In February 1856 he also commenced his own newspaper called the *'Western Standard'*, a weekly publication based in San Francisco.

At the time of the Utah War, George returned to Utah and was commissioned as a Lieutenant General in the Nauvoo Legion. He also served as the printer of the *Deseret News*.

In 1860 George Q Cannon returned to England where he presided over the European Mission of the church. During his time he edited the *'Millennial Star'* and developed a Welsh language periodical for the church called *'Udgorn Seion.'* However in 1862 he returned to America and was sent to Washington, D.C. to take charge of the church's promotion of Utah Territory's bid for statehood. In 1867 Cannon became the managing editor of the *Deseret News*. It was under his direction that the *Deseret News* was first published on a daily basis. He held this position until 1874.

On 8 April 1873, Cannon became a counsellor to Brigham Young, then President of the Church. He went on to serve as counsellor to three more presidents of the church until his own death on 12 April 1901 in California.

James E Talmage

James E Talmage was born in Hungerford, Berkshire on 21 September 1862, the son of Gabriel Talmage and Susannah Preater. He joined the church at age 10 on 15 June 1873 and emigrated with his family to Utah in 1874. He studied at the Brigham Young Academy, (later Brigham Young University) and graduated in 1880 receiving in 1881, the first ever collegiate diploma from the Scientific Department. James Talmage married May Booth on 14 June 1888. May was a native of Utah but the daughter of immigrants from Lancashire. She also studied at Brigham Young Academy where she met James who was one of her instructors. After completing her studies she worked as a teacher in Kaysville, Utah where James was involved in a project studying the Great Salt Lake. After a short relationship they married. James and May had eight children.

As well as James, later serving as the president of the European Mission, May oversaw the Women's organisation of the church, known as the Relief Society, throughout the mission. She also served for 40 years as a member of the General Board of the Young Women's Mutual Improvement Association of the LDS Church and whilst in Britain she oversaw the beginning of the Young Men's Mutual Improvement Association. Both of these organisations were specifically for the youth of the church.

May was also leader of the Utah Women's Suffrage Association, and was a delegate to the World Congress of Women held at the Chicago World's Fair in 1893.

James died on 27 July 1933 in Salt Lake City.

Charles William Penrose

Charles Penrose was born in London on 4 February 1832 the son of George William Penrose and Matilda Sim. It is said that he learned to read the Bible by the age of four. He joined the church at the age of eighteen on 14 May 1850 in London. He also met and married his wife Lucetta Stratford there. They had three children.

After joining the church, Charles Penrose served a seven year mission preaching throughout England. In 1861, he emigrated to Utah but shortly after his arrival he was sent back to England on a further mission. When he returned to Utah he settled in Ogden where he became involved in newspaper publishing, eventually becoming the editor of the *Deseret News* in Salt Lake City.

Charles Penrose was a professor of theology at Brigham Young Academy from 1897 to 1899 and again for a second term in 1901 and 1902.

He became an apostle on 7 July 1904 and later a counsellor in the First Presidency on 7 December 1911 where he served until his death in Salt Lake City on 16 May 1925.

It was not only the men of the church who enjoyed a prominent status. The following women are noted amongst British emigrants.

Ruth May

Ruth May was born on 16 November 1853 in Westbury, Wiltshire to James May and Mary Ann Harding. When Ruth was five months old her parents converted to Mormonism. Her mother died in childbirth when Ruth was 18 months old after which Ruth was sent to live with other Mormon families in the area. In 1865, her father James May emigrated to the United States and once established there arranged for the emigration of Ruth and her sister to Philadelphia. The family moved on to Utah in 1867.

On 8 May 1873, Ruth married Jesse W. Fox. Around the same time, Jesse lost his business, went into debt, and the Foxes ultimately lost their home. At this time they had 12 children.

She was active within the community being involved in several organisations. Ruth was president of the Utah Woman's Press Club, chair of the Second Precinct Ladies' Republican Club, treasurer of the Utah Woman Suffrage Association, and was a member of the Reaper's Club, the Salt Lake County Republican Committee, the Deseret Agricultural and Manufacturing Society, and the Traveller's Aid Society. In the late 1800s, she worked for the inclusion of woman suffrage in the Utah state constitution and helped draft the suffrage memorial presented and accepted by the 1895 Utah constitutional convention.

In 1905, Ruth became a counsellor in the general presidency of the Young Women's Mutual Improvement Association of the LDS church where she served until 1929 after which she became its president.

Ruth died in Salt Lake City aged 104 years on 12 April 1958.

May Anderson

May Anderson was born in Liverpool on 8 June 1864, the third child of Scott Anderson and Mary Bruce. She emigrated to Utah with her family after they became members of the church.

From October 1890, and for the next forty-nine years, May worked in the children's organisation (Primary) of the church. She was also the first editor-in-chief of 'The Children's Friend', the church's official magazine specifically published for the children.

May Anderson

During her tenure in the Primary organisation she set up the Primary Children's Hospital in Salt Lake City, and helped to establish many kindergartens in Utah.

The Primary Children's Hospital began in the early years of the twentieth century as a church-sponsored institution. The Primary Association (the children's program) opened a children's ward at Salt Lake's LDS Hospital in 1911 after May Anderson and a colleague were touched by the sight of a child on crutches struggling along a city street at which time they realised the need for special medical help for children.

The Primary Children's Hospital in Salt Lake City (LDS Church - Intellectual Reserve Inc).

On 12 May 1922, the Primary Association opened its own 35-bed facility in a large house at 40 West North Temple, Salt Lake City principally as a convalescent facility for the LDS Hospital. Children with orthopedic and chronic diseases were often hospitalised for several months and parents' visiting was restricted because of the threat of communicable diseases. Initially the hospital was part supported by donations of 'birthday pennies' by LDS Primary children, and by 'Penny Parades' held in surrounding area towns and farming districts.

May Anderson never married and died on 11 June 1946 in Salt Lake City.

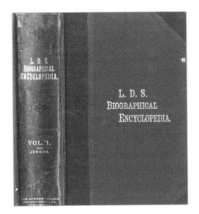

There are many published biographies of prominent church members from Britain and Europe within the LDS Biographical Encyclopedia (Andrew Jensen History Company).

CHAPTER TWO
Emigration of Church Members

The United States of America and the North American British Colonies had, for a long time, held an appeal for those wanting to emigrate and start a new life. Changes in employment conditions, the economy and rapid industrial growth in Britain did not always bring prosperity and security. Thousands of poorer working class families were unable to sustain themselves and desperately wanted some way of improving their lifestyle. The 1830s saw a large and sustained increase in the number of British families emigrating to America. 'The grimmest period of the nineteenth century' - the depression of the late 1830s, early 1840s, and the Irish potato famine encouraged (almost necessitated) such emigration.

The same factors which influenced nearly 100,000 working class people to emigrate to America between 1855 and the end of the nineteenth century also influenced 65,000 emigrants who were members of the Church of Jesus Christ of Latter-day Saints. These emigrants were ordinary people from agricultural labourers to blacksmiths, yeoman farmers to masons. The introduction of Mormon missionaries to England commencing in 1837, led by such prominent church leaders as Brigham Young, encouraged and initiated the Mormon emigration to America congregating first in Nauvoo and ultimately Salt Lake City. Although the church had been established in America in 1830, there was a period early in the next decade when there were more members of the church in Britain than in America.

The emigration of thousands of converts to America played a major role in the growth of the church in the United States throughout the nineteenth century. The massive emigration of church members ultimately made it possible for the Latter-day Saints to become a dominant economic, political, and religious force in Utah. In 1852 the British church publication *'Millennial Star'* published the following:

'For the Saints to get themselves to the Valley is a good thing. Few of them can be worse off there than they are here. Many of them here have not the necessities to say nothing of the comforts of life. There all would have the necessaries and most would obtain many of the comforts. As a whole the Saints in Utah are far better fed and clothed than their brethren and sisters in this country. Then how unwise is it for anyone to delay gathering till he gain sufficient means here to make himself what he thinks comfortable on the journey to and after he arrives at the mountains'.

Was this all the encouragement the British church members needed? The Star followed this with many different articles and admonitions including an article entitled 'Information for Emigrants' (transcribed below) which was noted by most church members who chose to emigrate through Liverpool. Its direction was a great help to those embarking on the voyages.

'We shall now proceed to give such particulars in regard to the journey as may be needful. Those intending to emigrate will do well to take no furniture with them except the necessary articles of beds, bedding, wearing apparel, pots, cooking utensils, etc., which will come in useful both on the ship and on the steam-boat, and after they arrive. Do not be encumbered with old bedsteads, chairs, tables, stands, drawers, broken boxes, worn out bedding, soiled clothings, rusty tools, &c., but provide a great plenty of good and substantial wearing apparel, bedding, &c., consisting of every necessary article of manufactured goods both for men and women, because these things are much dearer in Western America than in England, and no duties will be charged by the American government of wearing apparel already made up, even if each passenger has several suits of clothes. Every thing which is not designed for use on the passage should be carefully packed in strong boxes or trunks. Emigrants will not have to pay anything for freight of their usual household goods and furniture on the ocean; but it will cost something for freight up the Mississippi River for every article except a certain quantity which is allowed each passenger free as travelling luggage'.

In preparation for the onward journey on arrival in the USA the 'Star' also gave the following information.

'New Orleans is by far the cheapest route for emigrants to Illinois; and emigrating in large companies may save much more money. Those who wish to avail themselves of these advantages, and who are intending to emigrate this autumn, are informed that the name and age of each passenger, together with money to pay their passage to New Orleans and to purchase provisions, must be forwarded at least 10 days previous to the time of sailing, so that a ship may be chartered and provisions purchased according to the number of passengers, and thus avoid all hurry and confusion. The money and names being forwarded ten days previous to the time of sailing, the passengers and goods need not arrive till two or three days before the time of sailing. Thus when all things are prepared, they can go immediately on board, and begin to arrange the berths, beds, provisions, etc., and avoid the expense of living a while in the town of Liverpool. Perhaps the passage money and provisions for each passenger from Liverpool to New Orleans will be not far from four pounds. Children under fourteen years of age, half-price; under one year nothing. When the ship arrives in New Orleans the company will need to send their foreman, or leader, or committee, to charter a steam boat for Nauvoo or St. Louis, which will probably be from 15s. [shillings] to 25s. per head, and provisions to be purchased for about two weeks; so the whole passage money from Liverpool to Nauvoo will probably be from £5 to £7.33'

The object of the Latter-day Saints' emigration was the fulfilment of a divine command and not the betterment of life although this must have played a large part in the motive for emigration. Both the spiritual and temporal comfort of the emigrants was the ultimate aim of those who organised the journey. Consequently arrangements were made to assist the emigrants from the time they left their homes up to the time they arrived at their destination. An experienced church member was assigned to each vessel to superintend the voyage, in connection with the ship's masters, and also for the journey across the USA. Embarkation was, in the early days, between September and the following March or April, but once the migration to Salt Lake had commenced embarkation was generally between January and April which enabled the emigrants to arrive on the frontiers before June and early enough to cross the plains prior to winter. When the migration was to Nauvoo or Council Bluffs, Iowa, the prime objective was to pass New Orleans before the summer with its hot, humid and sickly climate.

The following explains how the emigration was undertaken by the church in the early period when most of the Saints departing Liverpool landed in New Orleans. Applications for emigration were received by the church agent in Liverpool, and when there were sufficient numbers a vessel was chartered and the intended passengers were notified by printed circulars containing instructions on how they were to proceed; when they needed to be in Liverpool to embark; what the fares were for the passage, which was normally steerage and details of the provisions and clothing allowed. In some instances one conference or district of the church would become a ships company so arrangements were made for them to all embark together.

The president of the conference would be required to contract with the railway companies for their conveyance to Liverpool, which for the church and its members generally meant a cost saving on fares. As a condition of the contract with the shipping company it was generally agreed that the passengers would go on board on the day of their arrival in Liverpool, or certainly no later than the following day. Such an arrangement, although sometimes considered inconvenient to the ship owners saved the expense of members having to lodge in Liverpool and also prevented members from being robbed by 'sharpers' (con-men) who considered the Liverpool docklands as rich pickings. When the passengers were on board, the agent, who was generally the leader of the Church in the British Isles, would visit with them and appoint a trio of company leaders. As a rule they were Elders who had travelled the route before, or at least had some experience of life on board a ship. They were appointed by common consent of the emigrants. The leaders would then proceed to divide the ships company into branches presided over by a priesthood holder. Watchmen were then selected from the adult passengers who guarded the ship day and night until its departure. Their prime role was to prevent any unauthorised person from descending the hatchways.

Whilst at sea, the leaders of the various branches saw that the passengers arose about five or six o'clock in the morning, that they cleaned their respective portions of the ship, and threw any rubbish overboard following which prayers were offered and after which the passengers prepared their breakfasts. During the remainder of the day the emigrants would occupy themselves with various on board duties, exercise and amusements. At eight or nine o'clock at night prayers were again offered, and all retired to their berths. Such routines were considered an excellent way of maintaining the general health of the passengers. In addition to this daily routine, when the weather permitted, worship meetings were held on the deck on Sundays, and also during the week. Schools for the education (secular and religious) of both children and adults were also conducted and lectures were also given. When missionaries were on board who had travelled in foreign countries they would often describe the scenes they had witnessed and relate incidents of their travels to the passengers. These activities helped to break the monotony of the voyage at the same time improving both the education and mental capacities of the passengers.

The way in which the passengers conducted themselves on board always seemed to leave a good impression on the crew and any non LDS persons on board. Because of this example fifty converts to the church occurred on the voyage of the *Olympus*, which sailed in March 1851 and forty eight including the captain on the *International*, which sailed in February 1853.

In the *Liverpool Morning Advertiser* of 2 June 1854 a report states:

'On Tuesday, says the London correspondent of the Cambridge Independent Press, I heard a rather remarkable examination before a committee of the House of Commons. The witness was no other than the supreme authority in England of the Mormonites (Elder Samuel W. Richards,) and the subject upon which he was giving information was to the mode in which the emigration to Utah is conducted. He gave himself no airs, but was respectful in his demeanour, and ready in his answers, and at the close of his examination he received the thanks of the committee in rather a marked manner. There is one thing which, in the opinion of the Emigration Committee of House of Commons, they the Latter-day Saints can do, viz., teach Christian ship owners how to send poor people decently, cheaply and healthfully across the Atlantic.'

Both the United States and the British governments undertook to establish laws and regulations looking primarily at the safety of passengers crossing the Atlantic, especially emigrants from the British Isles to America. The British Parliament introduced the Passengers Act in 1852, which, among other things, provided that every emigration agent shipping passengers to North America should supply them with seven days provisions if the ship sailed between the 16 January and the 14 October and eighty days' provisions if it sailed between the 14 October and the 16 January. The amounts were based upon the provisions that were provided by the LDS church to its emigrants. In addition to the requirements of the Act Latter-day Saint passengers were given two and a half pounds of sago, three pounds of butter, two pounds of cheese, and one pint of vinegar for each adult, and half the amount to children up to 14 years of age. One pound of beef or pork weekly to each adult was substituted for its equivalent in oatmeal. This quantity of provisions enabled many passengers to live better during the voyage than they did whilst at home in their native country. Passengers had to provide their own bedding, eating implements and cooking utensils. If any provisions remained unused on the arrival at New Orleans they were distributed amongst the passengers. If a vessel made good time then there would usually have been a considerable amount of food left which was used to aid poor emigrants on their onward journey. An example is the 'John M. Wood' which sailed 12 March 1854, and arrived in America ahead of its scheduled time. The amount of provisions saved the Perpetual Emigration Fund passengers one hundred and fifty pounds of tea, nineteen barrels of biscuit, five barrels of oatmeal, four barrels and four bags of rice and three barrels of pork. The ship provided the cooking apparatus and fuel, and the Passengers' Act required that every passenger ship carrying one hundred adults should have 'a seafaring person' who in the ship's articles was a passengers' steward, employed solely in administering the provisions to the passengers, and in assisting to maintain cleanliness, order and good discipline among them.

The Act also provided for the berthing of the passengers. It required each adult berth should be six feet in length, and eighteen inches in width. No two passengers unless members of the same family were to be placed in the same berth, and unless married no adult mixed sexes were to be placed in each berth. All unmarried adult male passengers were berthed in the fore part of the vessel, and were separated from the rest of the passengers by a strong bulkhead.

In 1855, two further Passenger Acts, one American and one British, were passed which introduced important changes in providing for the comfort and safety of emigrants crossing the Atlantic, The American Act came into effect in British ports 1 May 1855, and the British Act on 1 October 1855. In nearly all its main features as far as those relating to the carriage of church passengers between Great Britain and the United States were concerned, the Latter-day Saint agents were already complying with the requirements. The Act of 1855 was a considerable improvement on the Act of 1852 providing for more room and convenience on board and a better dietary scale, the provision of a doctor if the ship was carrying more than 300 adults and two cooks.

The first ships to sail under new legislation were the *Cynosure*, which sailed on 29 July 1855 after the American Act came into force and the *Emerald Isle* which sailed on 30 November 1855 after the British Act came into force. On arriving at New Orleans the emigrants were received by another church agent who procured steamboats for them to sail the Mississippi to St. Louis. It was the duty of this agent to send a report to the European Mission Office in Liverpool relating to the condition in which the emigrants arrived.

At St. Louis another church agent co-operated with the agent sent from England. The emigrants then continued their journey still by steamboat to the camping grounds and outfitting posts at Keokuk, Iowa two hundred and five miles from St, Louis, and later at Kansas City, Jackson County, Missouri which was located twelve miles west of Independence. At these outfitting posts emigrants found their teams, which the agents had purchased, waiting to receive them and their luggage. Ten individuals were allotted to one wagon and one tent. In 1854 the Perpetual Emigration Fund Company allowed one hundred pounds of luggage, including beds and clothing, to each person over 8 years old and fifty pounds to those between 4 and 8 years old. The wagons were ordered from coach builders based in either Cincinnati or St. Louis and were conveyed by steamboat to the outfitting posts. The cattle and oxen were purchased from cattle dealers in the area and they were driven there. A full team consisted of a wagon, two yoke of oxen and two cows. The wagon-covers and tents were made of good quality English cotton which was supplied to the emigrants before their departure from Liverpool, so they could make their covers and tents during the voyage. The material was twenty-seven inches wide, and forty-four yards were used for a tent and twenty-six for a wagon cover. The total cost of cover and tent was about two guineas. The poles for the tent and the cords were obtained in the United States. Each wagon in 1854 for Perpetual Emigration Fund emigrants was supplied with one thousand pounds of flour, fifty pounds of sugar, fifty pounds of bacon, fifty pounds of rice, thirty pounds of beans, twenty pounds of dried apples and peaches, five pounds of tea, one gallon of vinegar, ten bars of soap, and twenty-five pounds of salt. Fresh milk was obtained from the cows, and meat in the diet depended upon the game which was caught on the journey across the plains. They were dependant upon the many streams for their water. Emigrants who were self financing purchased their own supplies.

As soon as a sufficient number of wagons were ready the company or companies headed west under their respective captains. The agent remained at the outfitting posts until all the companies had began their journeys and then he would go forward, passing each company and arrive in the Salt Lake Valley first to resume his responsibilities on their arrival in Salt Lake.

The transportation of the emigrant Latter-day Saints from Europe to Salt Lake required the labours of hundreds of individuals besides the emigrants themselves, which in the early years of emigration cost in the region of £40,000 to £50,000 per annum.

Shipping Lines

The church member emigrants' stay in Liverpool was usually shorter than other emigrants although when the Morris & Co. shipping line had the original church contract their organisation was not the best. It often meant that many church emigrants spent from a few days to a few weeks waiting for their passage.

In the late nineteenth century church members crossed the Atlantic using vessels owned and operated by the Guion Line, a British shipping company registered in Liverpool in 1866 as the Liverpool and Great Western Steamship Company and operated by two brothers Stephen and William Guion along with John Williams. Stephen Guion was an American who moved to Liverpool in 1851 to work for the Black Star Line, where he had previously partnered John Williams and William Guion, who specialised in emigrant passages between Liverpool to New York.

Once the Liverpool based Guion Line took over the church emigration business the waiting period was greatly reduced to only one or two days and the service they provided was exemplary. The Guion Line became the prominent and most popular shipping company to the Church carrying over forty thousand church emigrants from Liverpool to New York up to 1890 which was by far the majority of LDS steamship passengers in the nineteenth century. The successful partnership between the Latter-day Saints and the Guion Line lasted for a quarter of a century and the relationship of Guion agent George Ramsden with the Church was considered extraordinary.

The Guion's worked in conjunction with the Hull based Wilson Line which met the need for bringing thousands of Scandinavian church members through Hull then to Liverpool before engaging a Guion steamship across the Atlantic. The emigrants would travel from Hull to Liverpool by railway which the dual shipping lines, along with Mormon agents organised. There is an excellent study of transmigration through Hull of the Scandinavian Latter-day Saints by Fred Woods and Nicholas Evans that can be viewed and downloaded from the BYU Studies website at: www.byustudies.byu.edu/showTitle.aspx?title=6807

Perpetual Emigration Fund

Most converts were from poor backgrounds and the majority did not have sufficient funds to emigrate. The church encouraged individuals and families to save and those who accumulated surplus funds after emigrating were asked to assist fellow converts to do the same. The Church introduced the Perpetual Emigration Fund (PEF) in 1849 to provide emigrants with loans with the concept that recipients would repay the loan when in a position to do so. These loan repayments and additional contributions by members to the fund would then aid others to emigrate thus making the fund perpetual. In most cases the loans were made available to individuals with the skills that were needed to establish communities in America. Loans were also available to those who donated to the PEF which also included donors' families and friends, or to faithful Church members of ten years or more. Between 1852 and 1887 the PEF assisted some 26,000 immigrants which was around one-third of the total LDS emigrants from Europe during that period. In the earlier days there were three categories of emigrants:

1. Those who were independent and paid for themselves to reach their final destination
2. Those who could only afford to pay to reach their destination port and then hoped to work or raise enough money for their onward journey across America
3. Those who were assisted by the Perpetual Emigration Fund

After about 1870 private assistance began to replace the PEF in the amount of aid rendered to emigrating church members. In the late 1880s - 1890s it was estimated that between 20 to 50 percent of the emigrants each year received such assistance. Enthusiasm amongst church members towards emigration appeared to be at its height in 1855, during the Crimean War, because more Latter-day Saints emigrated from Europe in that year than during any other year. 4,225 emigrants to the United States were Latter-day Saints and this was at a time when the total number was relatively low. Church membership in Great Britain and on the Continent was then just under 35,000. The American Civil War period also saw another high in LDS emigration.

Because general church funds, including the waning Perpetual Emigration Fund, were insufficient to help all those who wished to emigrate, the church leaders both in Britain and America utilised many other facilities. The large number of emigrants in 1855 virtually exhausted both church and PEF funds. Salt Lake City real estate was sold with the proceeds applied to the emigration fund. More significantly handcarts rather than large wagons were used for the overland journeys albeit only from Iowa to Utah, effectively cutting the costs of transportation to allow funds to be redirected to the emigration effort. Such a decision was not without tragedy as more than two hundred lives were lost in two handcart companies of 1856, because they departed late in the season and were caught in early snowstorms.

Although the PEF continued to assist with transatlantic voyages it did so on a very limited basis after 1856 because it was felt that more aid should be used to help those emigrating saints on the overland portion of their journey from East Coast America to the Salt Lake Valley. The church devised a 'train' system in 1861 to take the members overland. Teams of men together with wagons, drawn mainly by oxen, gathered in Salt Lake City ready to be deployed in helping church members across America. These men received wages paid in goods from local church storehouses or they received a credit for their tithing to the church. The latter actually meant that the Church's tithing system heavily subsidised the operation which also needed to be intricately planned and actioned. The principles of the PEF made it necessary for members who benefited to 'repay the loan' but it often took emigrants years to pay their indebtedness for emigration, and many actually failed to complete payment. By 1887 only about one-third of the emigrants had paid their debt in full to the PEF, another third had paid part and the remainder had paid nothing.

After the completion of the transcontinental railroad on 10 May 1869, emigrants could make the trip from Liverpool, England, to Salt Lake City in just over three weeks whereas without the railroad, the journey by ship and wagon usually took about six months. The nearest junction of the railroad was at Promontory Summit which was located to the north of Salt Lake City. Despite the advantages of such a journey in relative comfort it cost more to reach Salt Lake. The PEF still provided for more than a hundred emigrants annually from Europe until about 1881.

Local church leaders played important roles in organising the emigration from Europe. Clerks in each congregation had custody of individual emigration savings accounts and these were forwarded to the mission headquarters. Information and an application was made to mission headquarters for those who wished to emigrate and were determined by local leaders to be deserving cases in need of PEF help. The system expanded the original idea set up in the early 1840s when the early church leaders organised the first emigrant companies.

Perpetual Emigration Fund Debtors Index

The index which can be accessed at **www.mormonhistoricfoundation.org** contains information from the published list of 19,000 debtors who owed around 1 million US dollars and is a useful source for genealogical research. The list of debtors was sent out to the individual congregations in 1878 with a request that those appearing on the list, or their children, should pay the debt in cash. Multiple entries exist in some cases for females whose names changed and for sureties. Amounts owed are not included. As with any index it should be treated only as a finding aid because names were not necessarily recorded or transcribed accurately or consistently even in the original list from which the index is formed.

Using the index in isolation may result in more questions than answers but it provides a 'snapshot' of complex situations relating to many British emigrants who, after arriving in the West, found new opportunities and economic challenges, not least of which was a scarcity of money. Many never escaped poverty and as such could not repay their debt. Repayment of travel loans was essential to maintain the rolling fund and its ability to help other church emigrants.

Care, Agnes: 1863
Careless, Eliza: 1862
Careswell, Alfred D.—
Anna, Joseph, Anna,
Charles, Alice, Harriet,
Alfred Jr: 1869
Carlgren, Lars—Lena: 1864
Carlin, Elizabeth: 1864
Carlin, John—Ann, Ann,
Jane, Margaret, James:
1864
Carlisle, Ann—Willard,
Joshua, Georgiana,
Elizabeth: 1866
Carlisle, Mary Emma: 1862
Carlisle, Mrs. John
(Elizabeth Hocquar):
1855
Carlisle, Samuel Jr: 1868
Carlsen, Johan: 1868
Carlsen, Jorgen P.—Anna
E., Else, Caroline, Carl:
1868
Carlson, Anna Mari: 1874
Carlson, Hans—Maren,
Berthi Marie, Peter: 1866
Carlson, Johanna—Anna,
Carl Peter, Christina C.,
Christine: 1864
Carlson, Kersti—Christiana:
1863
Carlson, Niels Christian—
Kersti, Johan: 1862
Carlson, Niels—Ingrid,
Carl, Isaac: 1866
Carlson, Ole—Anna,
Bertha, Anna Maria,
Maren: 1862
Carlson, Peter—Anna,
Hans, Elma, Mari,
Anders: 1862
Carpenter, William: 1862
Carpenter, William: 1864
Carr, George: 1866

Carter, Eliza—Emmanda:
1868
Carter, Ellen—John: 1856
Carter, George: 1863
Carter, James: 1861
Carter, Jane—Samuel,
Anna, Frederick, John:
1862
Carter, John: 1854
Carter, John—Mary, Mary
A., William H.: 1868
Carter, Thomas P.: 1862
Cartledge, Wm. R.: 1863
Carver, Mrs. John (Sarah A.
Eames): 1868
Case, Andrew—Mary, Mary
An., Henry, Alford,
Ellen, Hyrum, William,
Johannah Spurl: 1868

Ann Jones Cash

Cash, Ann—Mary Ellen:
1855
Cashman, James: 1862
Cashmore, Isaiah—(Wm.
H. Royal, surety): 1869

W. Davis): 1868
Catherson, Sarah—James:
1869
Cato, Eliza: 1862
Cato, Ellen—Rebecca: 1868
Catt, Stephen—Lydia: 1868
Cave, Lydia—Frederik: 1869
Cazier, William: 1857
Cederloff, John: 1866
Chadburn, Henry: 1869
Chadburn, John—Ellen:
1856
Chadwick, James: 1860
Chadwick, John Sr.—
Elizabeth, Elizabeth Jr,
Alice, William, James,
John, Thomas: 1869
Chadwick, Mrs. Abr. (Mary
Ann Newby): 1866
Chalice, John—Ann,
Alexander: 1868
Chalmers, Ann: 1868
Chalmers, Margaret—
Elizabeth, Jane, Mary:
1875
Chalsworth, Ellen: 1872
Chamberlain, Mrs. (Francis
Turner): 1868
Chambers, Brigham: 1869
Chambers, Francis—Janet,
Euphemia, James,
William, Mary, Henry,
Jane, John, Richard:
1866
Champneys, Thomas: 1875
Chandler, Elizabeth A.:
1861
Chandler, Frank: 1864
Chandler, Frank—Sarah,
Sarah: 1864
Chandler, Jane—George:
1873
Chandler, Rose: 1869
Chandler, Ruth: 1862

The Perpetual Emigration Fund Debtors index sometimes contains photographs (LDS Church Intellectual Reserve Inc).

In order to fully understand the list it should be noted that the majority of those shown owed money to the PEF for their own travel. Although many received aid for their sea voyages, the majority of help from the fund was for overland travel especially during the early years of its operation when emigrants needed to purchase wagons and oxen for their journeys. Those who had repaid their debt before 1877 are not listed. The index groups families and those who travelled as small groups as well as those who travelled alone. Some of those listed were the 'sureties,' which indicates they had an obligation to guarantee payment for someone else. In many cases, however, the sureties assumed, rightly or wrongly, that the responsibility for payment would rest with the travellers themselves and that they (the sureties) would never be called upon to discharge the debt. Those who stood as sureties included relatives and friends and it would be incorrect to assume that the sureties received funding from the PEF for themselves. Some individuals only owed the fund for the transportation of their belongings rather than for their own passage. The fact that many emigrants stopped at locations on the route west before continuing to Utah is one explanation for the fact that the year recorded in the list is different from the year they actually sailed.

The Emigration Process

The British or European missions were responsible for giving notice to the local congregations of planned departures, detailing the fare costs and providing information about items passengers should take with them on their journey. In advance of the allocated departure date passenger agents from the missions made sure that deposits were collected in order to reserve places on particular vessels. In doing so the church cut out the shipping agent and therefore the fares were cheaper as there was no commission paid for ticketing. The passenger agents from the mission also made arrangements for food provisions and helped in the allocation of the passengers' berths once they had boarded the ship.

On every voyage the agent ensured that provision was made for a dietary based upon the following amounts each week for either each adult or for two children up to the age of 12years. (Beyond this age children were treated as adults). 3.5 lbs of bread, 1.5 lbs of flour, 1.5 lbs of oatmeal, 1.5 lbs of rice,1.5 lbs of peas, 2 lbs of potatoes, 1.25 lbs of beef, 1 lb of pork, 1 lb of sugar, 2 oz of tea, 2 oz of salt, ½ oz of mustard, ¼ oz of pepper, 1 gill of vinegar. Each person was also allowed 3 quarts of water per day.

10 gallons of water was allocated per day for cooking, based upon 100 people.

Men travelling with each group were appointed as leaders for the ship and were responsible for the conduct, welfare and morale of the church passengers and also for administering the spiritual needs of the ships company whilst on the voyage including the holding of religious services. A typical daily routine on board ship included holding prayer meetings, washing the decks, cooking (usually in groups or co-operatives), and holding meetings to discuss and resolve any problems that arose.

Although the process of emigration was successful for most of the members the threat of illness and possibly even death on the journey was a real risk. Travel during the nineteenth century was neither easy nor safe and many of the emigrating church members fell victim to sickness, disease, and injury despite the system set up to look after them. A number died on route but deaths of Latter-day Saint emigrants were less than those found among other emigrant groups travelling in the same period.

The possibility of debilitating illness or death was never far from the minds of most church emigrants as they accepted the challenges of the journey to America. Indeed many had been informed of such tragedies amongst family and friends who had preceded them.

As the Saints travelled as a 'Church family' and were subject to leadership and more importantly a well-organised emigration system they impressed nonmember observers as being orderly and civilised compared with the turmoil and unrest which often surrounded life on an emigrant ship.

The following is an extract from the LDS *'Ensign'*, magazine of March 1980, entitled *'The Voyage of the Amazon'* which relates to Charles Dickens and his encounter with the Mormons. The full Dickens article features in *'All the Year Round'* a journal published by Dickens, under the title *'The Un-commercial Traveller of 1863.'*

In June of 1863 the *Amazon,* a passenger ship with 891 Latter-day Saints aboard, set sail from London. Just before the voyage, many Londoners (government officials and clergymen included) came for a first-hand look at the Mormons and their travelling arrangements. Among the visitors was author Charles Dickens, who spent several hours on board the ship questioning British Mission President George Q. Cannon and quietly observing the Saints.

A month later Dickens published an account of his visit to a Mormon emigrant ship. He pointed out that these were primarily working-class people, including craftsmen in many trades. Though he remained sceptical about what the Mormons would find when they reached Utah, Dickens was impressed by their thorough organisation, their calmness, and their quiet self-respect:

'I went on board their ship,' he said, 'to bear testimony against them if they deserved it, as I fully believed they would; to my great astonishment they did not deserve it; and my predispositions and tendencies must not affect me as an honest witness. I went over the Amazon's side feeling it impossible to deny that, so far, some remarkable influence had produced a remarkable result, which better known influences have often missed.' Of the people themselves Dickens wrote that had he not known they were Mormons, he would have described them as, 'in their degree, the pick and flower of England.'

The *'Edinburgh Review'* also carried an article in the January 1862 edition:

'The ordinary emigrant is exposed to all the chances and misadventures of a heterogeneous, childish, mannerless crowd during the voyage and to the merciless cupidity of land-sharks the moment he has touched the opposite shore. But the Mormon ship is a Family under strong and accepted discipline, with every provision for comfort, decorum, and internal peace. On his arrival in the New World the wanderer is received into a confraternity which speeds him onwards with as little hardship and anxiety as the circumstances permit and he is passed on from friend to friend, till he reaches the promised home'

As the passengers arrived in America, they were met by another church emigration agent who assisted them with arrangements for transportation to the frontier outfitting point where they remained encamped until all arrangements could be completed for their overland journey.

In 1854 the church agent and passenger-broker, Samuel W. Richards, gave evidence to a Parliamentary inquiry on how the church organised the mass emigration of its members. He described how the Church chartered its own ships, charging passengers a fare of £3.12s.6d from Liverpool to New Orleans, and £20 for the full journey to Salt Lake City. The journey to Utah from New Orleans consisted of a 1,300 mile trip by steamboat on the Mississippi to St. Louis, then a further 800 miles on the Missouri River to Council Bluffs. From Council Bluffs they joined the wagon trains along the 'Mormon Trail' to the Salt Lake Valley, some 1,030 miles across the Rocky Mountains.

On arrival in Utah church emigrants were integrated into LDS communities. Those who did not speak English were well catered for as the church produced publications in their native tongue. The church also came up with the idea of producing a phonetic alphabet to make life easier for those who only spoke a foreign language. Unfortunately the alphabet was short lived as most became fluent in English as they lived amongst the English speaking Saints and this also played a role in reducing ethnicity amongst the European emigrants.

Because of a degree of adverse publicity in the late 1880s, LDS immigration was frowned upon by many in the United States. Many emigrants were still assisted by the church although not so much financially as being given guidance by church leaders. Church emigrants were asked to keep a low profile and not to form into

Mormon emigrant companies. During the 1890s church leaders began to discourage emigration because of prevailing economic conditions and the need to rebuild significantly depleted membership in both Britain and Europe. Church emigration had virtually ceased by the time of the great depression. However, following World War Two there was a further period of church emigration but nothing on the scale of the mid to late 1800s. By the early 1960s (when statistics were no longer logged) several thousand church members from all over Europe had once again emigrated, joined by many from Canada, and even as far afield as Australasia. To some extent emigration took a reverse effect as Britain benefited from church members coming into the country from the West Indies particularly and thus strengthening the church congregations here.

Who were the first

The first group of British Mormons to reach America numbered 41 who sailed on the 'Britannia' out of Liverpool in June 1840, arriving in New York on 17 July of that year. Francis Moon was amongst that company and was one of the first to arrive in Nauvoo, Illinois. He declared it 'a promising new settlement full of opportunity'. Being favourably impressed he called for other members of the church in England to 'come and help great things to pass'. This immediately encouraged large numbers of British Mormons to 'up sticks' and settle in the USA. They came from branches of the church which had been established all over England and Wales and this emigration set a pattern for several forward decades. Besides expounding the economies of emigration, the church also set a religious tone and in 1841, the following was amongst many similar proclamations made by church leaders:

'Latter-day Saints - particularly the poor - would have greater economic opportunities and better chances to achieve their individual potential in Zion (American) than in Europe.'

The Britannia on which the first church members sailed from Liverpool tor America (Illustrated London News 1847).

Within a year, over a thousand had emigrated, with ships being chartered specifically for such purpose. Most sailed out of Liverpool but they also sailed from Bristol and London. The voyage from Britain to East Coast USA arriving mainly at New York or New Orleans was possibly the easiest part of the journey for there were many additional trials encountered by emigrants as they crossed the plains to reach Utah.

Nauvoo which was strategically placed and was situated some 200 miles south west of Chicago became the primary gathering place of British church emigrants. As a young town, it lacked industry and manufacturing enterprises so many of the emigrants could not work because there was nothing to enable them to use their skills. A suggestion was adopted that a joint stock co-operative be set up to supply all that was needed. Complications and mis-management meant however, that it never secured a useful purpose and it was wound up in 1846 without achieving its aims. Because of the hardship caused by the company's failure church leaders in England petitioned Queen Victoria, requesting government assistance allowing the poorer LDS members to emigrate and to procure land grants in America. Although not an unusual request, the British Colonial Office rejected the idea and the petition, signed originally by 13,000 LDS members was never the subject of Parliamentary discussion. This was of course considered a set-back however; undiscouraged the British Saints turned their energies to developing and strengthening the church in England. In the ensuing years from 1841 to 1851 the church experienced the largest numerical growth of the century establishing branches in many areas of the country.

In February 1848, it was announced that the new permanent headquarters of the LDS Church was to be in Salt Lake City in Utah. At Council Bluffs, Iowa, the church organised a transport system to enable the emigrants to continue their journey to Salt Lake City.

The ships that followed

The table below gives basic information about the emigrant ships which sailed with companies of church members, not just from Liverpool but from other parts of the world. They relate mainly to the 'age of sail' and cover the period of main emigration between 1840 and 1868 and from 1869 to 1899 for the age of steam when travel was much quicker. The schedules form the basis of the Worldwide LDS Ships database. Passenger lists and voyage information are available for all of these voyages and also information for passengers and ships entering New York can be supplemented by using the Castle Garden and Ellis Island databases detailed later.

Vessel	LDS Pass	Departed	Date	Arrived	Date	Leader
Britannia	41	Liverpool	6 Jun 1840	New York	20 Jul 1840	J. Moon
North America	201	Liverpool	8 Sep 1840	New York	12 Oct 1840	T. Turley
Isaac Newton	50	Liverpool	15 Oct 1840	New Orleans	2 Dec 1840	S. Mulliner
Sheffield	235	Liverpool	7 Feb 1841	New Orleans	30 Mar 1841	H. Clark
Caroline		Bristol	1841	New York	1841	T. Clark
Echo	109	Liverpool	16 Feb 1841	New Orleans	16 Apr 1841	D. Browett
Alesto	54	Liverpool	17 Mar 1841	New Orleans	16 May 1841	T. Smith
Rochester	130	Liverpool	21 Apr 1841	New York	20 May 1841	B. Young
Harmony	50	Bristol	10 May 1841	Quebec	12 Jul 1841	T. Kingston
Caroline	100	Bristol	8 Aug 1841	Quebec	22 Oct 1841	T. Richardson
Tyrean	207	Liverpool	21 Sep 1841	New Orleans	9 Nov 1841	J. Fielding
Chaos	170	Liverpool	8 Nov 1841	New Orleans	14 Jan 1842	P. Melling
Tremont	143	Liverpool	12 Jan 1842	New Orleans	10 Mar 1842	
Hope	270	Liverpool	5 Feb 1842	New Orleans	1 Apr 1842	J. Burnham
John Cumming	200	Liverpool	20 Feb 1842	New Orleans	26 Apr 1842	
Hanover	200	Liverpool	12 Mar 1842	New Orleans	2 May 1842	A. Fielding
Sidney	180	Liverpool	17 Sep 1842	New Orleans	11 Nov 1842	L. Richards
Medford	214	Liverpool	25 Sep 1842	New Orleans	13 Nov 1842	O. Hyde
Henry	157	Liverpool	29 Sep 1842	New Orleans	10 Nov 1842	J. Snyder
Emerald	250	Liverpool	29 Oct 1842	New Orleans	5 Jan 1843	P. Pratt
Swanton	212	Liverpool	16 Jan 1843	New Orleans	16 Mar 1843	L. Snow
Yorkshire	83	Liverpool	8 Mar 1843	New Orleans	10 May 1843	T. Rullock
Claiborne	106	Liverpool	21 Mar 1843	New Orleans	13 May 1843	---
Metoka	280	Liverpool	5 Sep 1843	New Orleans	27 Oct 1843	---
Champion	91	Liverpool	21 Oct 1843	New Orleans	6 Dec 1843	---
Fanny	210	Liverpool	23 Jan 1844	New Orleans	7 Mar 1844	W. Kay
Isaac Allerton	60	Liverpool	6 Feb 1844	New Orleans	22 Mar 1844	---
Swanton	81	Liverpool	11 Feb 1844	New Orleans	5 Apr 1844	---
Glasgow	150	Liverpool	5 Mar 1844	New Orleans	13 Apr 1844	H. Clark
Norfolk	143	Liverpool	19 Sep 1844	New Orleans	11 Nov 1844	---
Palymyra	200	Liverpool	17 Jan 1845	New Orleans	11 Mar 1845	A. Fielding
Parthenon	10	Liverpool	30 Mar 1845	New Orleans	12 May 1845	---
Oregon	125	Liverpool	1 Sep 1845	New Orleans	28 Oct 1845	---
Liverpool	45	Liverpool	16 Jan 1846	New Orleans	25 Mar 1846	H. Clark
Brooklyn	235	New York	4 Feb 1846	San Francisco	31 July 1846	S. Brannan
Montezuma	10	Liverpool	15 Aug 1846	New York	17 Sep 1846	---
America	50	Liverpool	1 Feb 1847	New Orleans	10 Mar 1847	J. Taylor
Empire	24	Liverpool	6 Jul 1847	New Orleans	10 Aug 1847	L. Scovil
Carnatic	120	Liverpool	20 Feb 1848	New Orleans	19 Apr 1848	F. Richards

47

Vessel	LDS Pass	Departed	Date	Arrived	Date	Leader
Sailor Prince	80	Liverpool	9 Mar 1848	New Orleans	28 Apr 1848	M. Martin
Erin's Queen	232	Liverpool	7 Sep 1848	New Orleans	28 Oct 1848	S. Carter
Sailor Prince	311	Liverpool	24 Sep 1848	New Orleans	20 Nov 1848	L. Butler
Lord Sandon	11	Liverpool	30 Dec 1848	New Orleans	17 Feb 1849	---
Zetland	358	Liverpool	29 Jan 1849	New Orleans	2 Apr 1849	O. Spencer
Ashland	187	Liverpool	6 Feb 1849	New Orleans	18 Apr 1849	J. Johnson
Henry Ware	225	Liverpool	7 Feb 1849	New Orleans	8 Apr 1849	R. Martin
Buena Vista	249	Liverpool	25 Feb 1849	New Orleans	19 Apr 1849	D. Jones
Hartley	220	Liverpool	5 Mar 1849	New Orleans	28 Apr 1849	W. Hulme
Emblem	100	Liverpool	12 Mar 1849	New Orleans	4 May 1849	R. Deans
James Pennell	236	Liverpool	2 Sep 1849	New Orleans	22 Oct 1849	T. Clark
Berlin	253	Liverpool	5 Sep 1849	New Orleans	22 Oct 1849	J. Brown
Zetland	250	Liverpool	11 Sep 1849	New Orleans	24 Oct 1849	S. Hawkins
Argo	402	Liverpool	10 Jan 1850	New Orleans	8 Mar 1850	J. Clinton
Josiah Bradlee	263	Liverpool	18 Feb 1850	New Orleans	18 Apr 1850	T. Day
Hartley	109	Liverpool	2 Mar 1850	New Orleans	2 May 1850	D. Cook
North Atlantic	357	Liverpool	4 Sep 1850	New Orleans	1 Nov 1850	D. Sudworth
James Pennell	254	Liverpool	2 Oct 1850	New Orleans	22 Nov 1850	C. Layton
Joseph Badger	227	Liverpool	17 Oct 1850	New Orleans	22 Nov 1850	J. Morris
Ellen	466	Liverpool	8 Jan 1851	New Orleans	14 Mar 1841	J. Cummings
George Bourne	281	Liverpool	22 Jan 1851	New Orleans	20 Mar 1851	W. Gibson
Ellen Maria	378	Liverpool	2 Feb 1851	New Orleans	6 Apr 1851	G. Watt
Olympus	245	Liverpool	4 Mar 1851	New Orleans	27 Apr 1851	W. Howell
Kennebec	333	Liverpool	10 Jan 1852	New Orleans	14 Mar 1852	J. Higbee
Ellen Maria	369	Liverpool	10 Feb 1852	New Orleans	5 Apr 1852	I. Haight
Niagara	20	Liverpool	6 Mar 1852	Boston	19 Mar 1852	J. Taylor
Rockaway	30	Liverpool	6 Mar 1852	New Orleans	25 Apr 1852	E. Morris
Italy	28	Liverpool	11 Mar 1852	New Orleans	10 May 1852	O. Menster
Forest Monarch	297	Liverpool	16 Jan 1853	New Orleans	16 Mar 1853	J. Forsgren
Ellen Maria	332	Liverpool	17 Jan 1853	New Orleans	6 Mar 1853	M. Clawson
Golconda	321	Liverpool	23 Jan 1853	New Orleans	26 Mar 1853	J. Gates
Jersey	314	Liverpool	5 Feb 1853	New Orleans	21 Mar 1853	G. Halliday
Elvira Owen	345	Liverpool	15 Feb 1853	New Orleans	31 Mar 1853	J. Young
International	425	Liverpool	28 Feb 1853	New Orleans	23 Apr 1853	C. Arthur
Falcon	324	Liverpool	26 Mar 1853	New Orleans	81 May 1853	C. Bagnall
Gamillus	228	Liverpool	6 Apr 1853	New Orleans	7 Jun 1853	C. Bolton
Envelope	30	Sydney	6 Apr 1853	San Francisco	8 Jul 1853	C. Wandell
R. K. Page	17	Liverpool	1 Sep 1853	New Orleans	28 Oct 1853	Bender
Jessie Munn	335	Liverpool	3 Jan 1854	New Orleans	20 Feb 1854	C. Larsen

Vessel	LDS Pass	Departed	Date	Arrived	Date	Leader
Benjamin Adams	384	Liverpool	28 Jan 1854	New Orleans	22 Mar 1854	H. Olsen
Golconda	464	Liverpool	4 Feb 1854	New Orleans	18 Mar 1854	D. Curtis
Windermere	477	Liverpool	22 Feb 1854	New Orleans	24 Apr 1854	D. Garn
Old England	45	Liverpool	5 Mar 1854	New Orleans	26 Apr 1854	J. Angus
John M. Wood	397	Liverpool	12 Mar 1854	New Orleans	2 May 1854	R. Campbell
Julia Ann	63	Newcastle	22 Mar 1854	San Pedro	12 Jun 1854	W. Hyde
Germanicus	220	Liverpool	4 Apr 1854	New Orleans	12 Jun 1854	R. Cook
Marshfield	366	Liverpool	8 Apr 1854	New Orleans	29 May 1854	W. Taylor
Martha Whitmore	10	Liverpool	1854	New Orleans	1854	---
Clara Wheeler	29	Liverpool	24 Apr 1854	New Orleans	3 Jul 1854	---
Clara Wheeler	422	Liverpool	24 Nov 1854	New Orleans	11 Jan 1855	H. Phelps
Rockaway	24	Liverpool	6 Jan 1855	New Orleans	26 Feb 1855	S. Glasgow
James Nesmith	440	Liverpool	7 Jan 1855	New Orleans	23 Feb 1855	P. Hansen
Neva	13	Liverpool	9 Jan 1855	New Orleans	22 Feb 1855	T. Jackson
Charles Buck	403	Liverpool	17 Jan 1855	New Orleans	14 Mar 1855	R. Ballantyne
Isaac Jeanes	16	Liverpool	3 Feb 1855	Philadelphia	5 Mar 1855	G. Riser
Siddons	430	Liverpool	27 Feb 1855	Philadelphia	20 Apr 1855	J. Fullmer
Juventa	573	Liverpool	31 Mar 1855	Philadelphia	5 May 1855	W. Glover
Chimborazo	431	Liverpool	17 Apr 1855	Philadelphia	22 May 1855	E. Stevenson
S. Curling	581	Liverpool	22 Apr 1855	New York	22 May 1855	I. Barlow
Tarquinia	72	Melbourn	27 Apr 1855	Honolulu	5 July 1855	B. Frost
William Stetson	293	Liverpool	26 Apr 1855	New York	27 May 1855	A. Smethurst
Frank Johnson	10	Calcutta	29 May 1855	San Francisco	81 Sep 1855	---
Cynosure	159	Liverpool	29 Jul 1855	New York	5 Sep 1855	G. Seager
Julia Ann	28	Sydney	7 Sep 1855	Wrecked		J. Penfield
Emerald Isle	350	Liverpool	30 Nov 1855	New York	29 Dec 1855	P. Merrill
John J. Boyd	512	Liverpool	12 Dec 1855	New York	16 Feb 1856	K. Peterson
Caravan	457	Liverpool	14 Feb 1856	New York	27 Mar 1856	D. Tyler
Enoch Train	534	Liverpool	23 Mar 1856	Boston	1 May 1856	J. Ferguson
S. Curling	707	Liverpool	19 Apr 1856	Boston	23 May 1856	D. Jones
Thornton	764	Liverpool	4 May 1856	New York	14 Jun 1856	J. Willie
G. W. Kendall	9	Tahiti	5 May 1856	San Francisco	27 Jun 1856	Anderson
Horizon	856	Liverpool	25 May 1856	Boston	20 Jun 1856	E. Martin
Jenny Ford	20	Sydney	5-28-56	San Pedro	15 Aug 1856	A. Farnham
Wellfleet	146	Liverpool	31 May 1856	Boston	13 Jul 1856	J. Aubrey
Lucy Thompson	14	Liverpool	5 Jul 1856	New York	8 Aug 1856	J. Thompson
Columbia	223	Liverpool	18 Nov 1856	New York	1 Jan 1857	J. Williams
Escort	10	Calcutta	10 Dec 1856	New York	3 Mar 1857	M. McCune
George Washington	817	Liverpool	28 Mar 1857	Boston	20 Apr 1857	J. Park

Vessel	LDS Pass	Departed	Date	Arrived	Date	Leader
Westmoreland	544	Liverpool	25 Apr 1857	Philadelphia	31 May 1857	M. Cowley
Tuscarora	547	Liverpool	30 May 1857	Philadelphia	3 Jul 1857	R. Harper
Lucas	69	Sydney	27 Jun 1857	San Pedro	8 Oct 1857	W. Wall
Wyoming	36	Liverpool	18 Jul 1857	Philadelphia	3 Sep 1857	C. Harmon
Underwriter	25	Liverpool	21 Jan 1858	New York	11 Mar 1858	H. Harriman
Empire (II)	64	Liverpool	19 Feb 1858	New York	19 Mar 1858	J. Hobson
John Bright	89	Liverpool	22 Mar 1858	New York	23 Apr 1858	I. Iversen
Milwaukie	10	Melbourne	28 Dec 1858	San Francisco	18 Mar 1859	---
Gemsbok	5	Pt. Elizabeth	22 Jan 1859	Boston	18 Mar 1859	---
Alacrity	28	Pt. Elizabeth	9 Mar 1859	Boston	19 May 1859	J. Humphreys
William Tapscott	725	Liverpool	11 Apr 1859	New York	14 May 1849	R. Neslen
Antarctic	30	Liverpool	10 Jul 1859	New York	21 Aug 1859	J. Chaplow
Emerald Isle	54	Liverpool	20 Aug 1859	New York	1 Oct 1859	H. Hug
Underwriter	594	Liverpool	30 Mar 1860	New York	1 May 1860	J. Ross
William Tapscott	730	Liverpool	11 May 1860	New York	15 Jun 1860	A. Calkin
Manchester	379	Liverpool	16 Apr 1861	New York	14 May 1861	C. Spencer
Underwriter	624	Liverpool	23 Apr 1861	New York	22 May 1861	M. Andrus
Monarch of the Sea	955	Liverpool	16 May 1861	New York	19 Jun 1861	J. Woodward
Humboldt	323	Hamburg	9 Apr 1862	New York	20 May 1862	H. Hansen
Franklin	413	Hamburg	15 Apr 1862	New York	29 May 1862	C. Madsen
Electric	336	Hamburg	18 Apr 1862	New York	5 Jun 1862	S. Christoffersen
Athena	484	Hamburg	21 Apr 1862	New York	7 Jun 1862	O. Liljenquist
John J. Boyd	702	Liverpool	23 Apr 1862	New York	1 Jun 1862	J. Brown
Manchester	376	Liverpool	6 May 1862	New York	12 Jun 1862	J. McAllister
William Tapscott	807	Liverpool	14 May 1862	New York	25 Jun 1862	W. Gibson
Windermere	110	Le Havre	15 May 1862	New York	8 Jul 1862	S. Ballif
Antarctic	38	Liverpool	18 May 1862	New York	27 Jun 1862	W. Moody
Rowena	15	Pt. Elizabeth	14 Mar 1863	New York	22 May 1863	R. Grant
Henry Ellis	32	Pt. Elizabeth	31 Mar 1863	New York	28 May 1863	Stock and Zyderlaam
John J. Boyd	767	Liverpool	30 Apr 1863	New York	29 May 1863	W. Cluff
B.S. Kimball	657	Liverpool	8 May 1863	New York	15 Jun 1863	H. Lund
Consignment	38	Liverpool	8 May 1863	New York	20 Jun 1863	A. Christensen
Antarctic	486	Liverpool	23 May 1863	New York	10 Jul 1863	J. Needham
Cynosure	775	Liverpool	30 May 1863	New York	19 Jul 1863	D. Stuart
Amazon	895	London	4 Jun 1863	New York	18 Jul 1863	W. Bramhall
Echo	9	Pt. Elizabeth	5 Apr 1864	Boston	12 Jun 1864	J. Talbot
Susan Pardew	18	Pt. Elizabeth	10 Apr 1864	Boston	11 Jun 1864	W. Fotheringham
Monarch of the Sea	974	Liverpool	28 Apr 1864	New York	3 Jun 1864	J. Smith

Vessel	LDS Pass	Departed	Date	Arrived	Date	Leader
General McClennan	802	Liverpool	21 May 1864	New York	23 Jun 1864	T. Jeremy
Hudson	863	London	3 Jun 1864	New York	19 Jul 1864	J. Kay
Mexicana	47	Pt. Elizabeth	12 Apr 1865	New York	18 Jun 1865	M. Atwood
Belle Wood	636	Liverpool	20 Apr 1865	New York	31 May 1865	W. Shearman
B.S. Kimball	558	Hamburg	8 May 1865	New York	14 Jun 1865	A. Winberg
David Hoadley	24	Liverpool	10 May 1865	New York	19 Jun 1865	W. Underwood
Bridgewater	7	Liverpool	7 Jun 1865	New York	14 Jul 1865	---
Albert	15	Melbourne	17 Oct 1865	San Francisco	26 Jan 1866	J. Spencer
John Bright	747	Liverpool	30 Apr 1866	New York	6 Jun 1866	C. Gillet
Caroline	389	London	5 May 1866	New York	11 Jun 1866	S. Hill
American Congress	350	London	23 May 1866	New York	4 Jul 1866	J. Nicholson
Kenilworth	684	Hamburg	25 May 1866	New York	16 Jul 1866	S. Sprague
Arkwright	450	Liverpool	30 May 1866	New York	6 Jul 1866	J. Wixom
Cornelius Grinnell	26	London	20 May 1866	New York	11 Jul 1866	R. Harrison
Cavour	201	Hamburg	1 Jun 1866	New York	31 Jul 1866	N. Nielsen
Humboldt	328	Hamburg	2 Jun 1866	New York	18 Jul 1866	G. Brown
St. Mark	104	Liverpool	6 Jun 1866	New York	24 Jul 1866	A. Stevens
Hudson	20	London	1 Jun 1867	New York	19 Jul 1867	---
Manhattan	482	Liverpool	21 Jun 1867	New York	4 Jul 1867	A. Hill
John Bright	720	Liverpool	4 Jun 1868	New York	13 Jul 1868	J. McGaw
Emerald Isle	876	Liverpool	20 Jun 1868	New York	14 Aug 1868	H. Hals
Constitution	457	Liverpool	24 Jun 1868	New York	5 Aug 1868	H. Cluff
Minnesota	534	Liverpool	30 Jun 1868	New York	12 Jul 1868	J. Parry
Colorado	600	Liverpool	14 Jul 1868	New York	28 Jul 1868	W. Preston
Minnesota		Liverpool	2 Jun 1869	New York	15 Jun 1869	E. Morris
Minnesota		Liverpool	15 July 1869	New York	28 July 1869	G. Olsen
Colorado		Liverpool	28 July 1869	New York	10 Aug 1869	J. Pace
Minnesota		Liverpool	25 Aug 1869	New York	6 Sept 1869	M. Ensign
Manhattan		Liverpool	22 Sept 1869	New York	7 Oct 1869	J. Lawson
Minnesota		Liverpool	10 Oct 1869	New York	18 Oct 1869	J. Needham
Colorado		Liverpool	20 Oct 1869	New York	1 Nov 1869	G. Wilden
Colorado		Liverpool	28 Jun 1870	New York	12 July 1870	A. Carrington
Manhattan		Liverpool	13 July 1870	New York	26 July 1870	K. Maeser
Minnesota		Liverpool	20 July 1870	New York	1 Aug 1870	J. Smith
Idaho		Liverpool	7 Sept 1870	New York	22 Sept 1870	F. Hyde
Nevada		Liverpool	14 Sept 1870	New York	26 Sept 1870	D. Walter
Manhattan		Liverpool	16 Nov 1870	New York	2 Dec 1870	R. Thompson
Wisconsin		Liverpool	22 Mar 1871	New York	3 Apr 1871	
Wisconsin		Liverpool	28 Apr 1871	New York	9 May 1871	

Vessel	LDS Pass	Departed	Date	Arrived	Date	Leader
Wyoming		Liverpool	10 May 1871	New York	22 May 1871	J. Parry
Wyoming		Liverpool	21 Jun 1871	New York	3 July 1871	G. Lake
Minnesota		Liverpool	28 Jun 1871	New York	12 July 1871	W. Cluff
Wonga Wonga		Honolulu	4 July 1871	San Francisco	8 July 1871	E. Kearsley
Colorado		Liverpool	12 July 1871	New York	25 July 1871	H. Park
Nevada		Liverpool	26 July 1871	New York	7 Aug 1871	L. Smith
Minnesota		Liverpool	9 Aug 1871	New York	21 Aug 1871	W. Douglass
Nevada		Liverpool	6 Sept 1871	New York	18 Sept 1871	J. Hart
Nevada		Liverpool	18 Oct 1871	New York	7 Nov 1871	G. Peterson
Nevada		Auckland	20 Dec 1871	San Francisco	7 Jan 1872	
Manhattan		Liverpool	12 Jun 1872	New York	27 Jun 1872	D. Brinton
Nevada		Liverpool	26 Jun 1872	New York	9 July 1872	E. Peterson
Wisconsin		Liverpool	31 July 1872	New York	13 Aug 1872	G. Ward
Minnesota		Liverpool	4 Sept 1872	New York	17 Sept 1872	G. Wilkins
Minnesota		Liverpool	16 Oct 1872	New York	29 Oct 1872	T. Dobson
Nevada		Liverpool	6 Nov 1872	Queenstown	(see note)	
Manhattan		Liverpool	4 Dec 1872	New York	23 Dec 1872	D. Kennedy
Nevada		Liverpool	4 Jun 1873	New York	16 Jun 1873	C. Wilchen
Wisconsin		Liverpool	2 July 1873	New York	15 July 1873	D. Calder
Nevada		Liverpool	9 July 1873	New York	23 July 1873	E. Box
Wyoming		Liverpool	3 Sept 1873	New York	19 Sept 1873	J. Fairbanks
Idaho		Liverpool	22 Oct 1873	New York	5 Nov 1873	J. Hart
Nevada		Liverpool	6 May 1874	New York	21 May 1874	L. Herrick
Nevada		Liverpool	10 Jun 1874	New York	23 Jun 1874	J. Birch
Idaho		Liverpool	24 Jun 1874	New York	6 July 1874	P. Carstensen
Minnesota		Liverpool	8 July 1874	New York	21 July 1874	J. Keller
Wyoming		Liverpool	2 Sept 1874	New York	14 Sept 1874	J. Graham
Wyoming		Liverpool	13 Oct 1874	New York	26 Oct 1874	W. Fife
Wyoming		Liverpool	12 May 1875	New York	24 May 1874	H. Gowans
Wisconsin		Liverpool	16 Jun 1875	New York	28 Jul 1875	R. Burton
Idaho		Liverpool	30 Jun 1875	New York	14 July 1875	C. Larsen
Wyoming		Liverpool	15 Sept 1875	New York	27 Sept 1875	R. Morris
Dakota		Liverpool	13 Oct 1875	New York	26 Oct 1875	B. Eardley
Montana		Liverpool	19 Jan 1876	New York	1 Feb 1876	I. Coombs
Nevada		Liverpool	24 May 1876	New York	5 Jun 1876	J. Woodhouse
Idaho		Liverpool	28 Jun 1876	New York	10 July 1876	N. Flygare
Nevada		Liverpool	23 Aug 1876	New York	5 Sept 1876	
Wyoming		Liverpool	13 Sept 1876	New York	25 Sept 1876	W. Binder
Wyoming		Liverpool	25 Oct 1876	New York	4 Nov 1876	P. Barton

52

Vessel	LDS Pass	Departed	Date	Arrived	Date	Leader
Wisconsin		Liverpool	4 Jan 1877	New York	25 Jan 1877	J. Wilson
Wyoming		Liverpool	13 Jun 1877	New York	23 Jun 1877	D. Udall
Wisconsin		Liverpool	27 Jun 1877	New York	7 July 1877	J. Rowberry
Wyoming		Liverpool	25 July 1877	New York	4 Aug 1877	
Wisconsin		Liverpool	19 Sept 1877	New York	29 Sept 1877	H. Park
Idaho		Liverpool	17 Oct 1877	New York	29 Oct 1877	W. Paxman
Montana		Liverpool	7 Nov 1877	New York	22 Nov 1877	
Wyoming		Liverpool	8 Dec 1877	New York	19 Dec 1877	
Nevada		Liverpool	25 May 1878	New York	5 Jun 1878	T. Judd
Montana		Liverpool	15 Jun 1878	New York	26 Jun 1878	T. Brandley
Nevada		Liverpool	29 Jun 1878	New York	16 July 1878	J. Cook
Wyoming		Liverpool	14 Sept 1878	New York	25 Sept 1878	H. Naisbitt
Nevada		Liverpool	21 Sept 1878	New York	3 Oct 1878	J. Christensen
Wyoming		Liverpool	19 Oct 1878	New York	29 Oct 1878	A. Milner
Malay		Sydney	21 Feb 1879	San Francisco	11 May 1879	
Wyoming		Liverpool	19 Apr 1879	New York	30 Apr 1879	C. Nibley
Wyoming		Liverpool	24 May 1879	New York	3 Jun 1879	A. McDonald
Montana		Liverpool	21 Jun 1879	New York	2 Jul 1879	
Wyoming		Liverpool	28 Jun 1879	New York	9 Jul 1879	W. Williams
Montana		Liverpool	30 Aug 1879	New York	10 Sept 1879	
Wyoming		Liverpool	6 Sept 1879	New York	16 Sept 1879	N. Flygare
Arizona		Liverpool	18 Oct 1879	New York	28 Oct 1879	W. Bramhall
Wyoming		Liverpool	10 Apr 1880	New York	21 Apr 1880	J. Bunting
Nevada		Liverpool	17 Apr 1880	New York	April 1880	
Wisconsin		Liverpool	1 May 1880	New York	12 May 1880	
Arizona		Liverpool	8 May 1880	New York	17 May 1880	
Wyoming		Liverpool	15 May 1880	New York	25 May 1880	
Wisconsin		Liverpool	5 Jun 1880	New York	16 Jun 1880	J. Jones
Australia		Honolulu	13 July 1880	San Francisco	15 July 1880	L Higglan
Nevada		Liverpool	26 Jun 1880	New York	9 July 1880	
Wisconsin		Liverpool	10 July 1880	New York	21 July 1880	N. Rasmussen
Nevada		Liverpool	4 Sept 1880	New York	16 Sept 1880	J. Rider
Arizona		Liverpool	25 Sept 1880	New York	4 Oct 1880	
Wisconsin		Liverpool	23 Oct 1880	New York	3 Nov 1880	J. Nicholson
Wyoming		Liverpool	16 Apr 1881	New York	27 Apr 1881	D. Dunbar
Arizona		Liverpool	23 Apr 1881	New York	2 May 1881	
City of Sydney		Auckland	26 Apr 1881	San Francisco	17 May 1881	G. Batt
Wyoming		Liverpool	21 May 1881	New York	1 Jun 1881	J. Matthews
Nevada		Liverpool	11 Jun 1881	New York	23 Jun 1881	R. Runolfsen

53

Vessel	LDS Pass	Departed	Date	Arrived	Date	Leader
Wyoming		Liverpool	25 Jun 1881	New York	7 July 1881	S. Roskelley
Nevada		Liverpool	16 July 1881	New York	28 July 1881	J. Eyvindson
Wyoming		Liverpool	3 Sept 1881	New York	13 Sept 1881	J. Finlayson
Wisconsin		Liverpool	22 Oct 1881	New York	2 Nov 1881	L. Martineau
Wyoming		Liverpool	12 Nov 1881	New York	26 Nov 1881	
Wisconsin		Liverpool	7 Jan 1882	New York	19 Jan 1882	
Nevada		Liverpool	12 Apr 1882	New York	24 Apr 1882	J. Donaldson
Arizona		Liverpool	22 Apr 1882	New York	5 May 1882	
Alaska		Liverpool	13 May 1882	New York	21 May 1882	N. Farr
Nevada		Liverpool	17 May 1882	New York	29 May 1882	W. Webb
Abyssinia		Liverpool	3 Jun 1882	New York	17 Jun 1882	J. Fearn
Wisconsin		Liverpool	10 Jun 1882	New York	21 Jun 1882	J. Taylor
Nevada		Liverpool	21 Jun 1882	New York	3 July 1882	R. Irvine
Arizona		Liverpool	3 July 1882	New York	11 July 1882	J. Howell
Alaska		Liverpool	22 July 1882	New York	31 July 1882	S. Langdon
Wyoming		Liverpool	2 Sept 1882	New York	12 Sept 1882	W. Cooper
Arizona		Liverpool	9 Sept 1882	New York	18 Sept 1882	D. Moses
Wyoming		Liverpool	7 Oct 1882	New York	19 Oct 1882	A. Ballard
Abyssinia		Liverpool	21 Oct 1882	New York	4 Nov 1882	G. Stringfellow
Alaska		Liverpool	4 Nov 1882	New York	14 Nov 1882	N. Fransden
Abyssinia		Liverpool	25 Nov 1882	New York	7 Dec 1882	L. Spangberg
Abyssinia		Liverpool	30 Dec 1882	New York	15 Jan 1883	C. Smurthwaite
Wisconsin		Liverpool	6 Jan 1883	New York	22 Jan 1883	I. Bowler
Alaska		Liverpool	20 Jan 1883	New York	31 Jan 1883	D. Burnett
Nevada		Liverpool	11 Apr 1883	New York	23 Apr 1883	D. McKay
Nevada		Liverpool	16 May 1883	New York	28 may 1883	B. Rich
Alaska		Liverpool	2 Jun 1883	New York	11 Jun 1883	B. Bjarnason
Arizona		Liverpool	16 Jun 1883	New York	28 Jun 1883	W. Grosebeck
Nevada		Liverpool	20 Jun 1883	New York	2 July 1883	H. Magleby
Abyssinia		Liverpool	23 Jun 1883	New York	5 July 1883	R. Anderson
Wisconsin		Liverpool	14 July 1883	New York	25 July 1883	J. Sutton
Abyssinia		Liverpool	28 July 1883	New York	8 Aug 1883	J. Olsen
Alaska		Liverpool	11 Aug 1883	New York	20 Aug 1883	J. Watt
Nevada		Liverpool	29 Aug 1883	New York	10 Sept 1883	P. Goss
Abyssinia		Liverpool	1Sept 1883	New York	12 Sept 1883	J. Bird
Oregon		Liverpool	6 Oct 1883	New York	18 Oct 1883	J. Barber
Wisconsin		Liverpool	27 Oct 1883	New York	7 Nov 1883	J. Pickett
Arizona		Liverpool	3 Nov 1883	New York	12 Nov 1883	
Wisconsin		Liverpool	1 Dec 1883	New York	11 Dec 1883	J. Volker

Vessel	LDS Pass	Departed	Date	Arrived	Date	Leader
Wyoming		Liverpool	22 Dec 1883	New York	2 Jan 1884	W. F. Smith
Nevada		Liverpool	29 Dec 1883	New York	10 Jan 1884	W. Reeves
Wisconsin		Liverpool	4 Jan 1884	New York	17 Jan 1884	G. Barber
Wyoming		Liverpool	26 Jan 1884	New York	8 Feb 1884	N. Giles
Arizona		Liverpool	16 Feb 1884	New York	26 Feb 1884	J. Wild
Nevada		Liverpool	9 Apr 1884	New York	21 Apr 1884	F. Jeldsted
Arizona		Liverpool	17 May 1884	New York	26 May 1884	E. Williams
Wyoming		Liverpool	7 Jun 1884	New York		J. Cannon
Arizona		Liverpool	14 Jun 1884	New York	23 Jun 1884	E. Nye
Alaska		Liverpool	21 Jun 1884	New York	30 Jun 1884	J. Evans
City of Chester		Liverpool	24 Jun 1884	New York	5 July 1884	N. Anderson
Wisconsin		Liverpool	5 July 1884	New York	16 July 1884	
Australia		New Zealand	22 July 1884	San Francisco	11 Aug 1884	
Wyoming		Liverpool	26 July 1884	New York	6 Aug 1884	
Nevada		Liverpool	2 Aug 1884	New York	13 Aug 1884	H. Attley
Wyoming		Liverpool	30 Aug 1884	New York	10 Sept 1884	B. Bennett
Wisconsin		Liverpool	24 Sept 1884	New York	9 Oct 1884	? Dawson (Mrs)
Alaska		Liverpool	11 Oct 1884	New York	20 Oct 1884	W. Pack Jr.
City of Berlin		Liverpool	23 Oct 1884	New York	3 Nov 1884	C. Ek
Arizona		Liverpool	1 Nov 1884	New York	11 Nov 1884	J. Smith
Arizona		Liverpool	6 Dec 1884	New York	16 Dec 1884	
Wisconsin		Liverpool	27 Dec 1884	New York	8 Jan 1885	
Alaska		Liverpool	24 Jan 1885	New York	9 Feb 1885	J. H. Smith
Wisconsin		Liverpool	11 Apr 1885	New York	22 Apr 1885	L. Lund
Wisconsin		Liverpool	16 May 1885	New York	27 May 1885	N. Hodges
Wyoming		Liverpool	23 May 1885	New York	3 Jun 1885	J. Jennings
Wisconsin		Liverpool	20 Jun 1885	New York	1 July 1885	J. Hansen
Wyoming		Liverpool	27 Jun 1885	New York	8 July 1885	J. Morgan
Wyoming		Liverpool	1 Aug 1885	New York	11 Aug 1885	J. Bjarnason
Abyssinia		Liverpool	20 Aug 1885	New York	28 Aug 1885	S. Erickson
Wisconsin		Liverpool	29 Aug 1885	New York	9 Sept 1885	J. Thornley
Nevada		Liverpool	19 Sept 1885	New York		F. Jensen
Nevada		Liverpool	22 Oct 1885	New York	5 Nov 1885	A. Lund
Nevada		Liverpool	16 Apr 1886	New York	27 Apr 1886	E. Woolley
Arizona		Liverpool	15 May 1886	New York	24 May 1886	I. Gadd
Nevada		Liverpool	22 May 1886	New York	1 Jun 1886	M. Pratt
Mararoa		Honolulu	June 1886	San Francisco	14 Jun 1886	
Nevada		Liverpool	26 Jun 1886	New York	7 July 1886	C. Olsen
Alaska		Liverpool	10 July 1886	New York	19 July 1886	Icelandic Members

Vessel	LDS Pass	Departed	Date	Arrived	Date	Leader
Wyoming		Liverpool	21 Aug 1886	New York	31 Aug 1886	D. Kunz
Wisconsin		Liverpool	Sept 1886	New York	23 Sept 1886	
British King		Liverpool	13 Oct 1886	Philadelphia	27 Oct 1886	J. Green
Nevada		Liverpool	16 Apr 1887	New York	28 Apr 1887	D. Callister
Nevada		Liverpool	21 May 1887	New York	1 Jun 1887	E. Davis
Wyoming		Liverpool	3 Jun 1887	New York	15 Jun 1887	J. Nielson
Wisconsin		Liverpool	18 Jun 1887	New York	29 Jun 1887	Q. Nicholas
Mariposa		Honolulu	1 July 1887	California	9 July 1887	J. Smith
Wisconsin		Liverpool	27 Aug 1887	New York	8 Sept 1887	J. Hart
Nevada		Liverpool	8 Oct 1887	New York	19 Oct 1887	J. Wells
Nevada		Liverpool	8 Dec 1887	New York	18 Dec 1887	G. Taylor
Arizona		Liverpool	29 Oct 1887	New York		J. Long
Alameda		Hawaii	6 May 1888	San Francisco	13 May 1888	
Wisconsin		Liverpool	28 Apr 1888	New York	10 May 1888	F. Bramwell
Wyoming		Liverpool	19 May 1888	New York	29 May 1888	W. Wood
Arizona		Liverpool	26 May 1888	New York	4 Jun 1888	
Wisconsin		Liverpool	2 Jun 1888	New York	13 Jun 1888	C. Dorlus
Nevada		Liverpool	9 Jun 1888	New York	20 Jun 1888	J. Stucki
Wyoming		Liverpool	23 Jun 1888	New York	2 July 1888	H. Bowring
Wisconsin		Liverpool	7 July 1888	New York	18 July 1888	R. Lindsay
Wyoming		Liverpool	28 July 1888	New York	8 Aug 1888	H. Christensen
Wisconsin		Liverpool	11 Aug 1888	New York	24 Aug 1888	L. Naylor
Wyoming		Liverpool	1 Sept 1888	New York	11 Sept 1888	A. Johnson
Wisconsin		Liverpool	15 Sept 1888	New York	25 Sept 1888	W. Phillips
Wyoming		Liverpool	6 Oct 1888	New York	16 Oct 1888	N. Lindelof
Wisconsin		Liverpool	20 Oct 1888	New York	31 Oct 1888	J. Quigley
Arizona		Liverpool	17 Nov 1888	New York	27 Nov 1888	L. Moench
Wyoming		Liverpool	4 May 1889	New York	15 May 1889	N. Krumperman
Arizona		Liverpool	11 May 1889	New York	20 May 1889	H. Barrell
Wisconsin		Liverpool	18 may 1889	New York	29 May 1889	N. Dalley
Wyoming		Liverpool	8 Jun 1889	New York	20 Jun 1889	L. Anderson
Wisconsin		Liverpool	22 Jun 1889	New York	5 July 1889	J. Volker
Wyoming		Liverpool	17 Aug 1889	New York	27 Aug 1889	J. Welbye
Wisconsin		Liverpool	31 Aug 1889	New York	11 Sept 1889	W. Payne
Wyoming		Liverpool	21 Sept 1889	New York	1 Oct 1889	R. Larson
Wisconsin		Liverpool	5 Oct 1889	New York	17 Oct 1889	E. Bennett
Wyoming		Liverpool	26 Oct 1889	New York	6 Nov 1889	A. Skanchy
Arizona		Liverpool	2 Nov 1889	New York		J. Adams
Nevada		Liverpool	16 Nov 1889	New York	27 Nov 1889	R. Morse

Vessel	LDS Pass	Departed	Date	Arrived	Date	Leader
Wisconsin		Liverpool	29 Dec 1889	New York		H. Ballard
Wisconsin		Liverpool	19 Apr 1890	New York	24 Apr 1890	O. Worthington
Wyoming		Liverpool	3 May 1890	New York	13 May 1890	A. Anderson
Wisconsin		Liverpool	24 May 1890	New York	4 Jun 1890	J. Hayes
Wyoming		Liverpool	7 Jun 1890	New York	19 Jun 1890	E. Willardsen
Wisconsin		Liverpool	28 Jun 1890	New York	10 July 1890	A. Maw
Wisconsin		Liverpool	2 Aug 1890	New York	13 Aug 1890	L. Jordan
Wyoming		Liverpool	16 Aug 1890	New York	26 Aug 1890	J. Ostlund
Wisconsin		Liverpool	6 Sept 1890	New York	17 Sept 1890	J. Stucki
Wyoming		Liverpool	20 Sept 1890	New York	1 Oct 1890	J. Jensen
Wisconsin		Liverpool	11 Oct 1890	New York	23 Oct 1890	J. Golightley
Wisconsin		Liverpool	24 Jan 1891	New York	7 Feb 1891	J. P. Benson
Wisconsin		Liverpool	11 Apr 1891	New York	23 Apr 1891	J. Arnott
Nevada		Liverpool	25 Apr 1891	New York	6 May1891	J. Anderson
Wyoming		Liverpool	9 May 1891	New York	21 May 1891	R. Appendahl
Wisconsin		Liverpool	23 May 1891	New York	3 Jun 1891	W. Bonder
Alaska		Liverpool	3 Jun 1891	New York	22 Jun 1891	J. Bodmer
Nevada		Liverpool	6 Jun 1891	New York	18 Jun 1891	P. Abrahamson
Wyoming		Liverpool	17 Jun 1891	New York		
Wyoming		Liverpool	18 Jun 1891	New York	29 Jun 1891	H Arbosen
Wisconsin		Liverpool	15 Aug 1819	New York	26 Aug 1891	A. Anderson
Nevada		Liverpool	29 Aug 1891	New York	10 Sept 1891	C. Abergler
Wyoming		Liverpool	12 Sept 1891	New York	23 Sept 1891	M. Akerland
Wisconsin		Liverpool	26 Sept 1891	New York	9 Oct 1891	J. C. Anderson
Nevada		Liverpool	10 Oct 1891	New York	22 Oct 1891	C. W. Anderson
Wyoming		Liverpool	24 Oct 1891	New York	4 Nov 1891	C. Booth
Alaska		Liverpool	31 Oct 1891	New York	9 Nov 1891	
Wisconsin		Liverpool	7 Nov 1891	New York	19 Nov 1891	N. Hemingson
Nevada		Liverpool	21 Nov 1891	New York	2 Dec 1891	
Nevada		Liverpool	30 Jan 1892	New York	13 Feb 1892	
Wisconsin		Liverpool	20 Feb 1892	New York	3 Mar 1892	R. Bowling
Nevada		Liverpool	9 Apr 1892	New York	21 Apr 1892	
Wisconsin		Liverpool	6 May 1892	New York	19 May 1892	
Arizona		Liverpool	28 May 1892	New York	6 Jun 1892	O. Helgason
Nevada		Liverpool	12 Jun 1892	New York	22 Jun 1892	
Arizona		Liverpool	25 Jun 1892	New York	5 July 1892	
Wyoming		Liverpool	12 July 1892	New York	27 July 1892	A. Brandt
Nevada		Liverpool	2 July 1892	New York	14 July 1892	
Nevada		Liverpool	Aug 1892	New York	25 Aug 1892	

57

Vessel	LDS Pass	Departed	Date	Arrived	Date	Leader
Wyoming		Liverpool	27 Aug 1892	New York	6 Sept 1892	C. Aamodt
Alaska		Liverpool	3 Sept 1892	New York	14 Sept 1892	
Alaska		Liverpool	1 Oct 1892	New York	10 Oct 1892	A. Andersen
Nevada		Liverpool	5 Nov 1892	New York	17 Nov 1892	A. K. Anderson
Arizona		Liverpool	12 Nov 1892	New York	22 Nov 1892	J. Blackshaw
Wyoming		Liverpool	19 Nov 1892	New York	30 Nov 1892	A. Bauer
Teutonic		Liverpool	25 Jan 1893	New York	2 Feb 1893	J. Bench
Majestic		Liverpool	8 Mar 1893	New York	15 Mar 1893	A. Anderson
Aurania		Liverpool	11 Mar 1893	New York	20 Mar 1893	
Arizona		Liverpool	8 Apr 1893	New York	17 Apr 1893	E. Ashton
Alaska		Liverpool	22 Apr 1893	New York	1 May 1893	W. Bennion
Arizona		Liverpool	6 May 1893	New York	15 May 1893	T. Jansen
Nevada		Liverpool	13 May 1893	New York	24 May 1893	H. Ahl
Alaska		Liverpool	20 May 1893	New York	29 may 1893	A. Andersen
Arizona		Liverpool	3 Jun 1893	New York	13 Jun 1893	J. Hasenfratz
Arizona		Liverpool	1 July 1893	New York	19 July 1893	A. Bakker
Alaska		Liverpool	15 July 1893	New York	24 July 1893	
Alaska		Liverpool	19 Aug 1893	New York	29 Aug 1893	J. Smith
Alaska		Liverpool	14 Oct 1893	New York	24 Oct 1893	J. Anderson
Majestic		Liverpool	22 Nov 1893	New York	29 Nov 1893	J. Bell
Arizona		Liverpool	14 Apr 1894	New York	23 Apr 1894	A. Havert
Arizona		Liverpool	14 May 1894	New York	21 May 1894	N. Benson
SS Paris		Southampton	26 May 1894	New York	2 Jun 1894	F. Baugh
SS Paris		Southampton	16 Jun 1894	New York	23 Jun 1894	E. Anderson
SS New York		Liverpool	30 Jun 1894	New York	7 July 1894	J. Bulleter
Anchoria		Glasgow	10 Jan 1895	New York	21 Jan 1895	
Furnessia		Glasgow	7 Feb 1895	New York	19 Feb 1895	R. Hill
Furnessia		Glasgow	20 Apr 1895	New York	1 May 1895	G. Bradbury
Circassia		Glasgow	1 May 1895	New York	15 May 1895	
City of Rome		Glasgow	9 May 1895	New York	18 May 1895	J. Argyle
Warrimoo		Sydney	18 May 1895	California		B. Goddard
Furnessia		Glasgow	22 May 1895	New York	14 Jun 1895	M. Bridgewood
Furnessia		Glasgow	27 Jun 1895	New York	8 July 1895	A. Hohne
Furnessia		Glasgow	27 July 1895	New York	12 Aug 1895	C. Hohnchen
Anchoria		Glasgow	15 Aug 1895	New York	26 Aug 1895	A. Andersen
Furnessia		Glasgow	5 Sept 1895	New York	16 Sept 1895	
Furnessia		Glasgow	10 Oct 1895	New York	22 Oct 1895	K. Hemdt
Furnessia		Glasgow	22 Nov 1895	New York	3 Dec 1895	H. Anderson
Ethiopia		Glasgow	31 Jan 1896	New York	14 Feb 1896	J. Holden

Vessel	LDS Pass	Departed	Date	Arrived	Date	Leader
Island		Copenhagen	5 Mar 1896	New York	23 Mar 1896	J. Petersen
Anchoria		Glasgow	9 Apr 1896	New York	23 Apr 1896	E. Batt
Circassia		Glasgow	23 Apr 1896	New York	6 May 1896	J. Bichsel
Furnessia		Glasgow	30 Apr 1896	New York	11 May 1896	
Warimoo		Sydney	1 May 1896	Vancouver		
City of Rome		Glasgow	21 May 1896	New York	1 Jun 1896	M. Brenner
City of Paris		Southampton	26 May 1896	New York	June 1896	
Furnessia		Glasgow	4 Jun 1896	New York	15 Jun 1896	
Furnessia		Glasgow	4 July 1896	New York	15 July 1896	W. Behle
Anchoria		Glasgow	23 July 1896	New York	3 Aug 1896	A. Arnson
Furnessia		Glasgow	6 Aug 1896	New York	17 Aug 1896	
City of Rome		Glasgow	24 Sept 1896	New York	5 Oct 1896	W. Beresford
Furnessia		Glasgow	15 Oct 1896	New York	26 Oct 1896	C. Andersen
Circassia		Glasgow	2 Dec 1896	New York	17 Dec 1896	K. Iverson
Anchoria		Glasgow	13 Jan 1897	New York	29 Jan 1897	
Circassia		Glasgow	4 Mar 1897	New York	20 Mar 1897	T. Betty
Circassia		Moville	9 Apr 1897	New York	28 Apr 1897	F. Anderson
Furnessia		Glasgow	29 Apr 1897	New York	11 May 1897	M. Barton
Anchoria		Glasgow	14 May 1897	New York	May 1897	C. Hyberg
City of Rome		Glasgow	22 May 1897	New York	1 Jun 1897	L. Jackson
Furnessia		Glasgow	9 Jun 1897	New York	14 Jun 1897	H. Ahlquist
Island		Copenhagen	10 Jun 1897	New York	28 Jun 1897	C. Nilsson
City of Rome		Glasgow	19 Jun 1897	New York	28 Jun 1897	T. Best
Furnessia		Glasgow	3 July 1897	New York	13 July 1897	A. Ashdown
Furnessia		Glasgow	5 Aug 1897	New York	15 Aug 1897	A. Ahlquist
City of Rome		Glasgow	28 Aug 1897	New York	5 Sept 1897	J. Ayre
City of Rome		Glasgow	25 Sept 1897	New York		A. Affleck
Anchoria		Glasgow	7 Oct 1897	New York	18 Oct 1897	O. Anderson
Furnessia		Glasgow	14 Oct 1897	New York	25 Oct 1897	A. Newmann
Warrimoo		Sydney	18 Oct 1897			W. Baker
Anchoria		Glasgow	11 Nov 1897	New York	23 Nov 1897	
Furnessia		Glasgow	20 Nov 1897	New York	1 Dec 1897	M Anderson
Furnessia		Glasgow	10 Feb 1898	New York	23 Feb 1898	W. Anderson
Ethiopia		Glasgow	24 Feb 1898	New York	8 Mar 1898	U. Holmes
Furnessia		Glasgow	25 Mar 1898	New York	5 Apr 1898	
Furnessia		Glasgow	29 Apr 1898	New York	9 May 1898	A. Anderson
Anchoria		Glasgow	14 May 1898	New York	25 May 1898	R. Barrett
City of Rome		Glasgow	21 May 1898	New York	31 May 1898	F. Belling
Furnessia		Glasgow	2 Jun 1898	New York	13 Jun 1898	E. Billings

Vessel	LDS Pass	Departed	Date	Arrived	Date	Leader
Ethiopia		Glasgow	9 Jun 1898	New York	21 Jun 1898	A. Anderson
Anchoria		Glasgow	18 Jun 1898	New York	29 Jun 1898	C. Anderson
Furnessia		Glasgow	2 July 1989	New York	13 July 1898	O. Allen
Furnessia		Glasgow	4 Aug 1898	New York	15 Aug 1898	J. Alexander
Furnessia		Glasgow	8 Sept 1898	New York	19 Sept 1898	D. Archibald
Anchoria		Glasgow	6 Oct 1898	New York	18 Oct 1898	J. Badger
Furnessia		Glasgow	13 Oct 1898	New York	24 Oct 1898	J. Hermanson
Ethiopia		Glasgow	22 Oct 1898	New York	6 Nov 1898	A. Hart
Anchoria		Glasgow	5 Nov 1898	New York	16 Nov 1898	M. Austin
Furnessia		Glasgow	17 Nov 1898	New York	28 Nov 1898	J. Allbrand
Ethiopia		Glasgow	1 Dec 1898	New York	15 Dec 1898	R. Anderson
Furnessia		Glasgow	30 Dec 1898	New York	13 Jan 1899	H. Barrett
Furnessia		Glasgow	9 Feb 1899	New York	23 Feb 1899	F. Humphries
Ethiopia		Glasgow	23 Feb 1899	New York	3 Mar 1899	W. Boyer
Warrimoo		Sydney				G. Hirinorme
Furnessia		Glasgow	25 Mar 1899	New York	6 Apr 1899	
Ethiopia		Glasgow	6 Apr 1899	New York	20 Apr 1899	W. Adams
Anchoria		Glasgow	19 Apr 1899	New York		
Miowera		Sydney	25 Apr 1899			A. Lamnert
Ethiopia		Glasgow	11 May 1899	New York	23 May 1899	
Ethiopia		Glasgow	13 July 1899	New York	25 July 1899	
Anchoria		Glasgow	27 July 1899	New York	5 Aug 1899	D. Horsley
Furnessia		Glasgow	3 Aug 1899	New York	14 Aug 1899	E. Hopwood
City of Rome		Glasgow	28 Sept 1899	New York	8 Oct 1899	
Anchoria		Glasgow	9 Nov 1899	New York	22 Nov 1899	
Tainui		Glasgow	27 Nov 1899	New York	9 Dec 1899	E. Haynes
Ethipoia		Glasgow	7 Dec 1899	New York	22 Dec 1899	S. Harrop
Anchoria		Glasgow	14 Dec 1899	New York	27 Dec 1899	
Astoria		Glasgow	28 Dec 1899	New York	16 Jan 1900	

Note: The ship Nevada which sailed on 6 November 1872 from Liverpool returned to the port because of breakdown and the passengers transferred to the Manhattan for their onward journey.

About this database

Many ships also carried passengers form Scandinavian Countries who travelled principally from Copenhagen to Hull and then overland to Liverpool by rail before continuing their journey on LDS chartered ships.

From 1869 onwards the numbers of LDS passengers on the emigrant ships are not shown in the table but names and details can be found using the European Emigration Card Index or the Early Church Information File detailed later. The number of church passengers travelling varied significantly in the later years and in some cases there was perhaps only a family or even an individual travelling on any one ship. The Church however assigned a leader and that information is provided in the last column of the above database. Some names included relate only to sole passengers so it is necessary to search the passenger lists etc for details. There is no guarantee that all vessels which carried church members are included in the above.

It is known that several ships left Australia for the USA with church member emigrants that are not shown in the database including: *Envelope* in 1853, *Julia Ann* in 1854, *Tarquinia* in 1855, *Jenny Ford* in 1856, *Lure, Yankee* and *Lucas* in 1857, *Milwaukee* in 1859 and *Albert* in 1865.

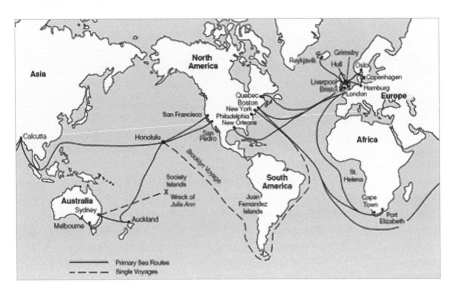

Church emigration Shipping routes from around the world (LDS Church Intellectual Reserve Inc).

The journal for the ship 'Lucas' can be searched on microfilm no. 928396, available via local Family Search Centres.

The arrival dates in New York or other destination ports are when the return was filed so if you are cross referencing to Ellis Island or Castle Garden then you will need to look for a couple of days either side of the date shown above.

Ports and sailing times

The church tended to charter ships or use vessels departing from the following ports:

Britain - Liverpool, Glasgow, Hull, Leith, Bristol
Scandinavia - Copenhagen
Germany & Switzerland - Gluckstadt, Hamburg, Kiel, Lubeck,
Australasia - Sydney, Melbourne
Others - Calcutta, Auckland (New Zealand), Port Elizabeth and Cape Town (South Africa), Tahiti

Average Sailing Times in the 'age of sail':

Liverpool to New Orleans	54 days
Liverpool to New York	34 days
Liverpool to Philadelphia	38 days
Hamburg to New York	47 days
Australasia to San Francisco	90 days
South Africa to Boston	64 days

Sailing times were significantly cut once steamships operated the routes.

Passenger arrival ports in the USA for LDS emigrants were used for very specific periods:

New York	1840 & 1855 - 1925
Boston	1852, 1856-1861 and 1864
Philadelphia	1840, 1856-1868
New Orleans	1840-1855
San Diego	1847-1868
San Francisco	1847-1868, 1880-1890.

Throughout Church history there has only been one disaster on emigrant ships. The '*Julia Ann*' on its way from Australia to San Francisco was wrecked.

Crossing the ocean

If your ancestor emigrated to the United States from any European country with a Church company, then to find more information about them you should consult one or more of the following:

European Emigration Card Index
The European Emigration Card Index covers the period 1840-1925 and is comprised of an alphabetical card index of most, but not all, LDS Church members who emigrated from European countries to the United States providing the names, ages, nationality; number of persons in group; name of ship; date and place of departure and arrival. These cards have been filmed by the GSU and can be accessed at LDS Family History Centres.

Microfilm by surname.

A - Bri	0298431
Bro - Dy	0298432
E - Ha	0298433
Ha - Jones	0298434
Jones - Mh	0298435
Mi - Peteersen	0298436
Petersen - Smith, O.	0298437
Smith, P. - Wh	0298438
Whi-Z	0298439

Once the information has been located in the card index the next step is to search the Church Emigration Registers under the date of departure (arranged in chronological order) and name of the ship. The passengers' names will appear on the list but not necessarily in alphabetical order.

The US Passenger lists also in chronological order by date of arrival will also show similar information. The ship's name should appear on each page of a passenger list.

Worldwide LDS Ships Register
This is a compiled index to microfilms of passenger lists of emigrating church members and is a comprehensive list of ships used by Church emigrants between 1840 and 1913 arranged chronologically by date of departure. Included are details of ships sailing from Liverpool, Glasgow, Copenhagen, Hamburg, Cape Town South Africa and other ports as shown in the above database.

If using this method of locating voyage information it will be necessary to record the name of the ship, date of departure (which will also narrow your search of the Church emigration registers) and the date of arrival together with the microfilm number of the United States passenger list given under the US Roster column.

DATE OF DEPARTURE	SHIP NAME	PORT OF DEPARTURE	LDS ROSTER	COMPANY LEADER or (passenger)	PORT OF ARRIVAL	DATE OF ARRIVAL	US ROSTER	ARRIVAL IN UTAH
1869	Argonaught			(John August Olsen)				
2 Jun 1869	Minnesota	Liverpool	0025,692	E. Morris	New York	15 Jun 1869	175,669	
10 Jul 1869		Copenhagen	0025,696		Hull	14 Jul 1869		
	Then sailed 15 July 1869 on the Minnesota from Liverpool							
15 Jul 1869	Minnesota	Liverpool		O. Olsen	New York	28 Jul 1869	175,671	?8 Aug 1869
28 Jul 1869	Colorado	Liverpool	0025,692	J. Pace	New York	10 Aug 1869	175,672	
	Swiss German saints sailed 25 Aug 1869 on the Minnesota from Liverpool. 949.4 B2ds							
25 Aug 1869	Minnesota	Liverpool	0025,692	M. Ensign	New York	6 Sep 1869	175,673	
22 Sep 1869	Manhattan	Liverpool	0025,692	J. Lawson	New York	7 Oct 1869	175,675	
6 or 10 Oct 1869	Minnesota	Liverpool	0025,692	J. Needham	New York	18 Oct 1869	175,675	28 Oct 1869
20 Oct 1869	Colorado	Liverpool		C. Wilden	New York	1 Nov 1869	175,676	

(LDS Church Intellectual Reserve Inc).

It lists date of departure and arrival date, ship's name, port of departure, microfilm number for the Church emigration register, name of company leader, arrival port, microfilm number for the United States passenger list, references to any written accounts of the voyage, and in many instances references to an illustration (drawing or photograph) and/or description of the ship. It does not show individual passengers. The register is available on microfilm number 1592753.

Church Emigration Registers

These are the register referred to in the Worldwide LDS Ships Register as 'LDS Rosters' and they record the departures from Liverpool of most British and many European church members who emigrated. They were administered by the Liverpool Office of firstly the British Mission and subsequently the European Mission after 1854.

The records include name, age, sex, occupation, marital status and nationality of the emigrant; conference to which they belonged, their address, or residence at the time of sailing; name of ship; departure date; and destination. Where a bond number is shown in the last but one column of page two of the register it means that the family were in receipt of funding from the Perpetual Emigration Fund although in many cases the actual amounts are not shown.

64

Emigration Registers - Page one of each entry shows important genealogical information (LDS Church Intellectual Reserve Inc).

Emigration Registers - Page two shows financial details relating to each person or family (LDS Church Intellectual Reserve Inc).

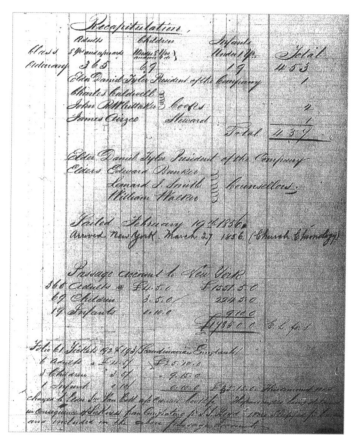

There is also a page relating to every Voyage which is a Recapitulation page.

This page at the end of each voyage register gives statistical information and includes Number of passenger, dates of departure and arrival, Names of leaders, cooks and steward and also shows a financial statement for the voyage. including costs of provisions etc. Each voyage was self sustaining. (LDS Church Intellectual Reserve Inc).

The Church Emigration Registers are available on microfilm according to date of sailing through local Family History Centres.

Rosters 1849-1855	25690
Rosters 1855-1863	25691
Rosters 1863 - 1874	25692
Rosters 1875-1885, 1899-1903, 1901-1914	25693
Rosters 1903-1914	25694
Rosters 1914-1923	25695

The Mormon Immigration Index CD

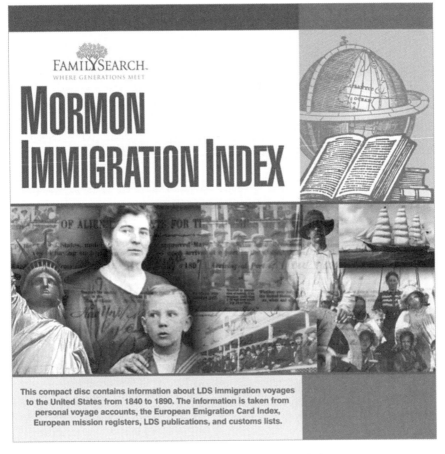

This compact disc contains information about LDS immigration voyages to the United States from 1840 to 1890. The information is taken from personal voyage accounts, the European Emigration Card Index, European mission registers, LDS publications, and customs lists.

(Mormon Immigration Index Intellectual Reserve Inc).

The database is available to purchase on CD via www.lds.org and includes records of more than 93,000 church members and their families who emigrated worldwide between 1840 and 1890 with the aim of making Salt Lake their final destination. The database includes name, age, country of origin, ports of departure and arrival, passenger list information, the leader assigned to each voyage, and general voyage information. There are four sections to the database - Individuals, Passenger Lists, Personal Accounts and Voyages accessible from the main menu tabs from the home page.

Individual	Passenger List	Personal Accounts	Voyages		
Name		**Born**	**Ship**	**Departure**	
LAYTON, Mary		<1820>	Swanton	1843	
Gender: F	Age: 23				
Note: "Spelled Leighton on ship's customs lists."					
LAYTON, Cristopher		<1821>	Swanton	1843	
Gender: M	Age: 22				
Note: "Spelled Leighton in the ship's customs list."					
LAYTON, William M.		<1843>	Swanton	1843	
Gender: M	Age: infant				
Note: "Born Mar 1843"					

By clicking on the Ship's name alongside the individual you will find the passenger list for the company will be revealed (see below) (Mormon Immigration Index Intellectual Reserve Inc).

Besides valuable statistical information, the personal journals, letters of approximately 1,000 passengers graphically detail the challenges faced on the journeys and bring home some of the comments detailed above.

Individual	Passenger List	
Name		**Born**
KELLY, Esther		<1810>
Gender: F	Age: 33	
KELLY, John		<1839>
Gender: M	Age: 4	
KELSELL, Samond		<1816>
Gender: M	Age: 27	
Note: "Edmond?"		
KELSELL, Ann		<1820>
Gender: F	Age: 23	

(Mormon Immigration Index Intellectual Reserve Inc).

There are detailed accounts of births, deaths, illnesses, weather conditions, and information on travel costs, food, and supplies. Many journal entries not only include details of the journey but also detail what their new life was like including descriptions of the new communities in which they settled, about land purchases, employment taken up and church ordinances performed.

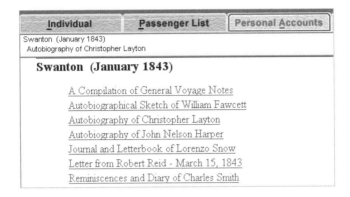

Swanton (January 1843)
Autobiography of Christopher Layton

Personal Accounts only exist for some of the Passengers (Mormon Immigration Index Intellectual Reserve Inc).

Personal journals etc. can be searched by either name of the ship on which they sailed or by individual name. Other names mentioned in entries are cross-referenced so you can link to other passengers.

Searching for an individual can be done using either a given name, last name, date of birth, and/or departure year. The results of the search will show name, year of birth (if recorded), the name of the ship and year of departure. Searches of the passenger and voyage lists include spelling variants. Searches can be undertaken using 'and' 'or' or 'not'. Wildcards and standardised names can also be undertaken.

Expanding the Personal Accounts or Voyages tab will enable a written report / autobiography/journal to be accessed. (Mormon Immigration Index Intellectual Reserve Inc).

Up to 100 records can be tagged for printing or saving to a GEDCOM file or directly into some of the popular family history programmes such as PAF, Family Tree Maker, Legacy and Roots Magic.

Some information from the index has been incorporated into the new Family Search website but currently using the CDs gives a much greater flexibility.

If your ancestor did not emigrate to the United States with a Church company, then it is necessary to use the records which were outside church organisation generation which to some extent involve different strategies of research. Some of the records detailed below will by their nature include information about emigrants who arrived in the USA as part of a church company so it may be worth searching those as well.

U.S. Passenger Lists

The U S Passenger lists are organised in two parts and it is likely that the majority of information relating to church member emigrants will be in the Customs Passenger Lists unless they emigrated after 1883 when it may be necessary to search both the Customs passenger lists and the Immigration passenger lists.

Customs Passenger Lists, 1820 to 1902.

These records include details for each immigrant including name, age, gender, occupation, country of origin, and place of intended destination which may not, in the case of church members have been their final address.

They were passenger lists that were submitted to U.S. Customs by the masters of passenger vessels when they arrived in the United States.

Immigration Passenger Lists, since 1883.

These ship manifests were submitted to the US Immigration Service (and its predecessors) by the masters of arriving ships. To some extent they are a duplication of the information submitted to customs between 1883 and 1902 but could also include additional information such as birthplace, last residence, marital status, and the names of relatives in their originating country and also any who were currently resident in the United States.

There are over 12,000 microfilms of passenger arrival records and the indexes are available through family history centres which are copies of those held by the National Archives in Washington. You will need to refer to the main Family Search library catalogue in order to obtain a film. To access the film index enter 'subject' in the 'search' field and 'Immigrant U S Passenger Lists' in the 'for' field of the catalogue on **www.familysearch.org**.

Between 1820 and 1923 over twenty three million emigrants sailed to New York, over two million to Boston and over 710,000 to New Orleans.

Hamburg Passenger Lists

The records of European passengers who emigrated through Hamburg have survived but those for other ports of Continental Europe including Bremen, Le Havre, Amsterdam,

Rotterdam, and Antwerp, have either been destroyed or are not available for research.

The Hamburg passenger lists relate to Europeans who departed from the port of Hamburg, between 1850 and 1934 (although none exist for the First World War period). Many European Church members also used Hamburg particularly post pioneer years. Like other lists those from Hamburg could provide important genealogical information including their home towns. There are extensive indexes to the lists which should be consulted in the first instance.

The Hamburg passenger lists are in two categories each with separate indexes.

The Direct Lists relate to voyages that sailed directly to their American destination. The Indirect Lists include about 25% of passengers who stopped over at a British or another European port before sailing to their American destination. Films of the Indirect Index 1855-1910 are available to view at the Society of Genealogists Library Ancestry.com has an index and images for both direct and indirect sailings for all years 1850-1934.

The Family History Library holds microfilmed records which can be obtained through Family History Centres. Refer to the main library catalogue for details.

Nauvoo Social History Index
This is a name index relative to emigrants who sailed on church sponsored voyages between 1840 and 1849. There are about 71,000 miscellaneous records which include information about Nauvoo property owned by many of the early church members before expulsion, tax lists, ship passenger lists, censuses, early members' family group records, and research notes. Each entry also shows the name, gender, and source information. Currently this is available on microfiche no. 6334931.

LDS Emigrant Roster and Voyage History, Crossing the Ocean, 1840-1869
This is a CD based index relating to various sources including Church Emigration Registers, Perpetual Emigration Fund lists, handcart pioneers, and Sons of Utah Pioneer records and focuses mostly on the church members who crossed the ocean for the later period between 1849 and 1869. Unfortunately the index is incomplete and only available at the main Family History Library in Salt Lake City.

Passenger Lists of Emigrants from Copenhagen to Hull, 1872-1894
The significance of this index is that it relates to a broken journey calling at Hull before proceeding to America. However the index text is in Danish not English. It shows name, age, occupation, residence and marital status of church emigrants from mainly Scandinavian countries and is available on microfilm no. 040994.

Castle Garden and Ellis Island - American Immigration Gateways

Castle Garden, is a fort at the southern tip of Manhattan in New York City. From 1 August 1855 until 18 April 1890, immigrants arriving in New York entered through Castle Garden which was America's first official immigrant examining and processing centre. The church members who emigrated and landed at New York would have been processed through this centre before being allowed to enter America.

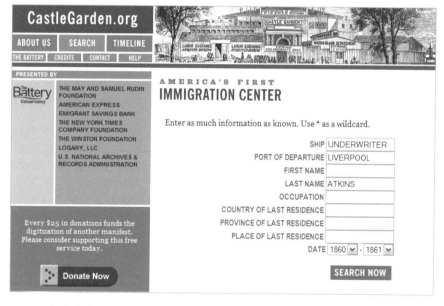

Castle Garden search page. Put as much information as you know into the search criteria boxes (Castle Garden.org).

After Castle Garden closed immigrants were processed at an old barge office in Manhattan until the Ellis Island Immigration Centre opened on 1 January 1892.

The CastleGarden.org database allows you to search by name and time period for immigrants who arrived in Castle Garden between 1830 and 1890. The site provides only a database but is in the process of digitising some of the ships manifests (passenger lists). Ancestry.com offers access to New York Passenger Lists, 1851-1891 and microfilms of the manifests can also be obtained through Family History Centres.

LAST NAME ▲	FIRST NAME	AGE	SEX	ARRIVAL DATE	PLACE OF LAST RESIDENCE
ADAMS	DAVID	24	M	22 May 1861	
ADAMS	WILLIAM	26	M	22 May 1861	
AGLASIA	SARAH	15	F	22 May 1861	
ALLDRIDGE	ANN	21	F	22 May 1861	
ALLDRIDGE	ANN	40	F	22 May 1861	
ALLDRIDGE	ELIZABETH	18	F	22 May 1861	
ALLDRIDGE	RICHARD	46	M	22 May 1861	
ANDREWS	MILO	48	M	22 May 1861	
ASHFORTH	SARAH	25	F	22 May 1861	
ASHFORTH	MARY	4	F	22 May 1861	
ASHFORTH	EDWARD	30	M	22 May 1861	
ASPINALL	ANN	32	F	22 May 1861	
ATKINS	WILLIAM	32	M	22 May 1861	
ATKINS	EMMA	21	F	22 May 1861	

This shows the passengers on the ship that William Atkins sailed on. Click Atkins to reveal data. (Castle Garden.org).

WILLIAM ATKINS			
FIRST NAME	WILLIAM	RELATIVE LEFT BEHIND	
LAST NAME	ATKINS	NAME OF RELATIVE LEFT BEHIND	
OCCUPATION	LABORER	ADDRESS OF RELATIVE LEFT BEHIND	
AGE	32	TICKET	
SEX	Male	PAID BY	Self
LITERACY	Unknown	IN THE US BEFORE	Unknown
SHIP	UNDERWRITER	IN THE US WHEN	
ARRIVED	22 May 1861	IN THE US WHERE	
COUNTRY	ENGLAND	GOING TO SOMEONE IN THE US	Unknown
PORT OF DEPARTURE	LIVERPOOL	RELATIONSHIP TO THAT SOMEONE IN THE US	
PLACE OF LAST RESIDENCE		NAME OF RELATIVE IN THE US	
PROVINCE OF LAST RESIDENCE	UNKNOWN		
CITY OR VILLAGE OF DESTINATION	UTAH	ADDRESS OF RELATIVE IN THE US	
PLAN	Unknown	CITY OF RELATIVE IN THE US	
PASSAGE	Unknown	COUNTRY OF BIRTH	ENGLAND
MONEY		PLACE OF BIRTH	

Details revealed in the database may be incomplete but is sufficient to enable identification (Castle Garden.org).

Its successor, Ellis Island, is a small island in New York Harbour which was the first Federal immigration station. Castle Garden had been administered by New York State authorities.

The Ellis Island Records database allows you to search by name, year of arrival, year of birth, town origin (which sometimes is the place of residence immediately before travel) or by ship's name for immigrants who entered the U.S. through Ellis Island between 1892 and 1924, which were the peak years of immigration. Results from the database provide a link to a transcribed record or a digitised copy of the ship manifest.

The Ellis Island immigrant records provide the following information, name, gender, age on arrival, nationality, marital status, last residence, date of arrival, ship on which they travelled and port of departure. It is also possible to obtain a photograph of the ship.

Many church emigrants were still entering the USA from Britain and Europe during the time that Ellis Island operated so you should be able to locate them or prove they did not enter the USA via New York. If you believe your ancestor landed in New York between 1892 and 1924 and you can't find him or her in the Ellis Island database, make sure all research options have been covered. The database is not without its transcription and spelling errors. Records of passengers that arrived at Ellis Island after 1924 aren't yet available on the Ellis Island database. These records are available on microfilm through your local Family History Centre. Emigrants could also have landed through the Port of New York and indexes exist to these passenger lists from June 1897 to 1948.

While the majority of immigrants during the peak years of immigration were processed through Ellis Island many others immigrated through other American ports including Boston, Baltimore, Galveston, and San Francisco. Some of the records of these immigrant arrivals can be viewed online, while others will need to be searched through more conventional methods.

The Julia Ann Shipwreck

The barque *Julia Ann* under the command of Benjamin Pond departed Australia on 7 September 1855 for San Francisco with a complement of fifty six passengers of which twenty eight were church members emigrating to Utah. Some of these passengers were born in Britain before emigrating initially to Australia. On 4 October the ship hit and lodged against a coral reef and began to break apart. A crew member swam to a rock on the reef and secured a rope. Many passengers crossed to relative safety using the rope or clung on to a piece of the ship, but five church members drowned. These were the wife and son of Edmund Harris, Maria and Mary Humphries and Martha Anderson. The surviving group managed to reach uninhabited islands where they found fresh water and were able to feed themselves on shellfish, turtle eggs and coconuts.

Captain Pond was faced with various options to try and affect a rescue. He could sail 1,500 miles west to the Navigator Islands or 300 miles east to Tahiti. Despite the vast difference in distance, the captain determined that sailing 1,500 miles westward was the most logical choice, for strong winds had been blowing continuously in that direction for weeks.

THE JULIA ANN WRECK.

Salt Lake City, April 22, 1886.
In your issue of the 4th inst. I read an article under the caption, "A Perilous Sea Voyage," written by Brother Amasa Potter of Payson, Utah county. The article gives some interesting details of the loss of the bark Julia Ann, on which a small company of Saints emigrating from Australia to Utah had taken passage, in 1855. But as Elder Potter obtains some of his information from the memory of another party, it is but natural that inaccuracies should occur. Permit me, therefore to present to your readers in brief what, in my historical researches, I have gleaned from the most reliable sources concerning the unfortunate Julia Ann, which represents the only case of shipwreck that has ever occurred in the long history of Latter-day Saint emigration from foreign lands to their gathering places in America.

The American bark Julia Ann, Captain B. F. Pond, sailed from Sydney, New South Wales, Australia, Sept. 7, 1855, bound for San Francisco, Cal., with 56 souls on board. Twenty-eight of that number, including Elders James Graham and John S. Eldredge, two American missionaries returning home, were Latter-day Saints on their way to Utah. Elder John Penfold Sr. had been appointed by President Augustus Farnham to take charge of the company. The bark left the Sydney Heads at 2 o'clock p.m. with the wind blowing from the northeast. Rather rough weather was encountered for a few days, with strong winds from the east northeast, which caused considerable sea sickness. Otherwise the voyage was successful until the 3rd of October, about 9 o'clock p.m., when the vessel struck on the reefs off the Scilly Islands. Captain Pond, expecting to pass between Moptia and the Scilly Islands, had set the watch in the foretop. The log was hove about 8 o'clock p.m., and the bark was found to be making 11½ knots per hour. Shortly afterwards the sea became broken, and in about an hour the vessel with a tremendous crash dashed head on to a coral reef. She immediately swung around with her broadside to the reef,

Various reports of the wreck of the Julia Ann were reported in Deseret News (Deseret News Publishing Company).

75

After repairing a small quarter-boat and using rescued 'nautical tools' Captain Pond and ten crewmen set out to try and secure help which they found three days into their journey on Bora-Bora, part of the Society Islands. Sixty days after the shipwreck the fifty-one surviving passengers of the Julia Ann were taken to safety. Despite the tragedy, the passengers spoke highly of Captain Pond and his leadership during the crisis.

Needless to say the reports of the shipwreck and the ultimate rescue reached the newspapers in Utah. The *Deseret News* reported on the disaster in some detail but not until some months later.

The Voyages
The following letter in the '*Manchester Examiner and Times*' available on the British Library Digitised Newspapers website accessed from **www.newspapers.bl.uk** gives a vivid account of a voyage from Liverpool to New Orleans and then onward on the Mississippi to St Louis. It is from John Chambers a church member born in 1818 in Manchester and was either not sent to the newspaper or not published until about 12 months after he arrived in the USA with his sister Maria.

'On the 15th February 1853, the ship Elvira Owen, Captain Owen, left the river Mersey, with a large number of passengers on board being chiefly Mormons, or Latter-day Saints, on their way to the general gathering place in the valleys of the Rocky Mountains, amounting to about 350 souls, including the crew, some from France, the isle of Jersey, Scotland, and the majority from England. We passed Holyhead at 10 p.m. sighted the Wicklow Mountains at 6 o'clock a.m. the following morning, and being highly favoured with a brisk east wind, we progressed rapidly, and passed Cape Clear at 8 o'clock p.m. on the 16th, our captain stating that we had traversed 220 miles in the first twenty-four hours, and in the second twenty-four 260 miles. In the evening of this day, as the vessel was cutting away through the great waters like a thing of life, the day being delightfully fine and most of the company on deck, a cry was raised, 'A man overboard!' 'Man the lifeboat!' All eyes were eager to catch a glimpse of the unfortunate man; but he was soon buried beneath the foaming waters. The boat was speedily manned, and they went in search of him, the ship being hove-to until their return, which was in about half an hour, without any success. The missing sailor, who lost his life so suddenly, was engaged in putting foot-ropes to a flying jib-boom, when his foot slipped, and he fell to windward.

Before I proceed to remark further on the progress of the voyage, I will take the liberty of giving an account of the organisation which is generally adopted by the Mormons in all their voyages. In the first place, there is a president appointed over the whole company, and he, in the next place, calls to his aid two individuals, of some experience, to act as counsellors. These are the first presidency on board the vessel, and take away from the captain all control over the company, leaving him simply to guide the ship into port. The council having been formed on board the Elvira Owen, they proceeded to form the company into eight divisions, and to each division a captain was appointed, who presided over all the men in his division. These divisions had duties to perform, such as clearing away all dirt between decks, keeping watch, and administering to the sick, &c. By this arrangement cleanliness and good order were maintained during the whole of the voyage. Prayers were conducted by the presidency during the passage - first, in the mornings, and afterwards, both morning and evening, when the weather became warmer. Divine service was conducted, also, three times a week, and the administration of the sacrament every Sunday; sometimes in the cabin, and on deck when the weather permitted.

As we proceeded in a southerly direction the weather became very agreeable, and our company began to take advantage of it by making their appearance on deck, but their looks betrayed anything but that of health. As I enjoyed excellent health (the motion of the vessel not affecting me in the least degree), I amused myself at times by looking at the various groups which occupied the decks. There was truly an abundance of matter for the exercise of the comic artistic skill of Cruikshank. Men and women were wrapped up in all kinds of garments, and of all colours; their heads were covered with variegated shawls, with a small portion of their sickly visages peering through a niche formed by the same, as though they were ashamed of showing the whole. Husbands might be seen nursing their wives, wives their husbands, children their parents, and parents their children; while the variety of expression produced on each physiognomy by the rolling of the ship was at once both pitiable and amusing.

On the 27th Feb. at noon, we came within the compass of the trade winds, being in long. W. 34° lat. N. 27-1/2°. the weather now became delightfully fine - these latitudes being very free from storms - and the captain assured us we would now have an onward progress, with little interruption, for upwards of 3,000 miles. During our passage in these parts we had many pleasant evenings; there were some musicians on board, and they afforded us a treat occasionally. This part of the voyage was really a pleasure trip. Sunset in this latitude is very beautiful, the sky presenting various hues of brilliant colours in rapid succession, until the refraction gives way to the light of the stars, which shine forth with great brilliancy, and many constellations are very distinct to the naked eye. It afforded me some pleasure on fine evenings to pace the deck with the mate, and glean all the information I could from him respecting this most interesting science - a privilege I could not obtain whilst in Manchester, as the atmosphere there was always overcast with the smoke that issued from its manufactories.

The Elvira Owen continued to keep up its speed, and we rolled and breezed away varying from eight to ten knots an hour, and everything went on well until the 4th March, when the smallpox broke out amongst the company on board, and the steerage being rather crowded, it was deemed wise to make an hospital on deck, to which all the sick were conveyed, and no one was allowed to pass the door or the windows, except the crew and other officers. The captain ordered the steerage to be visited three or four times a week with the tar-bucket, and the whole vessel smelled pretty strongly of tar; when the bucket made its appearance, there was a general rush upon deck, especially of the female portion of the company, escaping with all haste, with their garments partly on and partly in their arms, from the powerful gas escaping from the tar-bucket. The presiding elder of the Mormons proceeded to call meetings, and to give instruction to the people, and urged upon them the necessity of washing themselves, from the oldest to the youngest, in salt water. This was immediately attended to, - the females going to the stern, or quarter deck, the males to the forecastle, and the children all had a good ducking on the main-deck, and a fine stir it made, affording considerable amusement, for every bucket of water caused some of the little ones to dance and yell most vociferously. The president also appointed a fast-day to all except the sick, the aged, and those under eight years of age. All were urged to attend to their prayers, and to call upon the Lord to stay the plague. These things being attended to, and carried out with as much punctuality as though it were in the army or navy, the plague had little or no power (though in these climates the smallpox is a fearful visitor), only one young man dying of the disease.

As we approached the West India Islands, we spoke many small vessels. We spoke one brig on the 9th March in long. W. 63° 45' lat. N. 29° bound to Havana, 40 days out from London, and the Elvira 21 days out from Liverpool, and passed some others, showing the sailing qualities of the Elvira to be first-rate. About this time we entered the Caribbean Sea, passing the Island of St. Domingo, presenting a very rugged and mountainous appearance on the northern portion of it, which is said to have been caused by earthquakes. Jamaica we could not discern, as it lay about 40 miles to the south of our track. Soon after this we caught a glimpse of the isle of Cuba, and we coasted along it for two full days, and had the pleasure of beholding the green verdure which clothed its sloping banks. This was truly a treat after being on the wide ocean, surrounded by nothing but water, and being restricted to a floating house of about 300 by 40 feet, for a period of about four weeks. The Isle of Cuba is of considerable length, lying at the mouth of the Gulf of Mexico, running east and west, and is very fertile.

In the waters of the West India islands many curiosities are to be seen. We saw large numbers of porpoises and dolphins, the former affording some amusement to the company on board, by their curious gambols in the water, coming, as they did, in large droves, and turning their huge bodies over on the surface, gave the waters a very lively appearance. One was struck with a harpoon by one of the sailors, but in hauling it on board, the rope broke, and the fish sallied off with the harpoon. We also saw great numbers of flying fish; large flocks of these would rise from the waters, and skim along the surface for some distance; they were somewhat larger than mackerel, and of a beautiful silvery appearance. One day I was looking over the side of the vessel, when I beheld what I conceived to be a nautilus floating along, spreading its beautiful 'sails' to the soft breeze that was then blowing. Its appearance to me was that of a lady's cap, - of the same size and form; it was of a red colour, tinged with pink, and in the rays of a West India sun, it looked very beautiful. I also perceived on one occasion the waters disturbed by the gambols of a whale was thrown up to a considerable height in two distinct streams, but it did not come near enough to be seen from the vessel. I thought it singular to meet, in so warm a climate, with this animal.

We now began to tack in order to make the western point of the Isle of Cuba. The evening was a pleasant one - the 15th March - as I sat upon the quarter-deck, and watched the sun set in a West India sky, and looking from the vessel, there lay before me, an immense expanse of the beautiful waters, tinged with the golden rays of the setting sun, the silvery moon being directly over head, about to lend its aid to the mariner, shining forth with a brilliancy unknown in England. It was on such an evening that we entered the Gulf of Mexico, in full sail, and after rounding the western point of Cuba, we had the full play of the breezes from the great Atlantic, and we cut away at a modest rapid rate, making 260 miles in 24 hours. Suffice it to say, we reached the bar off New Orleans in 35 days; and what a change was presented to us, from that which we left behind us in England! The mouths of the Mississippi being three in number, extending over a surface of three miles - the principal one crowded with shipping - steamers of immense power, which are capable of tugging four vessels of large burthen up to New Orleans in 48 hours, - these too darting about in all directions - caused no little bustle in the great waters, and was truly a sight well worthy crossing the Atlantic to see.

New Orleans has a magnificent appearance as you sail along its quays, wharves, and pier heads. It is very extensive, and has a frontage to the river of seven miles. Spring is the finest and most healthy time of the year to arrive at this port. Like most seaports, this place is infested with a band of ruffians, who board all emigrant ships immediately on arrival, and if the passengers are not prepared to receive them, they will rush below into the steerage and ransack and pillage everything they can lay their hands on. The captain has not power to prevent this; - the deck and bulwarks of the Elvira were covered with these characters, whose looks were more like those of demons than anything else. The greatest number of them were Irishmen. The Mormons were aware of all this, and the president provided for it by doubling the guards at each hatchway, and they had instructions not to allow anyone to go below without knowing his business. This plan completely thwarted the object of this desperate gang of loafers, and for some time they sat upon the bulwarks of the vessel, grinning like fiends. They tried to effect an entrance by stratagem: one of them dressing himself in the garb of a female, came about sundown, and said he wanted to see one of the passengers named 'Mary Ball,' but the guards were on the alert; they knew no such person in that ship. The ruse being discovered, the mate was informed, who told them who he was, and that if they did not go ashore right away, he would pretty smartly call the policemen on board, and give them in charge. The bold front displayed by the mate, put a check on the audacity of the Orleans land pirates, and they retired, apparently much mortified at the failure of all their projects to plunder the Mormons. Where no organisation exists, they make common plunder; from this cause, the Irish emigrants suffer greatly, as they are generally in disorder.

New Orleans (Franklin Richards Publishers).

A steamer having been engaged to convey this company of Mormons up to St. Louis, we were soon steaming our way up this beautiful river, which was a great treat to one who had been pent up within the bulwarks of a ship for some time. There is a great sameness in the scenery on the banks of the Mississippi, until we reach the northern portion of it, where the banks begin to be more mountainous and rugged, but there is plenty to feast the eyes all the way up. The Negroes working in the rice and cotton plantations look fat and happy, and are seemingly much better provided for than many of the operatives in England. The woodland scenery is very extensive and very beautiful, and affords employment for large numbers of woodcutters, who provide the steamboats with fuel, by cutting immense piles of wood, and selling it to the captains as they pass to and fro in the river. On arriving at St. Louis, we were again visited by loafers but a sharp eye was kept upon them by the guards, and they were, as before, completely frustrated in all their attempts to obtain booty. On leaving St. Louis we took the steamboat Die Vernon, to proceed to the camping ground of the Mormons, which was at Keokuk, about 200 miles north of St. Louis. In this boat we were rather pinched for room; the berths were given to the females, and the men had to seek the best place they could find to sleep in. I slept with a young man in a wagon that was fixed at the bow of the boat, wrapping ourselves in blankets.

I had often heard of the 'snags' of the Mississippi, and the danger from them to the steamboats, sometimes causing them to sink in a very short time. Up to this period we had progressed without any mishap of this kind, but, on this occasion, just as I had got into a pleasant nap, the boat struck, not on a snag, but on a small island in the midst of the river - (as was afterwards ascertained). I was awoke by the concussion, and called out to my friend, with some degree of alarm, to pick up his boots and hasten to the stern, as we had struck on a 'snag.' Of this I was positive, as large branches of trees covered the wagon in which I slept; but before we had time to get out of the wagon, the engine was reversed, and we were again afloat, it being ascertained that no damage had been sustained by the boat. We arrived at Keokuk after being absent from England about eight weeks, and here it was intended to camp all the Mormons, to prepare for crossing the plains.

As this letter is of greater length than I at first anticipated it would be, I shall here conclude, leaving my description of the journey across the plains for the next mail. If you deem these items worthy of a place in the *Manchester Examiner* and *Times*, you are at liberty to make any use of it that you may think proper; they may be useful to other emigrants. - I remain, sir, with much esteem,'

The next part of the letter is appended to the chapter relating to the Overland Journey below.

CHAPTER THREE
The Overland Journey

As the long trek west began the emigrating church members had to leave Missouri during the winter of 1838-1839 because they were threatened with extermination. On 27 October 1838, Lilburn W. Boggs the then Missouri Governor signed his Mormon 'extermination order' declaring that the Mormons must be treated as enemies, must be exterminated, or expelled from the State. This directive meant that 10,000 men, women and children had to leave their farms and homes in the approaching winter. The action is referred to as the Mormon War in Missouri.

Primary migration routes for LDS members journeying to the Salt Lake Valley (author's sketch).

The records relating to 'Mormon Papers 1838-1842' include affidavits of the Mormon War payroll of the Missouri men and soldiers. The originals are held by the Missouri State Archives but a copy is available from Family History Centres on microfilm no. 984920.

Interestingly enough, and obviously much too late to have prevented such action, the extermination order was rescinded on 25 June 1976 when Christopher S. Bond the then Missouri Governor issued an executive order because of the original order's legal invalidity and formally apologised on behalf of the state of Missouri for the suffering it had caused the Latter-day Saints.

The expelled Saints established a settlement in Illinois on the banks of the Mississippi River which they called Nauvoo and this became the gathering place for an estimated 16,000 church members. The choosing of this location was no accident as Nauvoo became one of the largest riverside townships of the time and also an important commercial centre. The Church members were pragmatic and the establishment of Nauvoo tends to show this; they drained the swamps, devised and wrote a governing city charter, established a university, established a city 'militia', and constructed their first temple.

Nauvoo was to be the gathering point of most emigrating church members and other converts from Canada and the USA for the next seven years. Around 1846 when an additional 20,000 church members resided in the city it rivalled Chicago in size and status. Because of its environs and population it earned the nickname of 'Nauvoo, the Beautiful.'

Nauvoo Legion and the Mormon War in Illinois (1840-1846)
In 1840 the Nauvoo City Council was authorised to establish a militia which at its peak in 1844 numbered 5,000 men. Officers of the militia were commissioned by the governor. Other rank members were required to conform to all military duties as though they were regular state militiamen. The legion disbanded in 1846 but was reformed in 1852 under the same name in Utah after the emigrant church members had settled.

The papers relating to the Officers Commission records for the Illinois State Militia which includes those commissioned to the Nauvoo Legion show names, dates of commission, rank, and the date so appointed and in which company. The records are available on microfilm no. 908142.

The records of Miscellaneous Petitions 1839 - 1853 includes claims against the state for supplies furnished in the war at Nauvoo. It only shows the names and amounts claimed but could be a useful tool in identifying those who served irrespective of rank. This record is also available on the above microfilm no. 908142.

Some LDS Military Records between 1840 and 1847 are available in an on line database at Ancestry.com which contains information on nearly 1,000 men. The database lists those who served in the Nauvoo Legion between 1840 and 1844. It also contains a listing of the men of the Mormon Battalion mustered in July 1846. Each entry provides the soldier's name, rank and commission date and can be a useful aid for those researchers of early Mormon ancestors. The source material for the Nauvoo Legion was taken from the *Illinois State Militia Commission Records, 1834-1855* and the records for the Mormon Battalion were taken from *A Concise History of the Mormon Battalion* by Daniel Tyler.

Regretfully the peace and prosperity which existed in Nauvoo was short-lived because Nauvoo was seen as both a political and economic threat by many in the neighbouring communities. At the height of these tensions a local newspaper called for mob action against the church residents but the city council immediately responded by destroying that newspaper's printing presses. However, the damage was done as the 'mob' wanted the church members removed from the city. The surrounding native communities continued to persecute the members of the church and on 27 June 1844, Joseph Smith the president of the church and his brother Hyrum were killed. A few days before the shooting Joseph Smith and other church leaders went to the town of Carthage, some 20 miles southeast of Nauvoo to answer charges of civil disturbance. Until their trial they were held in the jail and were guaranteed protection from the mob violence by the Governor of Illinois. It was while they were in the jailer's bedroom that the murder took place.

Despite this double tragedy the church members continued with their resolve of building a temple at Nauvoo. They even continued to build it between February and September 1846 as they prepared to flee the unrest and head west. They were ultimately forced to abandon their homes and their newly built temple. Today many of the buildings in the original town have been rebuilt or restored and are a Church Historical site which is open to the public.

Few people in history have suffered as much persecution for their religious convictions as the early Latter-day Saints. The church was growing rapidly and its doctrine was questioned by many to the extent that Mormonism was treated with contempt virtually from 1830 when the church was first established. It seemed that for the first twenty or so years until the church found its permanent home in Utah that members were subject to a continual round of migration and expulsion, hence the long journey across the USA. Over a period of 17 years, Latter-day Saints moved from established bases in New York State (1830-1831), Kirtland, Ohio (1831-1838), Jackson County, Missouri (1831-1839) and Nauvoo, Illinois (1839-1848). During the winter of 1846, they began the gruelling journey to the Salt Lake Valley.

In 1845, the repeal of the Nauvoo City charter, which gave the church community the right to keep a standing militia for their own protection, signalled the end of their residency in Illinois. These events were of no surprise to the church members because as early as 1840 Joseph Smith had stated that their place of safety was towards the Rocky Mountains. By the autumn of 1845, the whole community was well advanced with its plans to leave Nauvoo in the spring of 1846. However, all did not go to plan as the 'mobs' forced them to leave earlier. On 4 February 1846, during the cold and bitter winter when even the Mississippi River was frozen over the Saints were driven from their homes and hurriedly journeyed west. The frozen Mississippi withstood oxen and wagons by the hundreds and was an absolute godsend at this point enabling a quick exodus from Nauvoo.

For seven or eight months from February 1846, the Saints systematically abandoned Nauvoo, heading Westward across the Mississippi River. Many who crossed in late February did so in sub-zero temperatures using the frozen river as their route. Later they used ferries to cross the wide expanse. The majority, however, left between March and May. By September only six or seven hundred remained in Nauvoo. The last church members to leave were known as the 'poor Saints,' because they were either physically or financially incapable of travelling by themselves to join the main body, which by then were approaching Iowa. Mobs again forced this last group from the city in September, 1846, in the 'the battle of Nauvoo.'

On the morning of 10 September 1846, the watchman in the tower of the temple noted a mob of over a 1,000 ready for battle and armed with a canon and plenty of ammunition. There were only one hundred and twenty-three men left in Nauvoo able to defend themselves against the mob.

A peacemaking committee from nearby Quincy arrived to try to mediate in the troubles without bloodshed but their efforts were futile as the mob virtually ignored them.

Against all odds the battle of Nauvoo commenced. A man called Benjamin Clifford took command of the militia, and Captain William Anderson organised the 'Spartan Band' (the marksmen of the militia). They improvised cannons made from two hollow steamboat shafts which they plugged at one end and because they had no cannon balls improvised by using scraps of iron and lead tied up into bags.

The following day having been met by the Saints militia, the mob were stopped in their tracks because they were not expecting to be confronted by the cannons and on the Saturday a flag of truce was taken into the city along with a note to the Nauvoo commander stating that if the Saints did not surrender they would suffer the consequences.

The Nauvoo troops had held their position and the next day fought a fierce battle which prevented the mob from entering the City. Unfortunately both sides suffered casualties. It is deduced from the available records that about a dozen mobsters were wounded or killed and the first casualty amongst the defenders was a 14 year old young church member called Augustus Anderson. He was the son of the Militia Captain, William Anderson who was also wounded in the skirmish. Another defender, David Norris was also killed.

The battle continued for six days but on the 16 September a treaty was made. The defenders were forced to surrender but the treaty gave the church members immunity from molestation and the sick and helpless were to be protected. The church members were however required to leave as soon as possible.

Illustration of the ruined Nauvoo Temple after the Saints had been expelled from the city (Frederick Piercy drawing 1853).

The mob actually entered Nauvoo the following day completely ignoring the terms of the treaty and rampaged through the city looting and abusing the people. A gang of mobsters showed total disregard by ransacking the temple (dedicated as a sacred building within the Mormon community) and from the tower they rang the bell, yelled and shouted abuse. The 'poor Saints' scattered in all directions as quickly as they could. Most crossed the river and camped on the banks of the Mississippi in Iowa.

The first 300 miles across Iowa really tested the stamina and courage of the Latter-day Saint pioneers. A few weeks into their journey through searing winter weather it became apparent to Brigham Young, their leader that they would not reach the Rocky Mountains in the time or manner that they had hoped and planned for.

This first Iowa campsite was at Sugar Creek about seven miles west of the Mississippi. It was known as the 'Camp of Israel', and was established in February. The severe winter weather, sickness and death, together with problems regarding supplies and equipment prevented the departure of the advance party westward until spring. During the spring of 1846 they continued across the Iowa prairies, preparing the way for those who were to follow. The party constructed bridges, erected cabins, and cropped the land but despite this advance there were still 12,000 Saints encamped in Iowa in mid June having made little progress west.

Moving on from Sugar Creek the main body of the pioneers remained at Chariton River Crossing until the worst of the weather passed. The wait allowed many travellers behind the main body to catch up.

At Locust Creek some 100 miles west of Nauvoo, Brigham Young redirected the saints northwest so that the 'taggers-on' (those who had joined the trains but were not church members) would be left behind. Church leaders created a temporary campsite at Garden Grove to serve members who were yet to travel. They again erected cabins and cultivated crops. Individuals volunteered to remain at Garden Grove to manage the site whilst the remainder moved on. This was also the site of one of the first trail cemeteries known as The Cow Yard. Garden Grove was finally vacated in the spring of 1848 because it became impractical in providing for all the increasing number of the Saints still crossing Iowa. A more permanent settlement was therefore established at Mount Pisgah and it was here that volunteers for the Mormon Battalion were called upon to enlist.

Now some 230 miles west, the crossing of the Nishnabotna River, which is a tributary of the Missouri River, was marked by the meeting of the Saints and the Potawatomie Indians. The Potawatomie were another group fleeing persecution of a different kind. They stayed only temporarily on their journey primarily to Canada, but the Saints travelled across the area for some time on their way to Council Bluffs. Close by was the grand encampment which was an obvious stopping place for pioneer companies as they approached the Missouri River and was where the Mormon Battalion volunteers were officially mustered for service in the war with

Mexico. Captain James Allen of the U.S. Regular Army was seeking 500 volunteers for the six-week-old war with Mexico. The volunteers would be paid standard fare for their services. Because the Latter-day Saints were essentially fleeing the United States for refuge in the then Mexican Territory Allen's approach was at first perceived as an affront. Brigham Young, who had long sought redress from the federal government for losses sustained by his people while under its jurisdiction, saw in the action the hand of providence.

Due in no small part to the efforts of the Mormon Battalion, the Salt Lake Valley switched from Mexican to United States control.

On arrival at Millers Hollow later known as Kanesville and then a few miles further at Council Bluffs the Saints established a major encampment and outfitting point that was to become one of the most significant settlements and which was also used by other groups heading west during most of the overland emigration period.

Council Bluffs before the establishment of the settlement (Frederick Piercy drawing - date unknown).

Orson Hyde, a prominent church leader in the area, established a community newspaper, the 'Frontier Guardian', which became the official source of information for the church members as they moved west. At the time there were over 80 established Latter-day Saint settlements in Potawatomie County, Iowa and it was from Kanesville, the most important settlement, that the Mormon Battalion began its march to San Diego in July 1846.

The Mormon Battalion

The Mormon Battalion which served for a short period (one year from July 1846) during the Mexican - American war was the only wholly religious unit that served in the United States army. It was comprised entirely of volunteers numbering between 534 and 559 men led by Mormon officers but commanded by regular US army officers. During its service, the battalion undertook one of the longest marches in military history at nearly 2,000 miles from Council Bluffs, Iowa to San Diego, California.

The Mormon Battalion at Gila River Arizona (from a painting by George Ottinger.)

The Battalion which never engaged in armed conflict was instrumental in helping the US secure much of the American Southwest, especially areas of Southern Arizona and at the same time opening up a strategic wagon route to California.

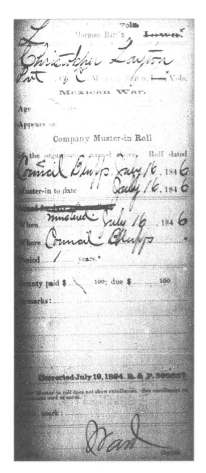

Extract from the Mormon Battalion Service Records showing record in three different variants of the surname Layton. (A brief case study for Christopher Layton follows later) (Genealogical Society of Utah Microfilm - Intellectual Reserve Inc).

The Battalion arrived at Fort Leavenworth on 30 August 1846 where they were formally organised into a combat battalion and received their guns. They also took the uniform allowance in cash. There was little time for training and instilling discipline. Newly promoted Lieutenant Colonel James Allen ordered the battalion forward along the Santa Fe Trail to overtake Kearny's Army of the West. On 23 August, Allen died and was the first officer buried in what became Fort Leavenworth National Military Cemetery.

The Battalion was divided into five companies each with four laundresses who were wives of Battalion members. 34 women and 51 children accompanied the Battalion, most of which remained at the winter camp at Fort Pueblo; however it is known that four women and six children completed the march to the Californian coast. All but one, who died in childbirth in San Diego, then completed the journey to Salt Lake City.

The Battalion's only armed engagement of the war was with, believe it or not, a herd of cattle. On 11 December 1846, wild cattle stampeded into the rear companies, colliding with some of the wagons and scaring the animals, so the Battalion's hunters shot at the beasts killing about 15 bulls but with three men wounded in the process. The action became immortalised as the 'Battle of the Bulls.'

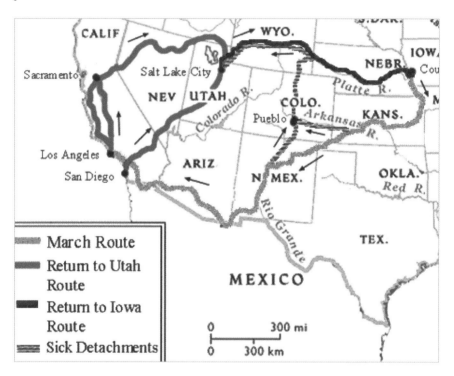

The Mormon Battalion March route (extracted form a map drawn by Brian Cole)

The Battalion arrived in San Diego on 29 January 1847 where for the next few months until their discharge in Los Angeles on 16 July 1847 they trained and performed other duties throughout Southern California. The most significant service was to block various mutinous bids to control California principally by constructing a fort at Fort Moore. Twenty two Mormon men died from disease or other natural causes during their service and about eighty men re-enlisted for a further six month period of service. Members received a campaign medal for their service.

Mexican War medal awarded to members of the Mormon Battalion
(the family of Donald E Davis Capt E Co.).

During its short lifetime the Battalion achieved a great deal viz: It established the first wagon trail across the southern desert to California; secured the fortified base at San Diego; established a U.S. presence in Tucson (originally in southern New Mexico but now part of Arizona).

This led seven years later to the Gadsden Purchase named after James Gadsden, the American Ambassador in Mexico at the time. This was a massive area of land virtually the size of Scotland and located in present-day Southern Arizona and Southwestern New Mexico that was purchased by the United States in a treaty signed by President Franklin Pierce on 24 June 1853, and ratified by the U.S. Senate on 25 April 1854.

Perhaps one of the least known achievements but obviously valuable to both the Church and the USA was that individuals in the Battalion helped in the discovery of gold at Sutter's Mill and the establishment of another wagon road this time over Cajon Pass and east from California to Salt Lake City.

The Mormon Battalion was a financial boon to the pioneers. Each of the battalion members received a $42 clothing allowance, paid in advance, for their one-year enlistment which was immediately given to a general Church fund from which wagons, teams, and other essentials for the pioneers were purchased. Similarly the wages of each man over the next year amounting to around $30,000 was also paid over.

Sutters Mill c1850 - the start of the Gold Rush.

A few discharged battalion members worked in the Sacramento area for James W. Marshall at Sutter's Mill where they effectively started the Gold Rush by discovering gold there on 24 January 1848 and when they returned home contributed a further $17,000 in gold to the economy of the church's Salt Lake Valley communities.

The original records of service for members of the Mormon Battalion are held by the National Archives in Washington but films of the records can be obtained through Family History Centres.

The service records are for all the volunteer soldiers in the Mormon organisations that served in the Mexican War and relate to the Mormon Battalion Volunteers, organised at Council Bluffs, Iowa, in 1846. They cover all five companies who enlisted for one year. Also included are the service records of those who re-enlisted in 1847 into what became known as Captain Davis' Company A, Mormon Volunteers, who served for a further six months.

The records are arranged by unit and are alphabetical by soldiers' surnames.

Each record consists of an envelope for each soldier labelled with his name, rank, and unit. All of these records should also contain abstracts and details from muster rolls and returns. There is also a microfilmed card index of the records which in itself provides the name of a soldier, his rank, and the unit or units in which he served. The main records can be found on the following microfilms and for those wishing to research in the National Archives of Washington their film numbers are also shown below.

Mormon Battalion volunteers - Surnames A-G	Film 471465
Mormon Battalion volunteers - Surnames H-R	Film 471517
Mormon Battalion volunteers - Surnames S-Z	Film 471518

National Archives, Washington catalogue reference M351 - 1 (A-G), 2 (H-R), 3 (S-Z).

Case study of a British Mormon Battalion Soldier

A humble Bedfordshire agricultural labourer, a pioneer, a military officer, a church leader, a farmer and business man, a politician now immortalised on a monument....

Christopher Layton was born on 8 March 1821 at Thorncote a hamlet in the parish of Northill, Bedfordshire. He was baptised in the parish church on 12 August 1821, a son of Samuel Layton a labourer and Isabella (known also as Elizabeth) late Wheeler and was the youngest of five children.

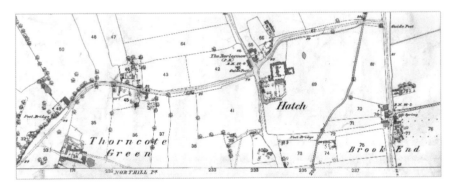

Thorncote is a hamlet within the parish of Northill, Bedfordshire. In some documentation Christopher is said to be from Hatch (Representative Map dated 1880 TNA ref OS26/126).

Christening entry for Christopher in the Northill parish baptism register (GSU Microfilm No. 1279127).

Like many males in his rural village, he became an agricultural labourer. Previously belonging to the Wesleyan Methodists he joined the Mormon Church on 1 January 1842 along with his future wife Mary Matthews.

Christopher Layton (known also to be spelt as Leighton) was around 6 feet tall, had blue eyes and light hair, he was deliberate in speech and sometimes outspoken. On 10 July 1842 Christopher married Mary Matthews in Northill Parish Church after which the couple prepared to emigrate to America under the church emigration scheme.

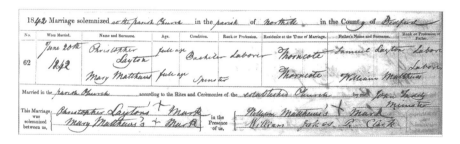

First marriage to Mary Matthews in Northill Parish Church. (GSU Microfilm No. 1279127).

They left Liverpool on board the Swanton in the company of 212 other church members led by Lorenzo Snow on 16 January 1843 after a two week wait in Liverpool to enable repairs to be made to their ship. They had travelled from Bedfordshire to Liverpool via Wolverhampton with the Coleman family who it is believed Christopher worked for prior to leaving Northill. The Swanton landed at New Orleans in March 1843. Their journey was not without disaster for the Laytons because their son, who was born on the voyage on 14 February 1843, died before they reached St Louis. They arrived in Nauvoo on 12 April 1843, and spent a few days lodging with Philemon Merrill. During their stay and while looking after an elderly woman with typhoid fever, Mary became ill with typhoid and died in September 1845, leaving Christopher a widower with an infant daughter, Elizabeth their second child who was born in Nauvoo on 17 August 1844.

Christopher and Elizabeth were amongst the first to leave Nauvoo and they crossed the Mississippi in February, 1846. It was while they were at Mount Pisgah on 16 July 1846 that the call came for volunteers to form the Mormon Battalion. Christopher was eager to serve and arranged for friends William Smith and his wife to look after Elizabeth while he was with the battalion. Christopher enlisted as a private in C Company whose commanding officer was Captain James Brown. The account of the battalion is given previously and Christopher was discharged in Los Angeles on 20 July, 1847.

After only 3 days digging for gold at Sutters Ranch (the start of the gold rush), he returned to San Francisco because the work did not suit him and whilst there he purchased a ticket to sail for England. He sailed home on 'James Pennel' via Cape Hope arriving at Liverpool in March, 1850. He returned to his Bedfordshire home, to be greeted by the sad news that his mother had died just two weeks earlier.

POSTERITY OF CHRISTOPHER LAYTON

FIRST FAMILY

CHRISTOPHER LAYTON, married July 10, 1842, at Thorncut, England, by Rev. Taddy, MARY, daughter of William MATTHEWS and Elizabeth Roundy, born ——, England; died Sept. —, 1845 at Big Mound, Ill.

THEIR CHILDREN

WILLIAM, born on Atlantic ocean, Feb. 14, 1843; died March 28, 1843, on Mississippi river, near St. Louis, Mo.

ELIZABETH, born Aug. 17, 1844, at Nauvoo, Ill.; married to WILLIAM GALBRAITH, April 11, 1861, at Kaysville, Utah, by Christopher Layton; died, Feb. 13, 1908 at Raymond, Alberta, Canada.

Her Children
(All born at Kaysville, Utah)
William L., b. Jan. 12, 1862; m. (1) Ann Elizabeth Bodily, Dec. 22, 1886 (d. May 19, 1904) ; (2) Annie Pearl Curtis, Feb. 10, 1909.
Mary L., b. Sept. 24, 1864; m. (1) Chas. C. Hyde, March, 1883; and (2) Elijah Laycock, Nov., 1889; d. Jan. 14, 1908 at Raymond, Canada.
George, b. Nov. 6, 1866; d. Oct. 4, 1868.
Christopher, b. Feb. 28, 1869; m. Mary Heva Johnson, March 23, 1895 at Diaz, Mexico.
Peter, b. Sept. 16, 1871; d. June 4, 1873.
David, b. March 30, 1883.

SECOND FAMILY

CHRISTOPHER LAYTON married, May 3, 1850 at Sandy church, Thorncut, England, by Rev. Cook,
SARAH, daughter of John MARTIN and Mary Ann Price; born, Nov. 29, 1822 at Thorncut, England; died, Oct. 25, 1864 at Kaysville, Utah.

THEIR CHILDREN

WILLIAM, born May 1, 1851 at St. Louis; died August —, 1851 at St. Louis.
CHRISTOPHER, born Jan. 1, 1853, at Salt Lake City; married Jane E. Bodily, Jan. 18, 1874 in Salt Lake City, by Daniel H. Wells.

His Children
(All born in Kaysville)
Frank B., b. Sept. 1, 1876; m. Emma Diana Ellsworth, June 12, 1901, at Safford, Ariz., by Andrew Kimball.
Christopher B., b. July 6, 1878; m. Margaret B. Flint, Apr. 23, 1902, in Salt Lake City, by John R. Winder.
Lawrence, R. B., b. Nov. 14, 1880.
Maggie B., b. Aug. 7, 1882.
Mary B., b. Feb. 13, 1885; m. to Albert B. Barton by President A. H. Lund, in Salt Lake City, Jan. 25, 1911.
Delbert Edwin, b. Aug. 19, 1887; d. April 18, 1891.
Jennie B., b. Sept. 25, 1889.
Roy Vernon, b. June 22, 1891; d. Jan. 30, 1892.
Eveline B., b. Mar. 19, 1893; d. Mar. 27, 1893.
Vernon Cecil, b. Feb. 12, 1896.

Details of the family of Christopher Layton taken from his autobiography (Deseret News Originally Published 1911).

Whilst back in Bedfordshire he met and married Sarah Martin at Sandy Parish Church on 3 May 1850 after which he prepared to return to Utah. Finding that there were many Saints wishing to emigrate but lacking sufficient funds, he paid all or part of the fare for the passages for 66 persons, including his new wife, father, six relatives and forty-six friends. They sailed again on 'James Pennel' leaving Liverpool for America on 2 October 1850 with 252 church members on board.

Christopher was appointed the leader of the company and arrived at New Orleans on 22 November 1850. On arrival he then spent two years at St. Louis where he helped new emigrants financially to cross the plains. In the spring of 1852 he became a train captain and led a company of 52 wagons to Salt Lake, arriving in September 1852 and taking with him the first threshing machine and 100 head of cattle.

In the spring of 1856, he journeyed to Carson Valley, Nevada, where he figured prominently in establishing a strong church community. In the autumn of 1857 Christopher Layton returned to Utah and became a successful arable farmer in Kaysville where he spent much of the remainder of his life.

Besides his agricultural pursuits, he also built and operated grist mills, a saw mill, small chain of butcher's shops, a milk house, and an ice plant. He was also involved in public life and was elected twice to the Territorial Legislature. He was also instrumental in establishing railroads, wagon roads, and canals and spent some time in Arizona. Whilst in Arizona, he contracted with the Government to supply flour to the San Carlos Indian Reservation.

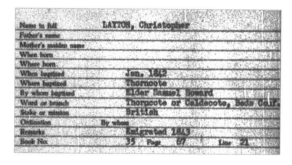

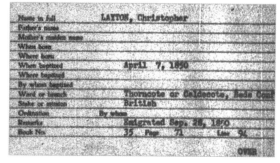

Utah Immigration Card Index entries for Christopher Layton's two emigration voyages
(LDS Church (Intellectual Reserve Inc).

He also continued his military connection by being active in the Nauvoo Legion in Utah, and was commissioned a Lt. Colonel in 1866. Along with his public responsibility he also fulfilled many prominent local positions within the church.

In June 1898, Christopher Layton went to Utah for an operation but died on 7 August 1898 at age 77 years never having really recovered from the effects of the surgery. His funeral service took place on 13 August that year and afterwards he was interred in Kaysville Cemetery. As a fitting tribute Christopher Layton is commemorated on the Mormon Battalion Monument constructed in El Presidio Park, Tucson, Arizona.

Christopher Layton obituary notice (from the Salt Lake Herald 9 August 1898). His final resting place and the Mormon Battalion Monument in Tucson, Arizona upon which he is remembered. (author's photographs).

This is the life of a humble agricultural labourer from a small Bedfordshire hamlet. His full biography written in 1911 by John Q Cannon, a close friend, is available as an e-book on **www.openlibrary.org**

British Members of the Mormon Battalion
The following is a list of those church members who were born in Britain and served in the Mormon Battalion. Information is at the time of enlistment.

NAME	RANK	COMPANY	BORN	PLACE
Joseph W Bates	Private	E	16 Jan 1827	Dudley, Staffordshire
William Beers	Private	E	30 Apr 1827	Banbury, Oxfordshire
James Bevan	Private	A	19 Oct 1821	Kings Capel, Herefordshire
John Borrowman	Private	B	13 May 1816	Glasgow, Scotland
Richard Brazier	Sergeant	E	6 Dec 1793	Biddenden, Kent
Daniel Browett	Sergeant	E	18 Dec 1809	Gloucester, Gloucestershire
George Coleman	Private	A	2 Mar 1817	Winford, Norfolk
Robert H Collins	Private	D	Dec 1822	England
John Cox	Private	E	10 Aug 1810	Deerhurst, Gloucestershire
James Davis	Private	D	26 May 1826	Llanfrothan, Monmouthshire
Joseph Dobson	Private	A	26 Aug 1804	Oultonlow, Cheshire
Ralph Briggs Douglas	Private	D	28 Dec 1824	Downham, Lancashire
William Evans	Private	B	1 Mar 1818	Herefordshire
James Ferguson	Sergeant	A	28 Feb 1828	Belfast, Ireland
John Fife	Private	C	18 May 1825	Leith, Scotland
Peter Muir Fife	Private	B	5 Apr 1806	Pathead, Midlothian
Robert Harris	Private	E	28 Dec 1808	Hucclecote, Gloucestershire
Charles T Howarth	Sergeant	E	7 Jun 1801	Upholland, Lancashire
Thomas C Joic	Private	C	17 Jun 1813	Eton Socon, Bedfordshire
Thomas Karren	Private	E	1 May 1810	Isle of Man
William Kelly	Private	A	6 Apr 1828	Isle of Man
Thomas Kirk	Private	B	18 May 1815	Staffordshire
Christopher Layton	Private	C	8 Mar 1821	Thorncut, Bedfordshire
Edward Martin	Corporal	C	18 Nov 1818	Preston, Lancashire
Thomas Morris	Private	B	16 Oct 1799	Swansea, Glamorgan
Daniel Moss	Private	A	17 Sept 1818	Newtown, Yorkshire
William Smith Muir	Corporal	A	19 July 1822	Bannockburn, Stirling
James Pollock Park	Private	B	21 Dec 1821	Cambuslang, Lanarkshire
John Perkins	Private	C	28 Jun 1821	Bath, Somerset
George Pickup snr	Private	C	16 April 1821	Manchester, Lancashire
Robert Pixton	Private	E	27 Feb 1819	Manchester, Lancashire
Jonathan Pugmire	Private	E	7 Dec 1823	Carlisle, Cumberland

Peter F Richards	Private	B	6 April 1808	Edinburgh, Scotland
Thomas Richardson	Private	E	21 Feb 1804	Wigan, Lancashire
Levi Roberts	Private	E	26 Feb 1815	Apperly, Gloucestershire
William J Robinson	Private	D	28 Feb 1828	Dublin, Ireland
John Roylance	Private	D	20 Nov 1807	Peover, Cheshire
Jospeh Shipley	Private	C	1 Nov 1813	Burton Latimer, Northants
Richard Swater	Private	E	2 Feb 1812	Lancashire
William Squires	Private	C	26 Sept 1816	Linton, Devon
Henry Standage	Private	E	26 Feb 1818	Southwark, Lancashire
John Steele	Private	D	21 Mar 1821	Holyrood, Co. Down
John S Watts	Private	E	4 Jun 1810	England
David Wilkin	Sergeant	C	1 Aug 1819	Inniskillen, Ireland
William Wood	Private	C	2 Feb 1823	Hereford, Herefordshire
Charles Wright	Private	B	12 Jun 1822	Cheshire

There were also two British women who were with the battalion, *Eliza Bridget Allred*, born 23 Nov 1831 in Herefordshire and *Catherine Campbell Steel* (wife of John Steele), born 10 Nov 1816 in Belfast, Ireland.

Winter Quarters
In the first year of migration only 2,000 people migrated to the Salt Lake Valley. However thousands remained in Iowa on their farms to prepare for those yet to migrate. The Latter-day Saints as they travelled built permanent roads and bridges and established river ferries.

Winter Quarters (The Winter Quarters Project).

Becoming an instant city Winter Quarters served as the headquarters of the Church for about a year, until the leadership moved west in 1847. By late December 1846, about 700 homes had been constructed. For many, however, the rigours of the migration across Iowa proved too much and several hundred Saints died during that winter, the result of exposure, and poor sanitation and nutrition.

Soon after the first pioneers reached Utah in 1847, the Church began encouraging its converts in the British Isles and elsewhere in Europe to emigrate. Between 1849 and 1855 about 16,000 European Latter-day Saints travelled to Salt Lake City Utah firstly by ship and then by ox and wagon.

The initial stages of the trek across Iowa saw the pioneers encounter blizzard conditions and their journey was continually hampered by heavy mud. At one point it became clear to Brigham Young that the Saints would never reach the Rocky Mountains in the time most had hoped for.

Entry to the Salt Lake Valley was postponed as nearly 12,000 Saints were still scattered across Iowa. On 5 April 1847 Brigham Young took an advance party of 143 men, 3 women, and 2 children from Winter Quarters and headed west. Their journey of about 1,050 miles was a reasonably easy one, considering the trials they had already encountered. The advanced party entered the Salt Lake Valley on 21 July but Brigham Young did not arrive until three days later as he contracted 'mountain fever'. Before he even saw the valley he declared from the back of the wagon in which he was travelling that, 'This is the right place' and by October of that year, a further 2,000 pioneering church members had reached the valley.

Thirty two days after his arrival in Salt Lake, Brigham Young instructed some of his members to head back to Winter Quarters to aid the remaining Saints with their journey. This trail became the first 'Inter-state Highway' of the time across Western America. Within a few weeks a constant stream of wagons was moving in both directions on the trail. It was in Brigham Young's Vanguard Company on 11 May 1847 that a 'road meter' (milometer) was attached to a wagon driven by Philo Johnson. The 1847 pioneers did not 'invent' the road meter, but the version they created was accurate enough to use in conjunction with the recorded mileage in the Latter-day Saints' Emigrants' Guide. This was a small booklet compiled by William Clayton detailing the prominent way-points or landmarks together with their distance from Winter Quarters to Salt Lake and this acted as a route-guide for all later emigrants.

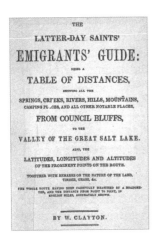

THE
LATTER-DAY SAINTS'
EMIGRANTS' GUIDE:
BEING A

TABLE OF DISTANCES,
SHOWING ALL THE

SPRINGS, CREEKS, RIVERS, HILLS, MOUNTAINS,
CAMPING PLACES, AND ALL OTHER NOTABLE PLACES,

FROM COUNCIL BLUFFS,
TO THE

VALLEY OF THE GREAT SALT LAKE.
ALSO, THE

LATITUDES, LONGITUDES AND ALTITUDES
OF THE PROMINENT POINTS ON THE ROUTE.

TOGETHER WITH REMARKS ON THE NATURE OF THE LAND, TIMBER, GRASS, &c.

THE WHOLE ROUTE HAVING BEEN CAREFULLY MEASURED BY A ROADOMETER, AND THE DISTANCE FROM POINT TO POINT, IN ENGLISH MILES, ACCURATELY SHEWN.

BY W. CLAYTON.

22

NOTES.

Note 1. If the Elk Horn river is fordable, you leave the main road a mile before you strike the river, and turn north. After leaving the road three-fourths of a mile, you will cross a very bad creek or slough, being soft and miry; but, by throwing in long grass, it will be good crossing. You then travel three-fourths of a mile further, and arrive at the ford. You will go up stream when fording, and gradually come nearer to the opposite above, till you strike a piece of low land on the west side; you then pass by a narrow, crooked road, through the timber, till you arrive on the open prairie. You will then see a post erected in near a south direction, about a mile distant. Go straight to that post, and you will find a good bridge over the creek—and there, again strike the main road. From here, you have before you near five hundred miles travel over a flat, level country, and a good road, with the exception of several sandy bluffs mentioned herein. The road generally runs from one to two miles from the Platte river, but not too far to turn off to camp in case of necessity. All camping places, which lay near the road, are mentioned in this work. You will find near two hundred miles without timber, but in that region you will find plenty of buffalo chips, which are a good substitute for fuel. Buffalo are numerous after you arrive at the head of Grand Island, and continue two hundred miles.

Note 11. The descent to the ford is steep, and at the bottom very sandy. Your best chance to ford will, probably, be to enter the river opposite to where you descend from the bluff; then go near a straight course, but inclining a little down stream, till more than half way over, when you will find a sand-bar. Follow this, down stream near half a mile, and you will then see a good place to go out on the south side. In this river the channels often change—the old ones fill up, and new ones are made—hence, the wisdom and necessity of having several men go across on horses, to find the best route, before you attempt to take wagons over. If this precaution is not taken, you may plunge your wagons from a sand-bar into a deep hole, and do much damage. If you ford up stream, and come out higher than where you enter, after crossing, strike for the bluffs, in a direction a very little west of south, till you arrive on the table land.

On arriving at Prairie creek, if you take a south-west course, a short day's drive will bring you to Wood river, six or eight miles above where the old road crosses; and by keeping the same course after crossing Wood river, you will strike

PROMINENT POINTS AND REMARKS.	DIST. miles.	FROM W Qrs. miles.	FROM C of G S L miles.
Winter Quarters, Lat. 41° 18' 53"			1031
The road good, but very crooked, following the ridges and passing over a continual succession of hills and hollows.			
Pappea, ten feet wide, high banks. -	18	18	1013
Some timber on the creek, but it is difficult to water teams. After this, the road is crooked and uneven to the Elk Horn.			
Elk Horn, nine rods wide, three feet deep.	9	27	1004
Current rather swift, and not very pleasant to ferry. Plenty of timber on its banks. (See Note 1.)			
Creek, ten feet wide, steep banks. -	⅜	27¾	1003¼
This creek has a good bridge over it, but little timber on the banks. There is a high post, erected near the bridge, for a guide to it.			
Platte river and Liberty Pole. - -	11¼	39	992
Plenty of timber, but you will probably have to go to the river for water—distance about a quarter of a mile. The nearest and best road to water is round the east point of the timber.			
Small Lake (narrow) south side the road.	3½	42½	988½
No timber on the Lake.			
Circular Lake, or pond, close to the road, (south.) - - - - -	⅜	43½	987¾
No timber. In the neighborhood of this, the road runs alongside a number of small lakes, or ponds, for two miles; but there is little timber near them.			
R. R. and T., road joins the river, Lat. 41° 27' 5" - - - - -	9	52½	978¼
This is a point where a branch of the river runs round an island, on which is plenty of timber. Not much water in the channel, but plenty for camping purposes.			
Indian Grave, north side the road. -	7½	59¾	971¼
This is a large pile of earth, about eighty yards north of the road.			
R. R. and T., road joins the river. -	⅜	60¼	970¾
Plenty of timber and water, without leaving the road			
Shell creek, 12 feet wide, three feet deep.	2	62¼	968¾
This creek is bridged, and a few rods lower is a place to ford. Plenty of timber on it. After this you will probably find no water for twelve miles, without turning considerably from the road.			
Small lake, south side of the road. -	5¾	68	963
Plenty of water in the Spring season, but none in Summer. It was entirely dry, October 18, 1847.			

The Emigrants Guide served as a route map for many thousands of emigrants on their overland journey
(Latter-day Saints Emigrants Guide - W Clayton).

On their journey, all emigrant Saints who left the Missouri travelled for hundreds of miles along the north side of the Platte River because by using this trail they faced fewer chances of unpleasant encounters with other emigrants who had been their former enemies from Missouri or Illinois. The north side of the river was also considered to be a healthier option than travelling on the south side would have been. Despite this it was often necessary to change to the other side when feed for livestock was in short supply or was non-existent. In 1849, 1850, and 1852, which were the heaviest migratory years a constant flow of traffic along the Platte used up all available supplies so times became desperate, so much so that lack of supplies and the constant threat of disease such as cholera, made the journey at best a gamble which most were still prepared to take.

Hundreds of thousands of Americans including the Latter-day Saints crossed the American Plains and the Rocky Mountains in the 1800s in their quest for a better life in the West. The most significant landmark on the overland trail was the 500 feet high Chimney Rock Nebraska. Not only did many Saints write about it in their journals, but it was perhaps the most sketched and painted landmark and many carved their names and dates of passage into it. Such memorials can still be found around the base of the rock.

To make the journey to Salt Lake all the migrating Saints were organised into companies, led by captains and with welfare and organising committees and they even organised choirs. These companies comprised of a hundred and fifty wagons, each one being allocated to a family or a group constituting a 'family' made up of individuals otherwise travelling alone as well as those widowed or orphaned whilst emigrating. These individuals were then adopted into another family so no one travelled alone. The organisation of committees was also paramount and each was designated for a specific purpose such as trail marking and road improvement. Everyone in the company had an assignment.

On the trek across the plains it was quite normal for many to walk for the majority of the journey and at the end of each day the Saints would gather round the campfire for evening entertainment, singing, music playing and even dancing would occur. Such entertainment was essential to the morale of the group and it was one of the ways that the companies looked after the spiritual and temporal welfare on the long journey.

The structure of the companies was centred around entire families (and sometimes an extended family), single adults, orphans and men with a multitude of skills and talents including professional men such as doctors and lawyers as well as skilled tradesmen including masons, carpenters, piano and organ makers. English, Welsh, German and Scandinavian travellers made the journey alongside each other. On the Trail they socially integrated, many learning each other's skills. As whole communities on the move they often had to improvise and became extraordinarily adaptable. For around 70,000 Latter-day Saint pioneers, it was a vision of a common future which brought and held them together.

After the initial arrival in the Salt Lake Valley a system of wagon trains was set up known affectionately as the 'Down and Backs' which ran between 1861 and 1868 each taking about 6 months to complete. Each wagon train departed Utah and travelled to the Missouri River, loaded with flour and grain which was sold in the East. On arrival the trains re-formed with newly arrived European converts, and headed back to the Salt Lake Valley. Everyone in a Utah settlement contributed to the cause with supplies or men.

The Handcart Companies

In 1856, the church inaugurated the handcart companies to facilitate poor British and European emigration. The two-wheeled carts were pulled by emigrants themselves instead of oxen because they were considered a faster, easier, and cheaper way of transportation to Salt Lake. Almost 3,000 Mormons, with 653 carts and 50 supply wagons, travelling in 10 different companies, made the trip to Salt Lake City. Each company consisted of about 500 people with 100 carts and 5 supply wagons.

A typical hand cart used by the Pioneers
(Public Service Broadcasting - Sweetwater Rescue re-enactment at Platte River).

The handcarts which could be either pushed or pulled were made mostly of wood and were around six to seven feet long but wide enough to span a narrow wagon track. They also incorporated a small box which could carry provisions and personal possessions.

The handcart companies were strictly organised into groups, basically one cart per five people together with a tent to sleep 20 people. Each person was only allowed to have, by weight, 17 pounds of clothing and bedding. The tent was round and supported by a centre pole. Five tents housing a total of 100 people were supervised by a 'tent captain'. The provisions for each group of one hundred emigrants were carried in a support wagon again under the control of the tent captain.

The Handcart Companies were made up of emigrants and the company journals state the name of the handcart company captain, the name and date of sailing of the ship from Liverpool and its destination and when the company arrived in Salt Lake, as follows:

CAPTAIN	SHIP'S NAME	DATE SAILED	DESTINATION PORT	ARRIVED SALT LAKE
Edward Elsworth	Enoch Train	23 Mar 1856	Boston	26 Sept 1856
Daniel McArthur	Enoch Train	23 Mar 1856	Boston	26 Sept 1856
	S Curling	19 Apr 1856	Boston	26 Sept 1856
Edward Bunker	S Curling	19 Apr 1856	Boston	2 Oct 1856
James Willey	Thornton	4 May 1856	New York	9 Nov 1856
Edward Martin	Horizon	25 May 1856	Boston	30 Nov 1856
Israel Evans	George Washington	27 Mar 1857 (originated Copenahgen)	Boston	11 Sep 1857
Christian Christensen	Westmorland	25 Apr 1857	Philadelphia	13 Sep 1857
George Rowley	William Tapscott	11 Apr 1859	New York	4 Sep 1859
Daniel Robinson	Underwriter	30 Mar 1860	New York	27 Aug 1860
Oscar Stoddard	William Tapscott	11 May 1860	New York	24 Sep 1860

Edward Bunkers' company was made up entirely of Welsh Church members and Christian Christensens' was wholly Scandinavian having sailed from Copenhagen to Liverpool before making the Atlantic crossing. The journeys were not without tragedies and two handcart companies suffered in 1856 due to severe weather.
All but two of the companies successfully completed the journey with few problems and no more than the normal number of deaths. However, the fourth and fifth companies, known as the Willie and Martin Handcart Companies respectively, encountered problems. Both companies left Iowa in July 1856, which was considered too late to make the journey across America without encountering severe weather as winter approached. They indeed met the severe winter weather as they crossed Wyoming and were severely hampered by deep snow and storms for the remainder of the journey. Food supplies ran out and it was necessary to instigate a rescue of both companies. Unfortunately because of the conditions more than 210 of the 980 emigrants within the two companies died.

The Perils of the Handcart Companies

The Willie Handcart Company, named after its leader James Willie, comprised of those emigrants who travelled form Liverpool to New York on board the Thornton, sailing on 4 May 1856. This company lost 68 members but eventually arrived in Salt Lake on 9 November 1856. The Martin Handcart Company named after its leader Edward Martin comprised of those emigrants who sailed on board the Horizon leaving Liverpool on 25 May 1856. This company suffered the most losses numbering 145 but did eventually arrive in Salt Lake on 30 November 1856. Because so many of the companies were British or European it is worth looking at how and why the disaster arose bearing in mind that each company was so well organised. Basically both companies were running out of food and encountering bitterly cold temperatures. On 19 October a blizzard struck the region, bringing both companies and the relief party to a grinding halt. The Willie Handcart Company was along the Sweetwater River where an advance party of rescuers found them, gave them some flour which they had just ran out of at the time and indicated that the main rescue party was close. The rescue party then tried to locate the Martin Handcart Company. To sustain themselves the Willie Handcart Company slaughtered their cattle but despite this sustenance the deaths continued. On 20 October James Willie and Joseph Elder set out at daybreak by mule to locate the supply train. They arrived at the rescue party's campsite during the evening, and a day later the rescue party reached the Willie Handcart Company where half remained to provide assistance.

One of the many modern memorials placed on the graves of those who died in the handcart companies' trek across the plains. (author's photograph).

The other half of the rescue party went on to assist the Martin Handcart Company. On 19 October the Martin Handcart Company was about 110 miles east, and making its last crossing of the North Platte River. As the company finished crossing the river they were hit by a blizzard. Many members of the company were suffering from frostbite after wading across the river, and being hampered by the snow they set up camp at Red Bluffs. The Martin Handcart Company remained at Red Bluffs for nine days where a further 56 members of the company died after which the emigrant company continued their journey.

George G Grant, the leader of the main rescue party, had this to say at the time *'that the sight is almost too much for the stoutest of us but we are doing all we can, not doubting nor despairing'*. This was in response to seeing people tired and worn out by struggling to pull hand carts through snow and mud; fainting by the wayside, children crying because their limbs had been stiffened by cold, their bare feet bleeding due to exposure to ground covered with snow and frost.

The rescue party unloaded the wagons of two of the companies that had been following the Martin Handcart Company so they could be freed up to transport the weakest emigrants. A small group of twenty men remained at Devil's Gate over the winter to guard freight unloaded there by the independent wagon companies. Devil's Gate is a narrow but deep cutting about a ¼ mile in length made by the Sweetwater River through an immense rock. On 4 November they crossed the Sweetwater River, which was hampered by floating pack ice. Many of the young men in the rescue party pulled the carts through and carried the weaker emigrants across the river which for some resulted in their deaths. The severe weather caused the Martin Handcart Company to remain for a further five days a few miles west of Devil's Gate at a place aptly names 'Martin's Cove'.

An almost daily occurrence on the handcart company trek was the burial of the dead (Intellectual Reserve Inc).

The rescue parties escorted the emigrants from both companies to Utah through more snow and severe weather. After the companies arrived in Utah, the residents opened their homes to them and cared for them over the remainder of the winter before they left to populate areas throughout the state.

The handcart companies continued until 1860 transporting many thousands of English and European saints across America. After 1860 the church abandoned the handcart companies but continued with the wagon trains until the completion of the Transcontinental Railroad in 1869, after which future emigrants were able to travel by rail.

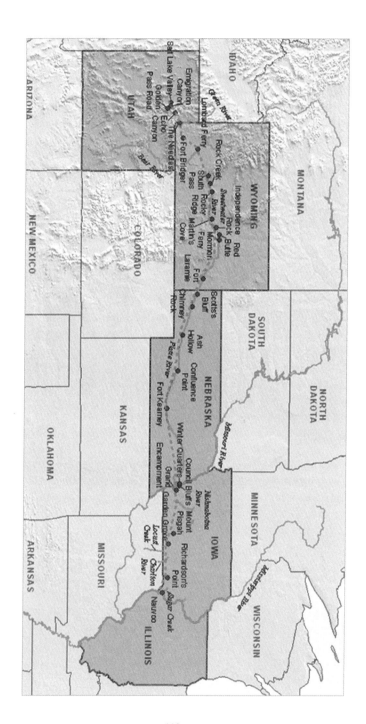

The Mormon Pioneer Trail used by both wagon trains and handcart companies.

The second letter to the *'Manchester Examiner and Times'* from John Chambers describes his view of the journey across the plains and is shown below.

'In my last letter I gave you an account of my journeys from England to Keokuk, a young but thriving city, beautifully situated on the banks of the Mississippi river, about 1,500 miles from the mouth of it. It was the place chosen by the Mormons for the starting point to cross the plains, it being considered a more healthful route to Council Bluffs than the one formerly traversed by them up the Missouri river to that place. I will therefore now proceed to give you a short description of the route from Keokuk to Great Salt Lake City. I travelled with a company of Mormons, and did not lose any opportunity of observing the order and discipline to which the whole body were subjected, and which enabled that singular people to achieve so much and overcome so many difficulties, a great deal of which is already known in part to your readers.

On the 1st day of June, 1853, the company with which I determined to travel moved from the city of Keokuk, Iowa, under the superintendence of Mr. Cyrus H. Wheelock. The train consisted of upwards of fifty wagons, drawn by ox teams; and a very imposing spectacle it presented, as it moved along over the black, loamy soil of Iowa, the white canvass of the numerous wagons affording a striking contrast. Away we went, somewhat joyfully, to see the wonderful city in the Valley of the Rocky Mountains, the rumbling of the wheels of the wagons, the cracking of the whip, and the shouting of the teamsters affording a little variety to the monotony which we had endured in camp at Keokuk.

The country through which we were passing was very fertile, and but thinly populated. The route through Iowa to Council Bluffs was crowded on the right and left with beautiful woodland scenery, and there were immense prairie lands covered with grass, varying from one to six or seven feet in height, affording good food for cattle. The rivers that intersected the territory were full of excellent fish, and many of the company employed themselves at the camping grounds on the rivers in fishing. Many times I thought of the English farm-labourers and operatives, and said within myself, 'Here is a land well fitted for such men to locate upon, and cultivate, and with a little industry raise their own crops, and their own stock, and live in comparative independence.' Here and there, as we moved along, we came up with settlers who were living in some degree of comfort, but it appeared to me that they indulged themselves in lazy habits, otherwise they might soon have considerable property around them.

Before I proceed to describe any circumstances of our travels, I will state here that the Mormons maintained a similar organisation across the plains as they did in crossing the sea. The whole were under the control of one captain, and he was empowered to elect others to assist him. There were captains of hundreds, of fifties, and of tens. These subordinate captains presided over a certain number of wagons, and had to see them over all difficult places; and to see that every man did his duty in watching, in herding the cattle, and in everything connected with camp life. There was also a captain of the guard appointed; his duty consisted in calling out the guard at the close of each day, when the company were camped. Officers were appointed to go ahead, and search out suitable camping grounds. A chaplain was also appointed; his duty consisted in calling meetings for prayer and public worship, every Sabbath Day being set apart for that purpose, the Mormons believing that the cattle required rest as well as themselves. The chaplain had also to see that all persons in camp attended the meetings, or to know the reason why they did not, and to see that all the sick were visited; it was his business to see that the sacrament was duly administered to every good member in the church, every Sabbath Day. Under this system, everything moved on in wonderful harmony among so large a number of individuals, from different parts of England, Scotland, and Ireland, and some from France. If anything wrong occurred - if there was any dispute or quarrelling among the members - or if any of them committed any crime that was unseemly and unbecoming a Mormon - a council was called of the whole camp, at which the president of the company presided, and the individual must confess his fault, if proved guilty, or be dis-fellowshipped. This procedure was fully carried out over the plains, until we arrived in the Valley of the Mountains, and every individual arrived in safety.

We proceeded on our tedious journey, under this kind of discipline, keeping the north side of the Missouri river until we reached Council Bluffs, where we camped for about one week, for the purpose of taking in our last supply of provisions, previous to leaving the last point of civilisation, as it was here the Mormons had arranged to have a large supply brought up by the steamboats to the city of Council Bluffs to provision all their companies for the remainder of the journey. I may just mention that Council Bluffs is a considerable city to be so far inland. It was first located by the Mormons, but is now occupied by numbers of Yankee speculators and half-breed Mormons, who made considerable progress during the emigration season.

It occupied considerable time to cross the Missouri ferry, but this done, we pushed forward through the remainder of the country occupied by the Iowans and the Omahans, but were not visited by either of these tribes. As we passed into the Pawnee territory, these natives soon paid a visit to our camp. Early one morning a party of Pawnees visited us, and conversed with Mr. Dykes (who was returning from a Mormon mission to Denmark), as he had crossed the plains at other times, and was somewhat acquainted with the languages of the Indian tribes. A pipe of tobacco being produced and lighted, the party sat down with Mr. Dykes and Mr. Wheelock, forming a circle upon the grass. The pipe was passed from one to the other, each one puffing three or four times, first to the right and then to the left, and lastly upwards, which was a sign that they were at peace with all around, and with the Great Spirit. The chief was made to understand that Mr. Wheelock was our chief, and he immediately embraced him, saluting him with the Pawnee kiss. The party then separated, taking with them many presents in the shape of biscuits, &c.; their object was to hunt buffaloes. This tribe is considered one of the most thievish of all the tribes on this route, but they did not exhibit any of these propensities in our company.

The company with whom I travelled were not at all annoyed by the Indians; perhaps we were too numerous for them. They frequently came and traded their skins and buffalo robes, moccasins, &c. for beads, trinkets, and bread or flour; but never showed any disposition to quarrel with us. I afterwards heard that a large party of Pawnees mustered on the route, and demanded large quantities of flour, more than the companies could well spare. They showed fight towards one company under Captain Brown, because they would not give them more than 200 lb of flour, and drew out in order of battle. When Captain Brown saw their determination, he gave orders to his 'boys' to get their rifles ready. But on the Indians perceiving this, they withdrew without further molestation. As a general thing, I may observe here, that the various tribes of Indians will listen to reason if you can possibly converse with them, and can be made to exercise kindness, and many of the virtues common to humanity.

Numerous and novel to me were the many scenes and trials in crossing the plains. Every two or three days we were visited by fearful storms of thunder and lightning, accompanied with tempestuous winds and torrents of rain and hail. Occasionally the force of the wind would overthrow a tent, and expose the inmates and the goods to the mercy of the storm; but help was soon at hand, and again the tent was reared. If a storm came on whilst travelling, orders were given to halt and turn the hind part of the wagon to the storm; the cattle unhitched, and permitted to graze, to prevent a 'stampede.' You in England can form little idea of the thunder storm on the plains. Its first approach is indicated by the rising of a small, dark cloud on the horizon, which gradually increases, and spreads with considerable rapidity over the plain. The thunder is heard booming along like the sounds of a large park of artillery, with a deep richness of tone that cannot be conceived in the narrow and confined streets of the towns and cities of England. These sounds seldom cease until the storm is over. Then comes the brilliant silvery flash of the lightning, which illumines the darkness of midnight with a light so pure that it would be possible to pick up a pin from the prairie ground, if one were there. Oft times have I experienced considerable pleasure in watching this awfully grand phenomenon of nature, as it lighted up my wagon, during the silent hours of the night; the shrill voice of the guard as he called the hour and 'all's right,' together with the pealing thunder, every now and again breaking the monotony of the hours of slumber. The rain fell in torrents, and hail came down upon our canvass as though the 'boys' above were pelting us with alabaster marbles; but the canvass withstood the battery in first-rate style. In all tempestuous storms which we passed through, I never observed any fear displayed by the Mormons; but every man was at his post, either at midnight or in the day time.

Previous to our arrival at Fort Laramie, we passed many places that were colonised by prairie dogs. These cunning little animals partake somewhat of the rabbit species, and burrow under ground, differing in their formation and in some of their habits. The nose and mouth are like the rabbit; the ears are short, and appear as though they had been cut. The other portion of the body is much like that of the dog, with the exception of the tail, which, I believe, is short and bushy. They generally occupy a large piece of sandy land; raise mounds by scratching a hole to burrow in, leaving the entrance at the top; and when anything disturbs them, there is one always on the watch, who raises the alarm by a sudden howl, and down they all go. It requires a smart marksman to shoot one, they are so exceedingly quick. At night, the howling of the prairie dogs and of the wolves around our camp was sometimes very great; and you might imagine them close upon your heels, so fierce and loud did they howl. If a horse or an ox fell or 'gave out' from fatigue, the wolves were soon upon the track, scenting out their prey, and by the light of the morning the bones of the animal were to be seen pretty well cleared of the flesh. These ferocious animals were very numerous, and at times very bold, attacking beasts in or near the camp at midnight unless the guard is keeping a sharp look-out; they invariably quit on the appearance of daylight.

Many rivers lay in our path, which we had to cross; some by ferry-boat, others we ran our teams through without stopping. Sometimes it was rather difficult to cross these streams by ferry boat, with heavily-laden wagons, owing to the sand-banks, snags, &c.; but these things appeared to be little in the way of the Mormons, for us soon as the difficulty presented itself, a dozen men were immediately at hand with spades, shovels, and pickaxes, to remove any obstacle that might be likely to retard our progress. In fact, a company of pioneers was formed - a man out of every twelve being required every morning. This party had a captain over them, and he called them out, and went ahead of the camp; and on perceiving any bad or difficult places, they endeavoured to smooth the path for the coming train, reducing, where possible, sudden descents and steep inclines, filling up sloughs and mud holes with prairie grass and brushwood, covering all with soil, thus giving a firmer footing for the cattle; forming bridges and repairing those that were broken down or carried away by the floods. In this manner the train met with little or no delay until they camped in the evening.

I must now hasten to give you a slight sketch of our journey from Fort Laramie, as we had up to this time been engaged in crossing rivers and plains, but now we were about to experience a change, - the Black Hills lay before us as we approached the fort - these we had to cross previously to our arrival at the Valley of the Great Salt Lake.

We reached Fort Laramie on the 24th August, and pitched camp on the north side of the river Platte - the same side on which we had been travelling. Here the company set about making repairs; fixing anything that was out of order, and tightening the tires on the wagon wheels, as we were about to experience a change in the character of the roads - from sand and mud to rocky mountains. Fort Laramie is but a small village, consisting of a store, a hotel, and some few houses. The inhabitants chiefly depend upon trading with the emigrants and Indians, and speculating with cattle. There is a mail station here also, and a company of the United States army to defend the rights of all travellers.

It was at Fort Laramie that we received a visit from the tribe of Indians called Sioux. These are a more noble looking race than the Pawnees, being taller and more athletic, with intelligent and rather handsome features. They went through the smoking ceremony with the chief of our company, and he made them some presents, one of whom received an old black dress coat, a hat, and a pair of pants; the coat he soon put on, and 'cut a dash' through the camp with the new garb, being a man upwards of 6 feet well proportioned and noble features. The pants he could not get on, and said they were 'no good,' as he could not walk or run in them. The female members of this tribe were of a beautiful appearance, though having a dark skin; they partake somewhat of the Spanish features, being brunette, with dark bright eyes. Two of these came to camp one morning, just as we were about to move, riding upon ponies, sitting cross-legged, and wished to trade their moccasins for bread, or trinkets, or jewels, but when we offered anything they could make no use of, they would smile, and truly their smiles were exquisite, enough to make an Englishman forget where he was. Many of this tribe followed us some distance, and seemed much attracted by a funeral ceremony that took place at Fort Laramie, which was the burial of one of the aged fathers of the company, who had come out from Ashton-under Lyne, near your city, with his family, and who was very desirous of seeing the valley in the far west.

But I am afraid I shall lengthen out too much, if I enumerate all the little circumstances that occurred on this journey. We now had crossed the Platte River and were running on the south side of it, leaving it to the right for a short time, and again coming to it. The hills that skirted our path on our left were covered with the dark foliage of the fir-tree, and, in the distance, appeared perfectly black. As the train advanced (which was a slow motion) we had ample opportunity of witnessing the varied mountainous scenery that now presented itself on every side. We would occasionally find ourselves running along a high ridge, from which we had an extensive view of immense basins or valleys, extending for miles every way, surrounded by lofty and rugged mountains. Next we would have to lock our wagon wheels, as we were descending a steep declivity into one of these beautiful valleys, and it would seem to the inexperienced traveller that we had got into a place from which there was no escape, as to all appearance we were locked in by impassable rocks of stupendous magnitude. But onward we pressed, until we came to a steep ascent, where it would require the doubling of teams to rush the wagons up to the next lofty ridge, and which again gave us a view of the apparently endless nature of our journey. On this part of our journey the company frequently refreshed themselves by the many springs of clear water that rushed from the foot of the mountains.

On the 29th of August we started on our journey as usual, but the day proved a rather eventful one. We had gone a short distance previously to camping for dinner, and for that purpose we turned a little out of our path, and proceeded towards the river Platte, where there was a deal of dry bunch grass, which is good feed for cattle. We halted; the cattle were unhitched from the wagons, and driven in a herd to the water. Orders had been given by the captain that no fires should be lighted, as, from the dryness of the grass; it was dangerous to do so. Two or three of the company did not hear the order, and without thought lighted fires. The inflammable nature of the prairie grass caused the flames to spread with considerable rapidity, being also aided by the brisk wind that was blowing. It appeared a critical moment. The flames, in some instances, reached the tops of the wagons, and set the canvas on fire. Horror was depicted on many countenances, and it seemed as though the whole company would be destroyed. Every exertion was made to put out the flames, men pulling off their coats, and women their shawls, to batter out the fire, but it was all to no purpose. The fury of the fiery element increased, and roared like thunder as it rolled along the ground, the heat being so great that it singed the men as they attempted to move the wagons to windward.

The captain, however, gave orders for the oxen to be brought up, and hitched in. A movement to an adjacent hill was commenced, and as soon as we got there out of danger, we again halted, and sat down on the grass to dine, watching the progress of the fire, which had by this time well-night reached the river, and there was presented to our view a large blackened surface - the effects of the destructive element.

Having recovered from the fright we had received from witnessing the prairie on fire, we again proceeded on our way over the Rocky Mountains; our course continuing much the same as previously described - over rocky and smooth ground, continuing to rise in altitude as we advanced, the highest elevation we attained being about 7,000 feet above the level of the sea.

Near to Independence Rock (an immense round rock, with a flat top on Sweetwater river, 300 miles from Great Salt Lake city, carved, and cut, and painted with all kinds of names of parties emigrating to and from California and Salt Lake) - near to this rock there is a fort and mail station, called Chambault Fort, and it is also a trading-post. Here also is a curiosity - the waters of the Sweetwater rush through, between two perpendicular rocks of considerable loftiness, and this is called Devil's Gate.

At Fort Bridger (113 miles from the city) there is also a trading-post. From this point to the city, the mountains take a great elevation - the highest being about 7,000 feet above the sea. The approach to the city is through canyons of eight or ten miles in length, being much cut up by creeks, and lined on either side by perpendicular rocks - a very dangerous passage for an army in a hostile country.

At the mouth of the Emigration canyon, through which we passed, we were five miles from the city, and as we approached it, the sun was just skirting the horizon in the west, on the 6th day of October, 1853'.

The two letters sent by John Chambers were meant to act as a motivation for other church members wanting to emigrate. Besides letters to relations and local newspapers, who did not always publish them, other emigrants sent information back to England, the most noted of which were the sketches drawn on route by Frederick Piercy. He was 23 years old when he sailed on the Jersey on 5 February

1853. He had the notion to document his journey through his talent as an artist and produced an illustrated travel guide to encourage British church members to emigrate to Utah. The result was that Piercy's illustrations were included in the book *Route from Liverpool* which also contains a detailed narrative of the journey. The illustrations show the prominent landmarks and vistas between New Orleans and Nauvoo and also between Council Bluffs and the Salt Lake Valley.

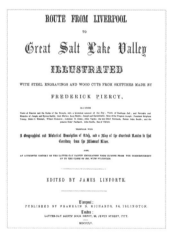

Piercy's Illustration of Salt Lake City taken from the 'Route from Liverpool'. (Franklin Richards Publications).

The book can be seen on Google Books and it is possible to download a PDF copy for personal use.

Finding information about your ancestor who crossed the plains

The Church's move from Nauvoo, Illinois to the Salt Lake Valley was the largest organised migration movement in American history spanning from 1846 until 1925. There are two compiled database sources which provide information about individuals:

The Early LDS Database
The Mormon Pioneer Overland Trail (referred to as the 'Crossing the Plains Index') It is recommended that both of these be consulted as you search for your ancestor because they contain slightly different fields of information.

Early LDS database

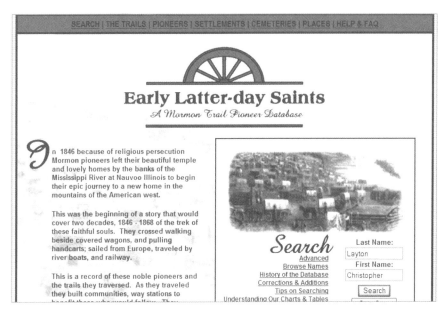

(Pioneer Research Group earlylds.com)

There is a very useful website which enables researchers to trace ancestors who actually crossed the plains. By using **www.earlylds.com** you should be able to trace your pioneers and supplement and enhance the information found on the Mormon Immigration Index referred to earlier. This database traces the lives of those who left Nauvoo and travelled to the west covering the important period of 1846 to 1868. It endeavours to give information about their lives and families, when and where their settlements were established and who lived and died in these then remote places.

It covers the journeys from Nauvoo, Illinois; Iowa City, Iowa and several other departure points across the plains of Iowa, some going through Garden Grove and Mount Pisgah to the east and west banks of the Missouri River at Kanesville (Council Bluffs) and the 90 or so other settlements towards Winter Quarters and Nebraska.

Matches 1 to 7 of 7 for Last Name equals LAYTON

	Last Name, Given Name(s) ▼	Born/Christened ▲		Person ID	Tree
1	Layton, Christopher	b. 8 Mar 1822	Thorncote Green, Bedfordshire, England ♀	I15554	Early Latter-day Saints
2	Layton, Eliza	b. 1826	, , England ♀	I15555	Early Latter-day Saints
3	Layton, Jona C.			I15556	Early Latter-day Saints
4	Layton, Jones	b.	, , Pennsylvania, USA ♀	I23426	Early Latter-day Saints
5	Layton, Leah			I34068	Early Latter-day Saints
6	Layton, Priscilla			I15521	Early Latter-day Saints
7	Layton, Sarah	b. 1816	, , England ♀	I32818	Early Latter-day Saints

An initial search will reveal names and data sufficient to identify the person you are looking for. By clicking on a particular name additional information will be available (Pioneer Research Group earlylds.com).

	Last Name, Given Name(s) ▼	Born/Christened ▲		Person ID	Tree
1	Layton, Christopher	b. 8 Mar 1822	Thorncote Green, Bedfordshire, England ♀	I15554	Early Latter-day Saints

Birth	8 Mar 1822	Thorncote Green, Bedfordshire, England ♀
Gender	Male	
Baptized (LDS)	1842	
Endowed (LDS)	31 Jan 1846	NAUVO ♀
Died	Aug 1898	Kaysville, Davis, Utah, USA ♀
Person ID	I15554	Early Latter-day Saints
Last Modified	07 Feb 2007	

Family 1	Mary Matthews, b. 20 Apr 1820, Thorncote Green, Bedfordshire, England ♀, d. Sep 1845, Nauvoo, Hancock, Illinois,USA ♀	
Married	20 Jul 1842	Thorncote Green, Bedfordshire, England ♀
Sealed S (LDS)	1 Mar 1973	SLAKE ♀ [9]
Family ID	F10721	Group Sheet

The information shown relates to Christopher Layton - the subject of the Mormon Battalion Case study earlier. The entry for birth shows how important it is to refer to original records as the year is inaccurate in the database. (Pioneer Research Group earlylds.com)

Individual and family information of real genealogical value can be found and is organised in family group, pedigree and descendant charts. Some contain photographs and biographies. There is also useful information relating to settlement histories, maps, cemeteries, and timelines that will help you gain a greater understanding of their lives and times.

The information contained within the cemetery section is particularly useful if your ancestor died on the journey. The cemetery database is ongoing but includes some of the major cemeteries in towns and settlements between Nauvoo and Salt Lake City and also layout plans of each burial ground.

718	⤺ Williams, John H.	b. 1 Mar 1841	Manchester, Lancashire, England ℗	d. 8 Apr 1847		I51839
719	⤺ Williams, Peter	b.	, Cheshire, England ℗	d. 22 Oct 1846		I5832
720	⤺ Williams, Peter	b. 15 Jan 1811	, Cheshire, England ℗	d. 22 Oct 1846	Winter Quarters (Florence), Douglas, Nebraska, USA ℗	I28131

The search results for persons who died on the journey provides, name, date of death and sometimes birth date. By clicking on the name additional information is available (Pioneer Research Group earlylds.com).

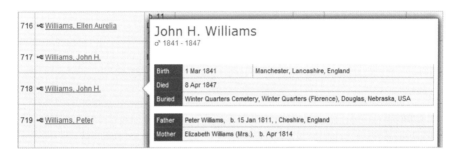

By looking at the entry it is clear that John is the son of Peter Williams who also died on the journey six months before John H Williams his son. Both are buried in Winter Quarters Cemetery.
(Pioneer Research Group earlylds.com.)

The Mormon pioneer overland trail (crossing the plains)

This internet database is still ongoing and relates to travel across the plains before the advent of the Transcontinental Railroad in 1869. The Church Historical Department is still adding information to this database (*Jan 2011*) from recently discovered rosters and other sources.

Each entry gives the name, age, gender, the year of the journey and which pioneer company they travelled with. Many entries also include other important genealogical information such as date and place of birth, date of death, or other identifying information.

Some information in this database may differ from that in earlier databases as the prime objective is to make this comprehensive and accurate. The database can be searched alphabetically (be aware of variants and alternative spellings), by surname which will provide information on all those travelling with the same surname irrespective of date, or by name of the pioneer company:

The original part of the database can be accessed on microfilm at Family History Centres on microfilm numbers 298440 - 298442 which although not complete is organised alphabetically. This part of the database is better known as the Utah Immigration Card Index, 1847-1868. It indexes pioneers alphabetically by the head of the family or group, in the case of single people, but includes names of other family or group members, who began their journey across the plains before the specific date of 10 May 1869 and only those who went in church sponsored companies. Each card gives the name of the company and the date of its arrival in Salt Lake City. In some cases a reference is given to the company roster which is a full list of people who were in the same pioneer company.

Many of the rosters can be searched on the internet at Ancestry.com under the heading of 'Heart Throbs of the West' and these include most of the 'They Came In...' volumes.

These publications by the Daughters of Utah Pioneers organisation contain information about pioneer immigration to Utah from 1847 to 1868 and include personal histories and accounts, the dates of emigrant ship crossings and also dates of overland journeys and sometimes names of pioneers in their respective companies. The information they contain was submitted by members of the organisation. The volumes form a useful resource for obtaining an overview of pioneer activity for a given year and are available on microfiche in Family History Centres.

Using the LDS Church website at **www.lds.org** it is also possible to access a full database of all those who crossed the USA as pioneers. The searchable database is part of the 'Church History' section of the website entitled '*Mormon Pioneer Overland Trail 1847-1868*'. Searches can be undertaken by individual family names, the name of the company, or the year. (See illustration below).

Home search page (LDS Church Intellectual Reserve Inc)

CHURCH HISTORY
The Church of Jesus Christ
of Latter-day Saints

Selection
Church History Library

LDS Home ▶ Church History ▶ Church History Library ▶ Resources Available ▶ Pioneer Details

Mormon Pioneer Overland Travel, 1847–1868

Search Index

Layton, Christopher

Alphabetical Company List

Birth Date: 8 Mar. 1821
Death Date: 7 Aug. 1898

Chronological Company List

Gender: Male
Age: 31
Company: Abraham O. Smoot Company (1852)

Submit Information

Pioneer Information:

About this Database

Captain of Fifty

How to use this Database

Sources:
Brockbank, Isaac, Autobiography, in [Stephen W. Brockbank], *Isaac Brockbank, Jr., 1837-1927: Autobiography* [1997], 9-15. **Read Trail Excerpt**   Source Locations

Wilson, James Thomas, "The Life of James Thomas Wilson," [1948], 43-55.   Source Locations

Woman's Exponent, 15 Feb.-1 Mar. 1901, 86   Source Locations

Alphabetical Company List

Chronological Company List

Submit Information

About this Database

How to use this Database

Abraham O. Smoot Company (1852)

Adam, Christmas (Unknown)
Adams, Emma Jackson (22)
Adams, Samuel Lorenzo (19)
Atkinson, Joshua Charles (28)
Atkinson, Mary Ann (29)
Aubrey, Jane (35)
Bailey, Elizabeth (22)
Bailey, John (22)
Bailey, John Henry (1)
Ballard, Hannah Russell (53)
Ballard, William (57)
Balser, Amelia Rhoda (Infant)
Balser, Emma Sarah Evans (28)
Balser, John (29)
Barnes, Sarah (25)
Beddoe, Daniel (1)
Beddoe, James (4)
Bonkitt, James (30)
Bonkitt [or Bowkutt], Susannah (27)
Brockbank, Agnes (1)
Brockbank, Elizabeth (13)
Brockbank, Elizabeth Mainwaring (43)
Brockbank, Isaac (46)
Brockbank, Isaac (14)
Brockbank, Joshua (4)

A search undertaken of a Company shows all the names of the members. By clicking on a name more information is available. (LDS Church Intellectual Reserve Inc.)

If you have difficulty locating your ancestor in either of the databases it would be worthwhile trying to determine the year or company in which they crossed the plains by looking at:

Biographies of each family member and also others who may have been travelling with them.

Obituaries of each family member in the local Utah newspapers as they will often provide that information.

Tax records. If you know where the family settled, study the tax lists (see later) and find the first year your ancestor appears. This helps identify about when he or she arrived in Utah.

Each of these are commented upon later.

Written accounts of voyages to and journeys across America
Many such accounts are included within the Mormon Immigration Index CD or can be found in the many biographies, journals and diaries left by the early emigrants and pioneers.

To locate written accounts of voyages:

Mormons on the High Seas: Ocean Voyage Narratives to America (1840-1890).
This is a bibliography of the many accounts of the voyages of church members arranged alphabetically by ship's name, and then chronologically by date of voyage and is available on microfilm no. 1592752.

To find written accounts of the journey across the plains see:

Mormon Pioneer Companies Crossing the Plains (1847-1868.) Narratives.
This is similar in content to the above volume with the Pioneer companies listed chronologically by year and by company leader and is also available on microfilm no.1592752.

Handcarts to Zion
This relates to the journeys of the ten handcart companies and is an excellent resource for accounts, journals and reports of the companies although the rosters are incomplete. This is available on microfiche no. 6031590.

Mormon Migration Patterns

Between 1840 and 1910 the largest numbers emigrated from the British Isles to the Salt Lake Valley. The following table shows the trend of emigration amongst members.

DECADE	CONVERTS	EMIGRATED
1840-1850	42,316	6,832
1851-1860	37,215	12,972
1861-1870	14,977	10,094
1871-1880	6,345	6,886
1881-1890	5,457	7,758
1891-1900	3,991	1,512
1901-1910	8,062	3,615
TOTAL	**118,363**	**49,669**

Throughout this period of church growth about 42% of the membership left the United Kingdom to emigrate to America.

In the early years of church emigration some migrant ships from Liverpool arrived at New York and Boston but most landed at New Orleans and the migrants then used the Mississippi to get to Nauvoo which was situated on its banks. After the Church moved to the Salt Lake in 1847, many church immigrants continued to disembark at New Orleans and travel up the Mississippi and then the Missouri before making their overland journey to Salt Lake. From 1855 the ports of entry to the USA used by the church were New York (the main port of entry), Philadelphia and Boston.

The reason for such a move was to some degree based upon health issues because it was noted that there was a high disease level amongst travellers using the Mississippi. From New York the immigrants used overland transport to the western trail heads, a journey which was often as harrowing as the pioneer trails.

Mormon pioneer emigrants experienced a journey fraught with difficulties and danger. Their journey also carried a real risk of illness, accident and disease and unfortunately many did not realise their dream of a new life in the west. The exact number of church members who died is not known, but it is thought that between 1846 and 1869, some 4,500 to 5,000 died during their journey of which 700 died at sea on the initial voyages, the remainder dying on the overland journey.

Because of the improvement to overland transport and particularly because of the expansion of the USA railroad system throughout the 1850s the trail head and outfitting stations changed locations in Missouri including St. Louis, Westport, Jefferson City, Alexandria, and Churchill to various locations in Iowa including Council Bluffs and even further west to Fort Leavenworth in Kansas, and Omaha, Nebraska. The outfitting camps also moved progressively closer to Salt Lake. With the completion of the transcontinental railway in 1869 Mormon immigrants generally travelled the whole way by train.

Not only was the journey usually arduous but each route was affected by its own unique health and safety challenges depending upon the mode of transport used and also the time the trip took.

The first leg of the journey across the Atlantic in the days of sail took anything form four to six weeks, sometimes longer depending upon the destination of the ship. Those travelling to New Orleans were frequently at sea for between eight and ten weeks. The full journey from Liverpool to Salt Lake often took up to six months to complete. Later migration journeys using steam ships and the railways could often be achieved in three to four weeks.

The amount of time travelling was a key factor in the health of Mormon immigrants and the risk of disease and illness was greater the longer they were 'on the trail'. In the days of pre steamship and railway there was a greater opportunity to fall ill because of the confinement of passengers on board, inadequately fitted out sailing vessels and the exposure they suffered from being in a wagon for the length of time it took to cross the plains.

Mormon immigration was only a small cog in the wheel of a much larger migration to the USA during the nineteenth century. However, health risks were the same for everyone so epidemics could occur. A voyage across the Atlantic was frequently uncomfortable, hazardous, and slow. Statistics show that in the age of sail and particularly between 1836 and 1853, two out of every hundred emigrants sailing to New York died on board or within a few hours of arrival.

The most common ailment amongst Mormon immigrants was seasickness, which was not life threatening but just plain uncomfortable and was not helped by overcrowding below decks and poor sanitation experienced on almost every vessel. Those suffering from seasickness would hardly be able to walk across the deck unaided. Rough seas inevitably meant that passengers remained below decks. Most of the church emigrants were steerage passengers and they were retained in an environment fostering putrid conditions. It was not surprising that disease was rife as sickness, vomiting, groaning and the overcrowding of the berths almost caused suffocation through lack of fresh air.

During the Atlantic crossings a significant number of deaths resulted from birth on board the ships. Often both women and babies died. The main reason was because of puerperal fever (relating to septicemia) caused in the main by inadequate midwifery care. Infants were more prone to deaths because of the inadequate diets of their mothers which meant that they did not produce sufficient milk as nourishment to the new born babies. Young children could not survive because of low protein in ship-board diets.

The same unsanitary conditions also contributed to more serious health problems. A number of other diseases are mentioned in journal entries of many emigrant passengers including malaria, TB, croup, measles and even typhoid and cholera. The most serious threat on board any ship was that contagious diseases could very quickly (and often did) reach epidemic proportions.

The most serious and feared disease encountered by emigrants was cholera. This was well illustrated in the log of the *'Germanicus'* which sailed in 1854 from Liverpool taking sixty nine days to reach New Orleans with 220 Mormon emigrants on board because it was becalmed in the Caribbean. The temperature peaked at 120 degrees and because of the unforeseen delay there was also a shortage of fresh water. Despite these setbacks, the passengers arrived at New Orleans in relatively good health, but they suffered four deaths en route. However, while the ship was docked at the quarantine island at New Orleans a major outbreak of cholera occurred affecting the final leg of the journey up the Mississippi. Twenty four of the 220 Mormon passengers died from the disease. This event was the main reason that the ports of arrival were changed to those on the eastern seaboard.

Cholera was one of the deadliest diseases that Mormon emigrants faced, not only at sea as indicated above but also during the overland journey. Cholera developed and became fatal sometimes in the space of only 24 hours. Most emigrants had this as their worst fear and because medical science was in the early stages of development doctors were unable to diagnose or know how to cure the illness. In fact at the time there was no known cure although there were a number of theories amongst the medical profession that attempted to explain the cause, prevention and cure for the illness. Cholera was not endemic and the first case in the USA was in 1832. The timing of the cholera outbreaks in the USA coincided with the heaviest period of Mormon emigration and as previously noted, the disease was present in the area around New Orleans and the Mississippi and was the cause of death for many European Mormon emigrants between 1849 and 1854.

Although the incidence of cholera among immigrants was controlled by stopping use of the New Orleans and Mississippi route, little could be done to prevent it taking hold on the overland trail. Cholera was the leading cause of death on the Mormon Pioneer Trail between 1840 and 1860.

Cholera was not the only medical challenge faced by the emigrants on their journey to Utah. It is very apparent that many died during the journey but others suffered from all manner of injuries and sickness. Broken bones, burns, snake bites, injuries sustained when wagons overturned and drowning in quicksand were just some of the injuries and amongst the other diseases were black scurvy, diphtheria, typhoid, mumps and smallpox.

On the modern day pioneer trail there is evidence of graves of those who died of Cholera. One such person was Rebecca Winters. She died on 15 August 1852 at Scottsbluff Nebraska, aged 53yrs. Originally a makeshift headstone made of an iron wagon tyre had words engraved on it but in the early 20th century a permanent monument was erected by Rebecca's descendants, after Railway surveyors found the iron marker and changed the track route in order to protect the grave. That was not the end of the story because as late as 1996 the grave was opened and repositioned because of a highway and railroad safety issue.

Rebecca Winters' Grave (Scotts Bluff County Tourism).   *Rebecca Winters memorial Park in Nebraska (Nebraska Landmark Country).*

Mountain fever, another mysterious illness which symptoms included nausea, severe headaches, and dysentery took hold as Cholera decreased. The illness was encountered in the area between the Platte and Sacramento rivers. The Mormon pioneers initially encountered mountain fever at South Pass in 1847. In itself it was not fatal and generally only lasted a couple of days but nevertheless it was somewhat debilitating. Some speculated that it was associated with Colorado tick fever, which was transmitted by the bite of a virus infected tick. Brigham Young also became a victim of mountain fever. His entry into the Salt Lake Valley was delayed because of the illness. The day he entered the Salt Lake Valley he was confined to bed in his wagon.

Deaths along the trail
Unfortunately there is no complete listing for details of those who died on the pioneer trail from Nauvoo to Salt Lake City. The following information has been extracted from an article which appeared in the Church publication *'Ensign'* in July 1998 by Susan E. Black

Estimated deaths

- Crossing Iowa and including deaths at Montrose, the Battle of Nauvoo, and the Poor Camps and on the trek to the Missouri River - between 295 and 385 died.

- On the 1846 voyage of the 'Brooklyn' from New York to San Francisco and then overland to the Salt Lake Valley - a total of 26 died including 11 at sea and 15 on the overland trail.

- At Winter Quarters Nebraska and the other settlements in the vicinity 1846-1853 - between 800 and 1,100 died.

- Mormon Battalion - 33 died.

- Voyages across the Atlantic or Pacific - between 670 and 700 died.

- In the St Louis area - estimated to be 125 deaths.

- On Mississippi Riverboats or trains 1846-1869 - unknown as there are few records. However 25 died as a result of the explosion on board the 'Saluda'.

- In wagon trains between Winter Quarters and Salt Lake Valley - between 1,950 and 2,275 deaths.

- In the 10 handcart companies - between 252 and 320 deaths.

The following lists have been compiled:

Mormon Trail Deaths 1847-1868
The Historical department of the Church has a database of Mormon Trail Deaths 1847-1868, the purpose of which is to record the documented deaths. The database is by year, then by company, and then by surname and entries include: name, gender, age, date and place of death, and source information. Personal searches are not allowed but the archive staff at the Historical department will undertake named searches on application.

Record of early members of the Church who died in Missouri, Kirtland, Nauvoo and on the Plains.
This is an alphabetical list of people who died along the trail and includes name, date and place of birth and death information. Information has been taken from various church published provincial newspapers and periodicals and is incomplete as at 1918. This database is available on microfilm no. 413034.

CHAPTER FOUR
Colonisation

The earliest settling of Mormon colonies took place at Kirtland, Ohio from 1830 but around the same time the early Saints settled in other areas of Missouri including Jackson County. Relatively few records exist from those early settlements. In the years up to 1839 the area around Nauvoo, Illinois began to be settled and by 1846 most Church members had crossed Iowa to Winter Quarters and established colonies around Omaha, Nebraska and Council Bluffs.

Upon arrival in the Salt Lake Valley in July 1847 exploration parties were sent to find other areas around the valley in which to settle (this is discussed later). One aspect of colonisation in the Salt Lake Valley was the establishment of communities according to skills and trades or professions but generally families settled with those they knew. These settlements grew as families who arrived later also joined them. Welsh, Irish and Scandinavian communities were also established. This colonisation did not occur overnight and it often took a couple of generations to establish the 500 or so settlements in the western United States. Some settlements have long been abandoned but many of these communities are still identifiable today.

Generally information about Church colonisation and settlement is not available on microfilm but copies of the *Historical Atlas of Mormonism*

detailed below can often be obtained at moderate prices through organisations such as Amazon or other on-line book sellers.

Historical Atlas of Mormonism: A comprehensive reference source exploring the impact of Mormonism on America, especially on the settling of the West, and offers seventy-four sections, each with maps, that describe migration routes and population distribution together with settlements and founding dates, colonisation, birthplaces of Church leaders, migration trails, and ethnic patterns.

A useful book found only in the main Family History Library is '*Mormon colonisation 1847-1900*' in which all known settlements are listed alphabetically under each year. This helps you determine the earliest date a member could have settled in a community.

Since the establishment of the church economic welfare has been an integral aspect of Mormon life. An 1830 revelation implied that every aspect of life had to do with spirituality and things eternal. For President Brigham Young it meant that spiritual and temporal aspects of the religion were inseparably connected.

This philosophy was frequently strengthened and supported by the social and economic experienced by the trials of the early Saints. The moving of the church headquarters and members from New York to Kirtland, Ohio, and then to Missouri was extremely important to the welfare of the Saints. The logistics of a mass move meant that leaders had to establish ways of helping members physically undertake the journey. This move involved Church leaders in buying land and formulating plans for community development and in introducing and establishing financial enterprises and industries to provide employment, thus planting the seed for the creation of an advanced society. Ultimately, according to LDS belief, the Church must establish Zion, the literal and earthly kingdom of God over which Christ will one day rule in person.

Perhaps of more importance was the Church's general reaction to persecutions it had to encounter. Church leaders had assumed responsibility for dealing with persecution and looking after the welfare of its members. The positive effect of such actions created community identity. The persecutions also necessitated frequent removals, forcing the Church to repeat its migration and establish more new settlements again purchasing land and initiating industry for member employment in the new areas. Economically all these aspects encouraged co-operation and prevented a rise in class distinction and selfishness.

The experiences of the pioneers and the social and religious origins of the Church resulted in a set of economic ideals and institutions that effectively became a permanent aspect of Latter-day Saint society setting it apart from many other groups of the time. These ideals contributed to the establishment the communities, the development of co-operatives and self sufficiency usually sponsored by the Church in maintaining economic equality.

The gathering together of like minded people into one place known as 'accumulating people' was prerequisite to the ultimate aims of the Church in 'establishing Zion'. It was all well planned, beginning in the 1830s with an effective missionary programme and a highly organised emigration service and by the establishment of a series of gathering places.

Establishing the Salt Lake Valley

Besides reaching the end of an arduous journey the arrival in the Salt Lake Valley had a special meaning to all the emigrants. They had endured many hardships which had tested their faith in their new religion and even for those who were not Latter-day Saints it provided a deeply emotional moment.

The journey totalling 7,840 miles, although taken in stages was perhaps the longest ever taken by such a great number of voluntary emigrants.

Liverpool to New Orleans	5000 miles
New Orleans to St Louis	1173 miles
St Louis to Kanesville	620 miles
Kanesville to Winter Quarters	12 miles
Winter Quarters to Salt Lake City	1035 miles

The pioneering days of these emigrant Saints was not yet over because they now had to establish their new homes. Within hours of their arrival in the valley, the Saints had organised work committees which staked out a 35-acre field for growing grain and produce. Another was laying out the temple site which started the construction of the renowned Salt Lake temple which took them 40 years to complete. A further group was surveying the area ready to lay out the streets and housing blocks. Engineering and public works were undertaken with the construction of irrigation canals. Individual homes and commercial properties were built, as well as kilns and quarries to provide the raw materials. Within a short space of time many were also called on missions to help develop 'some specific facet of territorial economy'. Missionaries were to serve in specific areas and so developed an iron mission, a sugar mission, a lead mission, a cotton mission, a silk mission, a flax mission, and a wool mission.

Others were, within weeks of the arrival in Salt Lake, sent out to colonise the far reaches of the American west which was to ultimately ensure self-rule, freedom from oppression and the establishment of a strong presence in the territory. Not all the pioneering Saints settled in the Salt Lake Valley. By the turn of the 20th century members of The Mormon Church had established over 600 communities in a vast area from Chihuahua, Mexico to Alberta, Canada and from Hawaii and California to southern Colorado.

When the Salt Lake Valley was populated, Church leaders were, according to the Assistant Church Historian at the time, B H Roberts (born Warrington, Lancashire), in his six volume *'Comprehensive History of the Church of Jesus Christ of Latter-day Saints'* - 'smarting under the sense of injustice and wrong permitted if not inflicted under quasi-sanction of the United States'. Despite this the Church leaders and the general community still considered the United States Constitution a fine document for political rule, so much so that the Church petitioned for statehood for the State of Deseret in July 1849. The proposals at the time included areas which now form the majority of the south western USA. They were not successful but were granted territory status (present day Utah) and Brigham Young was unanimously elected its governor.

The extent of the original State of Deseret and later the Utah Territory
(International Society Daughters of Utah Pioneers).

134

Because of the number of emigrant and mainly convert pioneers from Britain and Europe in mid to late 1800s, Utah today has 54% of its population claiming British ancestry but like most major conurbations now also claims a multi-cultural population.

So how was the Salt Lake area actually settled?

The establishment of settlements in Utah took place over time. Initially from 1847 to 1857, the 'valley settlements', as the pioneers called them, were established along the Wasatch Front, the Cache Valley on the Idaho to Arizona border. In addition to the early settlement of the Salt Lake and Weber valleys colonies were founded in the Tooele, and Sanpete valleys; and later in Box Elder, Pahvant, Juab, and Parowan valleys.

Thirty families settled in the Utah valley in early 1849 but the population of these communities reached over 2,000 by late 1850. Later in 1849 a further fifty families settled in the Sanpete Valley, south of Utah Valley, forming a nucleus for other settlements.

In 1849, a party of fifty persons was sent to survey the areas towards the northern border of Arizona, which was some 300 miles south of Salt Lake City. Their survey notes relate to identification of favourable areas for settlements, how the land could be utilised to sustain the settlements and the general topography of the area. There is also some mention of Forts needed for defence of the communities.

As a result of the survey additional settlements were quickly established in those areas during the late 1850 and within three years of the survey being conducted settlements were established on nearly all the identified settlement sites.

One of the most important colonies was established at Parowan which is near modern day Cedar City serving as a staging post between Salt Lake and southern California and supporting a local iron ore enterprise which was discovered during the survey. At the end of 1850, 167 people were sent to Parowan to farm in the 'iron mission' established at Cedar City. Soon there were a further dozen settlements made in the region.

Ninety settlements were established during the first ten years after the entry into the Salt Lake Valley in July 1847. The dates the communities were settled and which became major Utah settlements were (in date order), Salt Lake City and Bountiful in 1847, Ogden and West Jordan in 1848, Kaysville, Provo, Manti and Tooele in 1849, Parowan, Brigham City, Nephi, Fillmore and Cedar City in 1851, and Beaver, Wellsville and Washington in 1856.

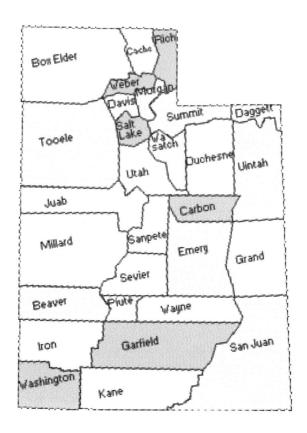

Locations of Counties within the State of Utah (Wiki.familysearch.org - Intellectual Reserve Inc)

Colonisation took two main forms: directed or non-directed. The directed colonies were those planned and organised by church leaders. The colonisation location was determined as described above. Families and individuals with appropriate skills were assigned to an area and a leader was appointed. Instructions were given on the particular type of missions of the colonies which were for specific reasons including the raising of crops, livestock farming, coal and iron ore mining, or to serve as way stations for travelling church members primarily on their way to California. On arrival at the designated settlement the colonists apportioned the land, erected fences, built a meetinghouse, a school and developed irrigation schemes etc. Homes were built on the 'fort' system which was in accordance with a set pattern of settlement that provided a balanced life style catering for religious, education, work and social aspects of family life. To aid the successful colonisation the State of Deseret also minted its own currency.

Currency minted and used by early Church members in their daily business in the State of Deseret.

Non-directed settlements were those settled by individuals, and families without church leader direction. Most of these types of communities were established along the Wasatch Front by the early arrivals to the valley.

An average of three thousand emigrants from Britain and Scandinavia arrived in the Salt Lake Valley each season in need of a place to live and although not under their control, Church leaders encouraged these types of settlements by offering assistance and establishing church units in them.

During the Utah War and Civil War periods church members from outlying areas as far afield as California and Nevada were effectively 'called back' for their own safety and security to consolidate in the Salt Lake Valley. This presented the church leaders with a small logistic challenge as these members had to be accommodated alongside the emigrants who also arrived during that time period. In the decade after the Utah War, (c1862-1873) one hundred and twelve new communities were established in Utah and after exploratory surveys new valley areas opened up for settlement. Expansion of both the established and new settlements continued until well into the 1890s. Prominent Utah cities established during this period include Logan, St George, Richfield and Morgan.

Church leaders were keen at this time to develop territorial self-sufficiency. New regions began to produce commodities such as cotton, flax, hemp, rice and sugar as well as establishing agricultural production. This self-sufficiency programme which followed the Utah War led Mormon leaders to expand the colonies of southern Utah such as 'Utah Dixie' and 'Santa Clara' which was originally called 'Big Bend'. These communities developed the grape and soft fruit industries which still exist today. Both of these centres expanded in the area around St George. The town of Mantua in Box Elder County was founded for the production of flax and twelve Danish families with the appropriate skills were appointed to settle in Flaxville in order to produce thread for use in making initially sacks for grain storage but diversifying into household linen and clothing. The town of Minersville, Beaver County, was established to work lead, zinc, and silver mines. This community was a large producer of lead for use in both paint and lead shot (bullet) manufacture. Under similar circumstances Coalville, Summit County, was also established to mine coal. These mines were an essential source of fuel for the church communities in the Salt Lake Valley.

In Salt Lake City newly arrived European emigrants were involved in creating a massive public works system which was centred on Temple Square. These workers built such useful structures as roads, walls, meetinghouses, railroads, telegraph lines, canals, the Salt Lake theatre, and of course the Salt Lake Temple and tabernacle. New arrivals were also organised into companies to settle in outlying agricultural villages. Property in these communities was allocated and regulated to ensure the highest possible use of resources. Each person had property sufficient to support his family, with any surplus land vested in the church storehouse system for the benefit of all. Initially the property rights were granted conditionally and were not protected if the owner refused to utilise or develop his land. Every man had his land measured off for both residential and farming purposes.

In general this directive seems to have been adhered to. Hoarding of land and money was strictly against Church rules.

After the settlement of villages and the determination of property rights, the Saints developed local resources. These were an economic necessity and in keeping with the self sufficiency aspect of church policy. The acceptance of this type of development and its associated accountability went a long way in explaining the passionate efforts of church members to develop their resources to their fullest extent.

The goal of both colonisation and resource development was economic independence as the Church needed to be financially self-sufficient. This was as a result of a religious revelation in the early years of the Church.

The Latter-day Saints were asked to become self sufficient in the manufacture of their own iron, mining their own coal, producing their own cotton and growing and milling their own grain. It was reasoned that self-sufficiency was a practical policy. As a result of applying this principle, Deseret and ultimately Utah were the only regions of the United States whose development was accomplished without recourse to outside capital.

Officially sponsored self-sufficiency projects included an 'iron mission' consisting of about 200 families assigned by the Church to develop the iron and coal resources near Cedar City. A 'sugar mission' was established in which several hundred people were required to establish the sugar-beet industry in Utah. A 'lead mission' was established near Las Vegas in which some fifty men were assigned to work lead mines for paint and bullet production. A 'cotton mission' which sent more than a thousand families to southern Utah grew cotton and as a sideline olives, grapes, indigo and figs. Other 'missions' included a silk mission involving the growing of mulberry trees and the establishment of a silk industry alongside a flax mission or a wool mission in every suitable community.

Unity of members and organisational ability were essential qualities required to successfully execute the economic programme of the Church which meant church wide cooperation centred upon the belief that unity was a Christian virtue. Group solidarity and a strong central organisation symbolised this effort.

The instigators of Church policy focused attention on production and good management of human and natural resources. The early Church was distinctly egalitarian in both theology and economics which to some extent was as a result of its own economic and Christian values.

From the beginning, there was always an attempt to conduct business with equality. When emigrant converts arrived at the Kirtland, Ohio, in May 1831, this was the governing principle for the allotment of property. The same principle was applied in all places that the church members resided but the core of the policy was very evident in the emigration system where those who could afford to do so donated money for the benefit of the poorer members who would otherwise have struggled to make the journey. The same principle applied to the establishment and running of the co-operatives which were characterised by a high degree of economic equality although many only existed for a short time.

During the late 1860s and early 1870s a further ninety-three new settlements were established in Utah adding to the economy of the area culminating in 1877 with an important colonisation of Emery, Carbon, Garfield and Wayne Counties. Other important new settlements were established in Northern Utah.

By the late 1870s those who had initially settled in the valley had now raised families resulting in an over-population. Work was not always available in these established areas apart from in some of the mines and also on the developing railways, so many of the younger generation began to move away to the contiguous states of Wyoming, Arizona, Idaho and Colorado.

A few new colonies were established in the outer areas of Utah up to the early twentieth century but the emigrants who arrived in this period also frequently settled in the surrounding states. Some even went as far afield as Canada and Mexico. The Church was by this time no longer involved in directing settlements and any migration tended to be sporadic. However, independent to, but with church as participating stock holders, the Deseret and Salt Lake Agricultural and Manufacturing Canal Company which was formed in 1889 established settlements mainly of emigrant church members in Millard County.

The real demise of the colonisation in the twentieth century was due to the fact that the Church leaders discouraged emigration suggesting to members that they build up their own communities in their native countries.

There was a great legacy from the colonisation period. Three hundred and twenty five permanent and forty four subsequently abandoned settlements were established and populated in Utah throughout the nineteenth century. Those that did not survive were the victims of modern farming techniques, improved transportation and the shift of rural to urban communities that occurred for economic reasons.

Intervention by the US Government had an adverse effect. Unemployment and low incomes particularly during the depression years of the 1890s adversely affected Utah's agriculture and mining industries. Church leaders used all the resources they could muster to expand and improve the areas' economy and as a result new enterprises came into existence. Two of these opportunities were the start of the hydro-electric power industry and the construction of the Saltair recreation resort. Railroads were also planned as were canals and new colonies showing that Church leaders did everything possible to expand their economic base.

Due to the success of the expansion of economic activity, national politicians and to some extent major business leaders, tried to force the Church to sell off its business interests. The Church's interests in the industries it established and developed throughout the latter part of the 19th century particularly the railroad and hydro-electric power, coal and iron and the sugar industry were systematically sold off because of this pressure.

Zions's Cooperative Mercantile Institution - ZCMI
The first departmental store in the USA was organised in 1868 as Zion's Cooperative Mercantile Institution (ZCMI) which was fully owned by The Church of Jesus Christ of Latter-Day Saints (LDS), until it was sold in 1999.

A renowned Mormon historian at the time, Martha Bradley, wrote the following to the Church leaders particularly Brigham Young; 'the railroad and the increased contact that it brought with national markets and the world outside presented a most serious threat to the cohesiveness and solidarity of the Saints'. Brigham Young anticipated that this would cause confusion and cultural and social diversity.

At the October 1868 Church Conference members were urged to cooperate economically. In late October many LDS businessmen from all over the territory met in Salt Lake City and organised a wholesale cooperative store to become known as the 'People's Store' or ZCMI whose directors were all Church leaders. The store's objective was to offer lower prices than the businesses belonging to non church members whilst at the same time promoting church unity.

Not all LDS merchants joined the new institution at first but in 1869 ZCMI's first store, known as the Eagle Emporium opened its doors for business selling clothing, dry goods, headwear, boots, and shoes. Shortly after a second store opened selling groceries and provisions, ironmongery farm implements, stoves, and hardware. From its establishment until 1924, ZCMI had eight departments, each with a retail and wholesale division: dry goods, grocery, butchery, china, shoes, carpets and men's clothing.

The exterior of the ZCMI department store in the early 1900s. (Utah Heritage Foundation).

141

ZCMI was incorporated in 1870 once the territory legislature passed the first incorporation laws. By that time around 150 cooperatives had been established extending into the adjoining states of Wyoming, Idaho and Nevada. Such co-operatives depended on the wholesale arm of ZCMI for many products as well as supplying locally made items. In line with economic self sufficiency encouraged by the Church its leaders encouraged home manufacturing and cooperative ventures to make the Mormons as self-sufficient as possible.

In its early years of trading ZCMI was financially successful. Within four years the Church and its members received dividends of over $500,000 almost doubling their initial investment. This led to ZCMI expanding in the early 1880s with new stores in Logan and Ogden, Utah. ZCMI also ventured into manufacturing when it bought the Deseret Tanning and Manufacturing Association in 1879. William Clayton served for many years as the company secretary and his journals contain some interesting background information. However, the Church's political troubles soon affected ZCMI. Because of federal laws and in the face of threatened government action against the Church it sold its ZCMI shares to private individuals.

The archives of ZCMI are held by the J Willard Marriot Library Special Collections Department within the University of Utah and consist of business records, annual reports and company history from its inception in 1868 to c2000. Access to some records may be restricted and at least one working day's notice is required for research. The catalogue can be searched at **www.content.lib.utah.edu**

Saltair - the resort
Saltair was completed in 1893 as a joint venture between the Church and the Los Angeles and Salt Lake Railroad Company but it was not the first resort to be built on the Great Salt Lake. It opened to the public on Memorial Day that year.

The concept behind Saltair was that it was a huge family resort, providing a safe and wholesome atmosphere for church members under the supervision of Church leaders. There were adequate direct train services between Salt Lake City and the resort. Interestingly enough it opened on Sundays and also sold tea and coffee! Its main attractions were swimming in the Great Salt Lake, and dancing. The resort also had a wide range of other attractions including a fairground with Ferris wheel, roller coaster and other amusements, bicycle races, touring theatre and musical companies, rodeos, boat rides and firework displays.

Saltair main pavilion c1900.

Saltair's main pavilion and some other buildings in the complex were destroyed by fire in April 1925 but a new pavilion was built and the resort was expanded at the same location although it did not achieve the success of the original complex. The advent of cinema coupled with the effects of the Depression of the 1930s subdued its activities. However it housed the world's largest ballroom and as such became renowned as a dance palace with the amusement park being secondary to its success. Many famous dance bands played there including Glenn Miller.

What records can help locate your ancestor?

As most of our emigrant ancestors would have lived a large proportion of their lives in the Salt Lake Valley area and almost certainly died in that locality part of your research must include searches of the records maintained by the Utah authorities, particularly in relationship to censuses, property ownership and death.

Utah Federal census returns
Besides the church census referred to later the Federal census was taken every ten years from 1850 although the 1890 census returns do not exist for Utah. Up to 1900 the operative date was 1 June but in 1910 it was taken on 15 April. All the available returns are indexed on **www.ancestry.com** for on-line research and each one should be checked to trace the family you are interested in. Information required for each census varied slightly.

The 1860 Federal census showing the family of Christopher Layton (US Federal Census Ancestry.com).

144

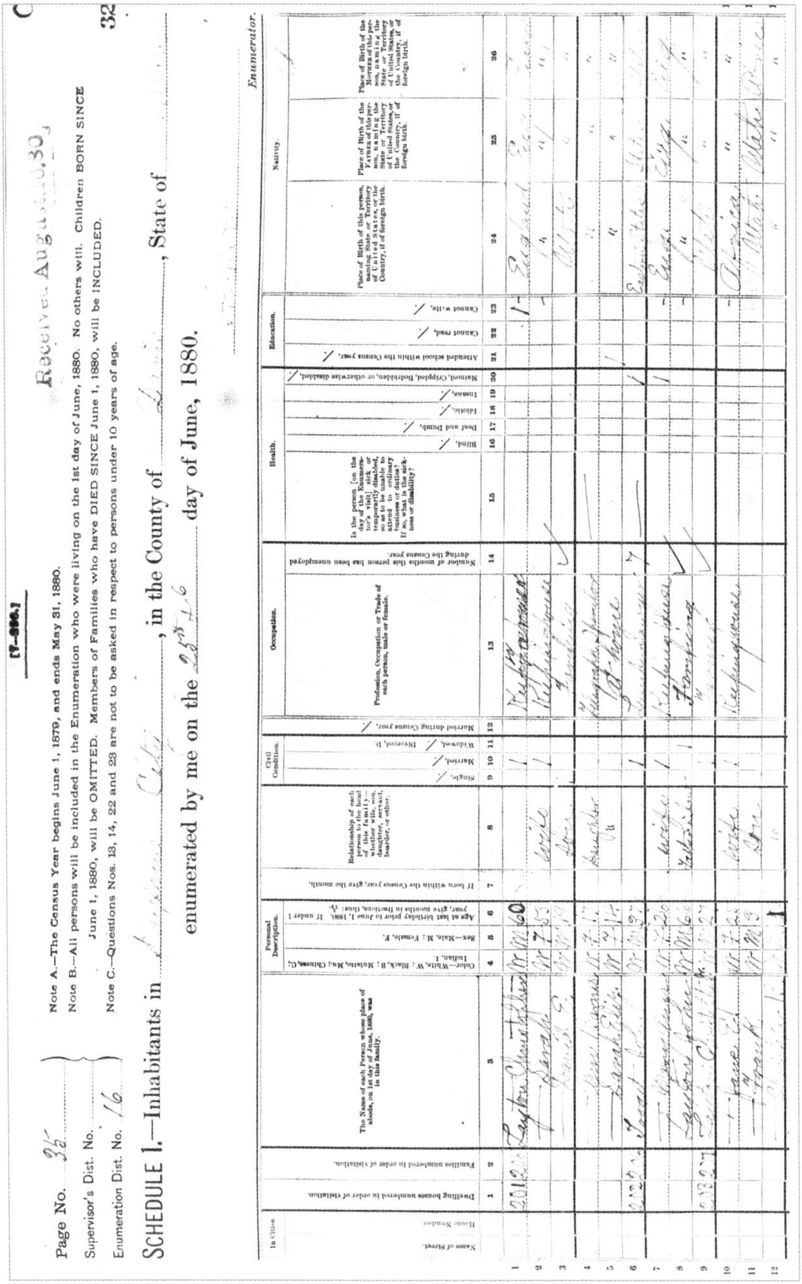
Page No. 35
Supervisor's Dist. No.
Enumeration Dist. No. 16

[7-296.]

Note A.—The Census Year begins June 1, 1879, and ends May 31, 1880.
Note B.—All persons will be included in the Enumeration who were living on the 1st day of June, 1880. No others will. Children BORN SINCE June 1, 1880, will be OMITTED. Members of Families who have DIED SINCE June 1, 1880, will be INCLUDED.
Note C.—Questions Nos. 13, 14, 22 and 23 are not to be asked in respect to persons under 10 years of age.

Received August 30,

SCHEDULE 1.—Inhabitants in ________, in the County of ________, State of ________, enumerated by me on the 25th day of June, 1880.

Enumerator.

The 1880 federal census showing the family of Christopher Layton (US Federal census Ancestry.com).

From the 1900 census, information about the birthplace of parents and the person's immigration and citizenship status was required along with information about property ownership. Such information will be very important in proving a connection. As images are available to download you will see the type of information that was requested which will enable you to piece together an idea of wealth and status of the family.

Utah Probate records
In order to locate a will of anyone dying in Utah it is necessary to look at two separate periods. The wills are filed by the dates that they were proved. The two periods are:

Territorial Period (1851-1896)
This covers the early period up to 1896 before Utah became recognised as a state. Probate records could exist in any one of several courts as they were kept by either the county probate court or the federal district courts.

The Utah Territorial Legislature established the county probate courts in 1851 and gave them authority 'to probate wills, administer the estates of deceased persons, and also to establish guardianships of minors, idiots, and the insane' During Utah's territorial period, these courts periodically also held jurisdiction over criminal and civil matters. Therefore early probate records may be mixed with other kinds of cases. When Utah became a state in 1896 the county probate courts were abolished and probate fell under the jurisdiction of the district court in each county within the state.

In the USA as in Great Britain, probate is the process by which a deceased person's property is identified and managed, his debts and taxes paid, and the property is then distributed to beneficiaries as specified in a will, or to heirs as required by intestacy law. Typically a probate case began when the court received a 'petition' to admit a will after which a hearing to establish its validity and appoint an administrator took place. The administrator asks any creditors to submit any outstanding bills, and the court obtains a full inventory of the estate. When all property in the estate has been properly accounted for and all outstanding debts paid, the court distributes the remaining property to the beneficiaries and the administrator has no further purpose. The probate process has remained the same throughout Utah's history. Guardianship was also the responsibility of the county probate and district courts. The courts have the responsibility to establish guardianships when a minor or an incompetent adult inherits a property. Guardianships are usually initiated under the terms of a will or by petition of a family member. A guardian is required to post a surety bond and remains accountable to the court for the management of a minor's property until that person reaches the age of majority.

Utah law makes provision for minor children to be adopted. The child, no matter what age, the adopting adults, and usually the persons offering the child for adoption must appear before or make written representation to the district court. Only when the court is satisfied that adoption is in the best interest of the child does it issue an 'adoption decree'. Such records are normally kept within probate minute records but are subject to a 100 year privacy rule.

Statehood Period (Post 1896)
After 1896 the earlier probate courts were abolished and the administration of probate became the responsibility of the new state district courts. The probate divisions of these courts exist in each county and handle all probate matters in virtually the same way as the territorial Courts did.

Availability of the records
The probate records comprise of different series including the minute books, probate case files and probate registers. The location of these records varies from county to county. Some probate records are still held locally at County Offices but the Utah State Archives also has certain records (refer to their on-line catalogue for details). The Family History Library has part copies of probate records for the majority of the Utah counties available on microfilm with the other parts retained by the county clerks. For Salt Lake county which covers the main area of Salt Lake City refer to District Court records 1852-1910 on 43 films commencing 425667 which includes an index for 1852 - 1890. There is also a Register of Probate Abstracts for 1876 - 1966 on microfilm no's 425623 - 425666.

Territorial Probate courts
The Utah courts generated various records including individual case files, court record books and minutes of proceedings as well as registers of action. Case files which were assigned a sequential number include petitions, court orders, notices, decrees, exhibits, wills, and inventories. Court record books are chronologically recorded copies of important documents found in the case files so documents relating to a particular case may appear in different volumes. Minutes record the daily actions of the court, and include information about the probate of an estate or guardianship. Registers of action sometimes referred to as 'registers of estates' are dated summary lists of outcomes and decisions taken by the court. Registers of action can usefully serve as guides to documents recorded in record books or information recorded in minutes.

The following is a summary of the records available for each Utah County during the Territorial period.

Beaver County
Probate case files, 1876-1894
Record Books, 1856-1897

Box Elder County
Record Books, 1856-1877

Cedar County
Minutes, 1859-1862.

Davis County
Estate Register of Actions, 1883-1896
Probate bonds record book, 1877-1895.
Record Books, 1853-1896

Garfield County
Probate record book, 1885-1892.

Iron County
Minutes, 1853-1868
Probate record book, 1868-1870.

Juab County
Minutes, 1859-1866.

Kane County
Record Books, 1864-1896
Millard County
Minutes, 1854-1862.

Rich County
Docket book, 1886-1887
Sanpete County
Minutes, 1852-1896
Probate docket book, 1889 - 1896
Probate record books, 1885 - 1897
Record books, 1855 - 1896

Summit County
Administrators' record book, 1883-1890.
Guardians and executors record, 1884-1888.
Record books, 1882-1913.

Utah County (Salt Lake City area)
Cost books, 1861-1896.
Divorce case files, 1863-1888.
Minute books, 1861-1876, 1885-1896.

Wasatch County
Administrator's Record Book, 1883-1898
Guardians record book, 1885-1894.
Inventory record book, 1885-1897.
Probate record, 1891-1901.

Washington County
Civil and Criminal Record Books, 1856-1886   Estate accounts registers, 1876-1895.   Estate claims register, 1882-1889.
Probate record books, 1877-1897

Weber County
Guardians record, 1884-1895.
Probate Minute Books, 1883-1896

The district court besides dealing with probate, guardianship and adoption also has jurisdiction for all other civil cases including divorces, child custody and support as well as criminal cases including homicides, assaults, sex and drug offences, forgery, arson, and robbery. Naturalisation cases were often handled by the courts also. After 1896 the records for each county were kept separately.

Cemetery records

The Utah Cemetery records are very comprehensive and include birth, marriage, and death information as well as clues to military service, religious affiliation and membership of societies or organisations for the person interred. They can be especially useful to identify young children who died or women who were not otherwise recorded in family archive information. There are many transcriptions available for Utah cemeteries and some of these have been indexed in the Early Church Information File on 75 microfilms beginning with film no.1750655.

However perhaps the best on-line source of information is the 'Names in stone' www.namesinstone.com website to which many of the city cemeteries submit information, and enable other family members buried in the same locality to be found (see illustration).

The results of a search for Christopher Layton (Namesinstone.com Gateway Mapping Inc).

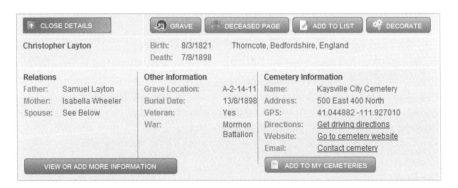

Details shown within the database identify cemetery and grave location as well as confirming other genealogical information. (Namesinstone.com Gateway Mapping Inc).

In the Utah State History **www.history.utah.gov** 'Find a cemetery in Utah' the records are listed by name of cemetery. This index does not include the Salt Lake City Cemetery. The records for the other cemeteries consist of 17 volumes available on microfilm no's 874340 - 874350. Each entry will provide the name of the deceased, location of the grave in the cemetery, date of birth, and usually information on the parents or spouse.

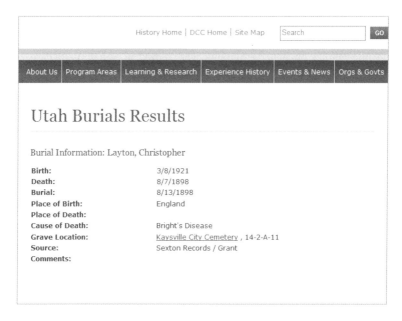

The Kaysville Cemetery website database also shows cause of death. Note the grave location is slightly different to that shown in the names in Stone database. Clicking on Kaysville City cemetery link will produce a cemetery plan for easy identification of locations of graves. (Utah State History Database - State of Utah).

The Salt Lake City Cemetery is separately recorded in sexton and interment books for the period between 1847 and 1976 and is available on 68 microfilms commencing with film number 1293881. (See library catalogue for full details). More than 100,000 burials are listed, many of which relate to the early pioneers from Britain and Europe. Each record is fairly comprehensive and includes the name of the deceased, date and place of birth, date and place of death, cause of death, doctor who certified death, burial date and grave location within the cemetery.

Tax Records in Utah
Tax records are an important element of any family history research, but to find more details of any ancestor who settled in the Utah area tax records will prove invaluable as a supplement to any census and land records. Their prime purpose is

to determine place and length of residence as they give a description of land and property holdings. The tax systems are fairly complex as they comprise of county property tax, county inheritance tax and lien records (in the USA a lien encompasses a wide range of encumbrances but is usually a form of security interest granted over an item of property to secure the payment of a debt or performance of some other obligation) and early federal taxes.

County Property Tax Records
These are the earliest sets of tax records commencing around 1850 and will obviously include information on many emigrants who settled in Salt Lake. These records which are organised on a county basis within the state give a description of the property, its value, and the tax payable. Most are held by the Utah State Archives but the Family History Library has copies of some of the records, particularly the 1865-1915 Assessment Rolls for Utah County (which covers the Salt Lake Valley area).

The Assessment Rolls not only cover property but also such elements as sheep tax, mine proceeds, school taxes and delinquency notices. They are available on microfilm no's. 175982 - 176103 plus some others so refer to the library catalogue for full details.

County Inheritance Tax and Lien Records
These records began in the early twentieth century but because they relate to taxes on inheritance can be a valuable family resource. The records are particularly useful for the names and addresses of individuals who share in an estate and their relationship to the deceased.

Inheritance tax and lien records are available at the Utah State Archives but the Family History Library has the Cache County returns which covers the area from Logan to the Idaho border north of Salt Lake City and commence in 1905 on microfilm no's. 431095 & 432096. These county films are indexed at the start of each section and this is followed by the actual record which gives the following information: names, addresses and relationships to the deceased, name of the estate with the executors, administrators, trustees, or grantees. Where a will exists, the volume and page numbers are given so you can locate the will in the probate records.

Federal Tax Records
Because it was necessary to finance the Civil War in the USA the Federal Government took over the responsibility for income tax for a short period from 1862-1872. The main records are held at the Utah State Archives but a copy of the Utah Territory assessment books for 1862, and 1867-1869 is available on microfilm no. 25780.

The books are not indexed and as such searches have to be done by locality so it is useful to know in which county your ancestor resided. The record gives the name of the head of household, the value of the property and amount of tax paid.

Additional Tax Records
Throughout Utah and introduced at different times are a variety of taxes including poll and road tax. These taxes were collected from the 1850's onward either in monetary payment or labour for the purpose of building and maintaining the road systems. Some records are in the Utah State Archives but many have not survived. The lists for Salt Lake exist for 1854 and 1861 and have been transcribed. Interestingly enough they include the name of the branch of the church to which the taxpayer belongs.

Utah military records

These Military records identify the individuals who served or in the case of the militia were eligible for service. Evidence that a church member actually served is often found in family papers, biographies, church and federal census records, naturalisation records, and the records of veterans' organisations. Military records provide important genealogical information including birth, marriage and death dates, names of spouse and children, and residence of the families.

Utah Militia
When the church members first arrived in the Salt Lake valley they set up a Constitution of the Provisional State of Deseret and created the Utah Militia in 1849 for their own protection. It stated that all men aged between 18 and 45 were to serve but there were also organisations for young men aged between 14 and 17 and for older men aged 45 to 75. In 1887 the Federal Government took over control of the Utah Militia.

Although the main records are held by the Utah State Archives the Family History Library holds amongst its collections microfilm copies of the musters and payrolls. *Utah Territorial Militia Muster Rolls, 1849 to 1870* arranged by military district and are found on microfilm no's. 485554 to 485558.

Alongside these records and of equal importance are the *Utah Territory Militia; Nauvoo Legion Correspondence Orders and Reports,* which include orders and reports, indexed by personal names, subjects or place. These records are available on microfilm no's. 497709 to 497711 with the indexes on microfilm no's 536223 and 536224.

The Utah War
The Utah War started when Brigham Young who had, up to that time, been the 'governor' was replaced by a state governor appointed by the Federal Government. In 1857 the US President ordered US troops to Utah, then still a Territory, rather than a State, to police the appointment and repel a so called Mormon rebellion. Although the troops arrived in 1858 and then built Camp Floyd the conflict was settled peacefully. Soldiers were stationed there up to the start of the American Civil War in 1861.

Information on some soldiers is found in the above mentioned Utah Militia records. The United States Army records contain information about soldiers who saw service in this so called 'war.' Registers of Enlistment of men into the U.S. Army between 1857-1861 are held by the US National Archives.

Utah civil and criminal court records

As early emigrant ancestors would have spent a large portion of their life in the developing areas of Utah it is possible that many of your ancestors can be found in court records in many guises such as plaintiffs or defendants in civil or perhaps even criminal cases, witnesses, or perhaps as jurors. There is a strong possibility that they may have been involved in a variety of cases such as probate (which is dealt with as a separate section), naturalisation, divorce, debt, appointment to public offices, taxes or property disputes to mention a few. Like many other records those generated by the courts can enhance your family history. From a genealogical aspect court records can establish family relationships, occupations, confirm places of residence and describe individuals enabling you to build a picture of your ancestors.

Utah's court system originated with ecclesiastical courts followed by the provisional state courts. Both courts existed side by side for a short period of time, after which the territorial courts were established. From about 1896 and throughout the twentieth century the courts have been under state control.

Ecclesiastical Courts
For only two years before the Provisional Government was organised in 1849, the Church provided the only government structure. Although church government officially ended in 1849, civil and criminal cases continued to be heard in Church courts as well as alongside the Territorial Courts until about 1890. Unfortunately because of the way in which church records are organised there is no separate court record system. They are filed with other Church records at the Church History Library of the Church of Jesus Christ of Latter-day Saints which means a personal visit or hiring a professional genealogist in Salt Lake to undertake the research on your behalf.

Provisional Government of the State of Deseret Courts
As the title suggests the Provisional Government was just that. No official recognition existed and the system lasted only between 1849 and 1850. The Supreme Court, justices of the peace, and county courts were created in January 1850 followed by municipal, and probate courts in January 1851. With a few exceptions the judicial court records for the provisional government era have not survived (if indeed they were formally kept in the first place).

Territory of Utah Courts
The Utah territory was established in 1850, and within a year the Supreme Court, district courts, county probate courts, and justice of the peace courts were up and running. This period was an era of conflict between church settlers and federal officials. Mormons were suspicious of the federal motives and tended to continue using the Church courts and local probate courts throughout the territorial period but many polygamy cases during the 1870s and 1880s were heard in the federal district courts. Like many court systems there was an established hierarchy.

Supreme Court.
The Supreme Court had jurisdiction over appeals from federal district courts. The majority of records are held by the Utah State Archives but the Family History Library has a copy of the National Archives, Washington film M0012 on microfilm no. 491567. Most of these records relate to appeals from the lower courts and it is advisable to research those to find more details.

Federal District Courts.
In 1850, the Territory comprised of three judicial districts with a fourth being established towards the end of the era in 1892. Those Courts were Salt Lake City, Ogden, Provo and Beaver. The district courts were held on a rotational basis with courts being held in different counties within each district at different times. The federal district courts had jurisdiction over criminal, civil, and common law cases, including disputes, estate settlements, divorces and as previously mentioned the violation of polygamy laws of which there are many case records and for which purpose the case files are worth researching.

Case Files of the U.S. District Courts for the Territory of Utah 1870-1896. The original records are held by the National Archives, Washington film M1401 but the Family History Library has filmed copies on microfilm No's 1616325 to 161359. The index is on the first film listed by name of both defendant and plaintiff and with the case file number alongside. The index lists the individual's name and the case file number. Without the number the case cannot be located without a search through all the films. The cases are alphabetical by the initial letter of the defendant's surname then numbered so they are not chronological.

In 1896 when Utah became a State the responsibilities of the federal district courts transferred to the state district courts.

Justice of the peace courts

The prime role of the Justices of the Peace was to perform marriages and deal with small civil and criminal claims. Until 1874 any appeals went to the probate courts and thereafter to the federal district courts. Justices of the Peace served either in a county, city or town. There is an overlap between the records of the territorial justices and the state justices. Many of the records have been destroyed or are difficult to locate. It is worthwhile checking with the equivalent State court to see if they still hold any records for the period. If they are not held by the courts they could be with the personal papers of the Justice of the Peace which may still be amongst collections held by descendants, in local libraries or at museums in the locality of court operation.

Utah Newspapers

The value of newspapers for genealogical purposes does not need an explanation. The Newspapers of Utah dating from the mid/late 1800s are available to search for free on the internet at **www.digitalnewspapers.org.** The site is dedicated to provincial newspapers from all over the state of Utah and can be searched either by name, event, place, date or newspaper.

The papers are a valuable resource for information about many of our pioneer ancestors who settled in Utah in the mid/late 1800s and include notable events, obituary notices etc.

The following is a listing of all the newspapers which can be searched on the above site, for which you will need Adobe Reader installed.

Utah digital newspaper collection

Title	Coverage
Beaver Southern Utonian	Sep 1881 - Jan 1896
Beaver City Press	Jan 1908 - Mar 1928
Box Elder Corinne Reporter	Jul 1871 - Nov 1873
Box Elder News	Jan 1904 - Dec 1926
Cache Utah/Logan Journal	Oct 1879 - Mar 1898
Carbon Eastern Utah Telegraph	Jan 1891 - Jan 1892
Eastern Utah Advocate	Feb 1897 - Jan 1916
Carbon County News	Dec 1908 - Apr 1915
News-Advocate	May 1915 - Dec 1932
Davis County Clipper	Mar 1892 - Aug 1971
Duchesne Myton Free Press	Apr 1915 - May 1925
Roosevelt Standard	Aug 1914 - Feb 1940
Duschesne Co. papers	May 1909 - Nov 1939
Emery County Progress	Sep 1900 - Jul 1910
Green River Journal	Jul 1955 - Mar 1956
Garfield Co. News	May 1913 - Mar 1950
Grand Valley Times	May 1896 - Aug 1919
Times Independent	Sep 1919 - Dec 1966
Iron County Record	Jan 1923 - Dec 1940
Parowan Times	Oct 1915 - Dec 1945
Juab Eureka Reporter	Nov 1902 - Dec 1922
Kane County Independent	Apr 1912 - Nov 1912
Kane County Standard	Jun 1929 - Dec 1951
Millard County Chronicle	Jan 1914 - Dec 1947
Millard County Progress	Jan 1894 - Dec 1939
Topaz Times	May 1942 - Aug 1945
Morgan County News	Apr 1910 - Dec 1954
Piute Marysvale Free Lance	Sep 1902 - Jul 1904
Piute Chieftain	Apr 1916 - Mar 1919
Piute County News	Oct 1924 - Feb 1949
Rich Co. News	May 1896 - Dec 1945
Salt Lake American Eagle	May 1897 - Feb 1905
Broad Ax	Aug 1895 -Jun 1899
Deseret News	Jun 1850 - Dec 1910
Intermountain Republican	Feb 1906 - Apr 1909
Murray Eagle	Jan 1927 - Sep 1960
Salt Lake Herald	Jan 1900 - Dec 1916
Salt Lake Mining Review	Apr 1899 - Mar 1929
Salt Lake Telegram	Jan 1902 - Aug 1952

Title	Coverage
Salt Lake Tribune	Apr 1871 - Jun 1899
Union Vedette	Nov 1863 - Nov 1867
Univ. of Utah Chronicle	Dec 1892 - May 1937
Valley Tan	Nov 1858 - Feb 1860
Western Light	May 1914 - May 1914
San Juan Record	Feb 1919 - Dec 1953
Sanpete Ephraim Enterprise	Sep 1891 - Dec 1972
Manti Messenger	Aug 1893 - Dec 1973
Sevier Richfield Reaper	Mar 1906 - Dec 1940
Summit Park Record	Jan 1881 - Dec 1970
Tooele County Chronicle	Jun 1947 - Dec 1948
Tooele Transcript-Bulletin	Sep 1894 - Dec 1924
Uintah Papoose	Jan 1891 - Feb 1892
Vernal Express	Feb 1892 - Dec 1982
Provo Daily Enquirer	Jan 1881 - Nov 1897
Wasatch Wave	Mar 1889 - Dec 1922
Washington County News	Jan 1908 - Dec 1923
Weber Ogden Standard-Examiner	
Ogden Junction	Jan 1879 - Feb 1881
Ogden Herald	May 1881 - Dec 1887
Ogden Standard	Jan 1888 - Dec 1908

more ...

y complime...

g of beauty is a ...

confer a favor by se...

...tion as soon as possible after ...

...from Zi...

...ollowing named missionaries

...rican line s.s. *Belgenland*, December 29...

...—Geo. A. Dixon, Salt Lake City; Wm.

...Joseph H. Downs, Logan; D. H. All...

...he Scandinavian Mission—Lars Chr...

... Mission—Geo. L. Weiler, Salt

...ay—Thos. P. Page, Riverto...

...were Kristian Jacobe...

...k, the former o...

CHAPTER FIVE
Church Growth in Britain and Europe

U p to 1850 there was a significant growth in church membership throughout Britain. In just 13 years after the introduction of the church in England the membership grew to 30,747. The organisational structure of the church in Britain at this time consisted of branches as the local unit and from 1840 between four and forty branches (depending upon geographical location) were grouped together for administrative purposes by the British Mission into what were called conferences.

British Church membership

YEARS	MEMBERS
1840	3626
1850	30747
1860	13853
1870	8804
1880	5112
1890	2770
1900	4947
1910	8202
1920	7830
1930	6491
1940	6481
1950	6375
1960	16623
1965	66371
1970	67849
1975	75692
1980	87776

Church Publishing in Britain

Because of this growth there was a need to publish church literature in this country. Up until the 1850s it had all been published in Salt Lake and shipped to this country but there was only a handful of members in Salt Lake with the skills and knowledge to operate printing presses on a large scale so it became impractical for literature to be produced in that country. Add to this the shortage and expense of paper in the USA and it made economic sense to transfer publication to Britain. Church scriptures and hymn books were published from Liverpool. The first publication was a collection of materials that dealt with ecclesiastical procedures and enlightened members on the gospel principles adopted by the church. It sold for one shilling.

The church publication business was not without its challenges particularly within the distribution operation. From Liverpool publications were shipped to many other parts of the world as the church growth developed. Agencies were set up at each conference of the church to distribute literature and collect payment which in itself proved to be a cumbersome process.

Millennial Star - the longest running church publication
As family historians we are surely aware of the value of 'parish magazines'. The Mormon Church has, over the years produced various periodicals, most of which were published in America, however *'The Millennial Star'* was the longest running church periodical which was published in England and ran from 1840 until 1970. It was inaugurated by Brigham Young just eight days after the start of his mission in the United Kingdom and was published monthly. The first publication announced that it *'will stand aloof from the common political and commercial news of the day and its columns will be devoted to the spread of the fullness of the gospel.'* Parley P. Pratt then church leader served as the editor until mid-July 1840, at which point Brigham Young and his colleague Willard Richards took over, with Richards doing most of the work. Their editorship was short-lived as Pratt resumed the editorship in October, until April 1842. At that point Thomas Ward a British member and convert to the church became editor until October 1846 when he was replaced by Orson Hyde, the then president of the British Mission and the British Mission continued the editorship from then on.

Initially the *Millennial Star* was a monthly periodical but on 15 June 1845, it was published twice a month and in 1852 it became a weekly journal. Even though the *Millennial Star* was published primarily for the members of the Church in England, it also became an important record for those in America.

That first issue set the standard format and contained an editorial; extracts of revelations given to the Prophet Joseph Smith, challenges to publications opposing the Church originating from other British (mainly nonconformist) churches, articles on different religions' beliefs, report of the conference (meeting) of the Church in Preston, history of the Church in America; letters and news from missionaries; poetry; and two hymns. Later issues followed a similar format but included information and articles about members. Its pages are an excellent source for the history and development of the Church. They also covered news from the states and abroad together with explanations of church doctrine, policy and gospel principles along with letters from members abroad and in Salt Lake City. These letters often illustrated the intricate details of events on a particular voyage. Many of the reports were historic in that it may have been several weeks after the actual voyage before a particular letter was published. Occasionally there may have been an article about preparing for emigration or a report of a particular company arriving in America or ending in Salt Lake City. You will need a degree of patience in searching this resource looking at all the letters and correspondence following the known date of an emigration.

Incorporated within each Millennial Star were lists of church appointments and important meetings (GSU Microfilm No. 1402725).

12   LATTER-DAY SAINTS' MILLENNIAL STAR.

C. R. SAVAGE of the famous Art Bazaar, Salt Lake City, sent us a beautiful calendar, a work of Art indeed, more fit for a parlor than for this office in dingy Liverpool; we can only compliment the donor, and referring to the old adage say, that "a thing of beauty is a joy forever."

CLERKS of Conferences would confer a favor by sending in reports of their conferences for publication as soon as possible after the close.

ARRIVALS.—The following named missionaries from Zion arrived in Liverpool per American line s.s. *Belgenland*, December 29, 1899: For the British Mission—Geo. A. Dixon, Salt Lake City; Wm. Stoddard, John T. Thain, Jr., and Joseph H. Downs, Logan; D. H. Allred and Chas. Munns, Lehi. For the Scandinavian Mission—Lars Christofferson, Salina. For the Netherlands Mission—Geo. L. Weiler, Salt Lake City, and M. Baker, Ogden. For Turkey—Thos. P. Page, Riverton.
With the company were Kristian Jacobsen of Ephraim and Mrs. Robina Thomas of Spanish Fork, the former on a visit to Scandinavia and the latter to Scotland.

APPOINTMENTS.—The Elders for the British Mission that arrived December 29 were appointed to labor in the various conferences as follows:
Geo. A. Dixon, Irish; Jos. H. Downs, Manchester; D. H. Allred and Charles Munns, Norwich; J. T. Thain, Jr., and Wm. Stoddard, Welsh.

The volumes are available on microfilm via local Family History Centres

1840-1847	film no.1402725
1848-1851	film no.1402726
1852-1853	film no.1402727
1854-1855	film no.1402728
1856-1858	film no.1402729
1859-1860	film no.1402730
1861-1863	film no.1402731
1864-1866	film no.1402732
1867-1868	film no.1402733

'The Star' (by which it became known) was nearly discontinued in 1841 and 1843 due to lack of subscribers and publication did actually cease for a time in World War Two. The demise of the Millennial Star happened in 1970 when it was absorbed into the current worldwide publication known as 'The Ensign' which is still published today.

MARRIAGES

★ James Gray, formerly a building missionary from Scotland who worked on the Nottingham Chapel and then stayed on in the Ward, was married on April 14th to Madeleine Joan Buxton. The bride wore a long dress and coat of pale pink chiffon and carried a white Bible. The honeymoon was spent in Italy.

The couple went to the Temple the following day, and spent their honeymoon in Surrey. They have now settled in Middlesbrough.

★ Joyce Storrow of Middlesbrough was married to Robert Robson of Newcastle on March 26th. The wedding took place at the Middlesbrough Chapel and was attended by many of the members from the two wards.

The bride wore a blush-pink suit and carried a Bible and a spray of flowers. The two young bridesmaids, Pauline Richards and Adrienne Henweed, wore velvet dresses in a shade that matched the bride's suit, and the Matron of Honour, Mrs. Joyce Hurren, wore a deep green velvet dress.

Joyce Storrow and Robert Robson after their wedding at Middlesbrough Chapel.

JUNE 1969

The Millennial Star of June 1969 like other editions includes details of birth, marriages and deaths of British members (Deseret Enterprises Ltd. Mitcham, Surrey for the LDS Church in the UK)

Besides the above filmed copies later editions of 'The Star' can be searched on line at www.contentdm.lib.byu.edu/cdm4/browse.php?CISOROOT=%2FMStar.

The British Library Newspaper Library in Colindale, North London also holds a complete run of the journal to 1970. You will need to be aware of the planned move of low-use items to Boston Spa in West Yorkshire in 2012 and also the digitisation programme for old newspapers and periodicals which is now underway. When the Library closes at Colindale access will be through the main British Library at St Pancras.

The Journal of Discourses

George D Watt, the first convert to the church in England had been recording on a voluntary basis many of the sermons and addresses given to gatherings of the Church in Utah and he sought permission to publish these. The Journal of Discourses as they became known began publication on a fortnightly basis in Liverpool in November 1853. Each edition comprised of sixteen pages and Watt himself described them as 'a source of light, information and joy and will be most valuable as a gauge of doctrine, a square to life and a repository of historical information'. The Journal continued to be published up to 1886 and has since continued as a 'handbook' used even to the present day.

They are available on line at www.journalofdiscourses.com

The 1851 Ecclesiastical Census Returns

The Religious Census taken in March 1851 concluded that the lowest level of religious observance was in larger urban areas. To the Church's advantage it also concluded that new religions of which the Church of Jesus Christ of Latter-day Saints was one, had become more effective in the working class areas of larger towns and cities and that nonconformity generally was greater in number than those of congregations of the Anglican Church. The Anglican Church however was shown to be dominant in most rural areas.

The Religious Census was compiled from returns made by the incumbents of all places of worship and showed the following information:

- Name or title of place of worship.
- Where situated specifying the parish or place, district and county.
- Religious denomination.
- When the building was erected.
- Whether the place of worship was a separate and entire Building.
- Whether used exclusively as a place of worship
- Space available for public worship and the number of sittings and standing room.
- Number of persons attending Divine Service on Sunday, 30 March 1851, (split into morning, afternoon and evening meetings).

The report of the Religious Worship Census of 1851 can be seen at www.histpop.org. The actual returns are available at The National Archives, Kew in class HO129 covering England and Wales. Some returns are available on-line at www.origins.net and most County Archives will have copies relating to their own county. Any Family History Centre of the LDS Church has access to microfilmed copies of the 1851 religious Census in its entirety covering HO129/1 - 623. These are available on film numbers 2206646 - 2206719 inclusive.

The statistics taken from this census in relation to members of the Mormon Church showed that there were 222 separate meetings of which 7,500 members attended morning services, 11,100 afternoon services and 16,500 evening services and 60% of these were concentrated on London or the larger Northern and central England towns and cities. The largest congregation was in Birmingham and numbered 1,200 regularly attending evening services.

By 1890 however, and suffering from the effects of mass emigration, there were only about 2,750 members of the church in Britain. The decline had been gradual and was not only affected by emigration but other influences such as the wars fought in the Victorian period. Missionary numbers also declined for similar reasons and because of the opposition to the church from a political viewpoint both here and in America.

The church in this country was not without its persecution. In Birmingham in 1857 there was mass agitation against the church led by a Reverend Brindley who was a revivalist preacher. He held meetings opposite the main chapel in Birmingham and systematically interrupted meetings for several weeks. The chapel was almost burnt down by Brindley's mob and would have been razed to the ground had it not been for intervention by the local police.

A local newspaper the 'Birmingham Journal' supported the LDS and did more to quell the unrest than the law did. It stated that Mormons observed the law, lived decent moral lives and that the law of the land must give protection to ALL religions. It ended by stating 'There must be no more religious bonfires in Birmingham'.

Native members who had emigrated returned on short term missions including George Watt and the situation began to improve although there was still some opposition (but not by the press). There remained however a stubborn prejudice against Mormons by many of the English people and this seemed to exist even into the 20th century. Despite this many of the prominent church leaders who were natives of this country continued to visit and preach or talk to gatherings about the Mormon stance and eventually with the favourable help of the provincial press attitudes began to change. Joseph F Smith the President of the Church visited England in 1906 and used Finsbury Town Hall in London to address large numbers of church members. He also spoke in Blackburn and in Scotland during his tour which motivated members to continue in their endeavours to overcome adversity and to 'grow the church'. However with the disruption of two world wars and the depression of the 1930s this did not really come to pass until the early 1950s.

The Church in Wales

The establishment of the church in Wales was based in two areas at opposite ends of the country. Flintshire in the north and Glamorgan and Monmouthshire in the south saw the first real missionary efforts come to fruition.

The first Welsh convert to the church was believed to be Frederick G. Williams who joined in November 1830. The fact that Wales was only some 20 miles away from where there had been tremendous success in establishing the church in Herefordshire suggested that many of the Herefordshire converts may have had relations or friends 'across the border'. The first real efforts to establish the church in Wales took place from 1840 in the county of Flintshire. The first branch of the church was established in October 1840 at Overton with 32 members. Meetings were held in private homes as the church was unable to obtain a licence to preach because other local ministers were opposed to the establishment of the church. By February 1841 the membership of the church in Wales had grown to 150. Mysteriously the Overton Branch does not appear to have left any records.

Church growth in South Wales was slow as this area had a strong nonconformist 'chapel' influence. The first members in this region were from Skenfrith and after continued efforts 44 new members formed a branch of the church at Llanthony and it is estimated that by the start of 1841 there were over one hundred members of the Church in this part of Wales, as well as a handful in Monmouthshire which at the time was part of England.

The next branch of the church to be established in South Wales was at Pen-y-Darran, Glamorganshire on 25 March 1843 followed fairly shortly afterwards by Merthyr Tydfil, Aberdare and Tredegar which were all strong non conformist mining areas. Much of this was attributed to a Cornishman named William Henshaw who became a church member in Wolverhampton in 1841.

Perhaps one of the most significant advances in regard to the growth of the church in Wales was the arrival of 'the Father of the Welsh mission' Dan Jones in 1845. Jones was born in Halkyn, Flintshire on 4 August 1810, became a seaman at 16 years of age and emigrated to the USA in 1840 where he became the Captain of the 'Ripple', a Mississippi Steamship plying between New Orleans and St Louis. It was through his job that he first had contact with church members as he transported emigrating members. The success of Dan Jones was phenomenal and he is generally termed the 'Father of the Welsh Mission.' He served for about four years and by the end of 1848 the membership in Wales had increased to over 3,500.

When Dan Jones returned to the USA on 25 February 1849 he took with him 250 Welsh Saints as they emigrated to Utah on board the 'Buena Vista'. Dan Jones returned a second time to Wales in 1852 to serve as a prominent church leader returning again with another group of 560 Welsh church members emigrating this time on board the 'Samuel Curling'. This was in fact the last group of Welsh church members to emigrate en-masse.

From this point until the middle of the 20th century there were very few new church members throughout Wales and as such the publications gradually ceased and missionary work dwindled.

Prophywd y Jubili

To counteract some of the adverse publicity which was thrown at the church by other religious denominations who published periodicals which contained slights against the Mormons, Dan Jones initiated a periodical in the Welsh language specifically for the Welsh members called 'Prophywd y Jubili' which translated means 'Prophet of the Jubilee' and was first published in 1846. This journal contained information about new members sometimes with their conversion stories as well as topical information about the church at the time. The name was later changed to 'Udgorn Seion' which translated means 'Zion's Trumpet'. Alongside this periodical Jones also published various leaflets and tracts relating to aspects of the church, again in the Welsh language. By 1852 the church's main scriptures and hymn book were also being published in the Welsh language and were the first official publications of the church to be printed in a language other than English. It is probable that the language had been a barrier to growth as membership increased to well over 5,000 within a few months of the Welsh publications becoming available. A digital copy of the published editions of 'Prophywd y Jubili' translated into English can be viewed on-line at www.contentdm.lib.byu.edu.

There is also a very good Welsh Mormon History website developed by Dr Ron Dennis which contains details of many of the early Welsh church members and outlines the history of the church in Wales.

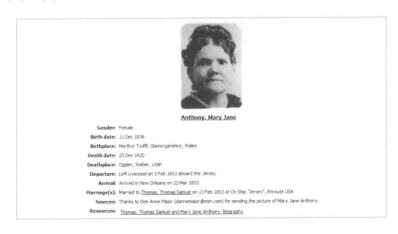

This is a list of the Welsh Mormon immigrants in our database. Click on an individual's name to see more information. Type a name (or a portion of a name) and click "Search" below to look for specific individuals.

Search: Surname: Given name: Search

6096 results found. This is page 4 out of 305

« Previous   Go to page: [   ] Go   Next »

Name	Birth date	Birthplace
Anthony, David John	12 Sep 1879	Tredegar, Monmouthshire
Anthony, Edmund	24 Dec 1880	Tredegar, Monmouthshire
Anthony, Evan Daniel	16 Aug 1885	Tredegar, Monmouthshire
Anthony, John	Abt. 1790	llanon, Carmarthen, Wales
Anthony, Mary Jane	11 Dec 1836	Merthyr Tydfil, Glamorganshire, Wales
Anthony, Rebecca Ann	6 Mar 1882	Tredegar, Monmouthshire

A search for Mary Jane Anthony in the Immigrants reveals basic information and a link to more detail. The presence of a photograph indicates that an illustration is included. (Welsh Mormon History website - Dr Ron Dennis)

Anthony, Mary Jane

Gender: Female
Birth date: 11 Dec 1836
Birthplace: Merthyr Tydfil, Glamorganshire, Wales
Death date: 25 Dec 1920
Deathplace: Ogden, Weber, Utah
Departure: Left Liverpool on 5 Feb 1853 aboard the *Jersey*
Arrival: Arrived in New Orleans on 22 Mar 1853
Marriage(s): Married to Thomas, Thomas Samuel on 13 Feb 1853 at On Ship "Jersey", Enroute USA
Sources: Thanks to Dee Anne Major (dannemajor@msn.com) for sending the picture of Mary Jane Anthony.
Resources: Thomas, Thomas Samuel and Mary Jane Anthony- Biography

Details of Mary Jane, her family and travel are shown in the expanded details (Welsh Mormon History website - Dr Ron Dennis).

167

THOMAS SAMUEL THOMAS AND MARY JANE ANTHONY

Thomas Samuel Thomas was born December 26, 1825 at Tredegar Iron Works in the Parish of Bedwellty, Monmounthshire, England. Mary Jane Anthony was born December 11, 1838 at Merthyr Tydfil, Glamorganshire, Wales. They both embraced the gospel in Wales. They met and were married, on board ship, while immigrating to Utah in the year 1853.

Thomas Samuel Thomas was the fifth son of eleven children born to Samuel Thomas and Margaret Watkins. As a young man he worked for a mining company, driving a horse-drawn coal car out of a mine. This job came to an end one day when the mine exploded. Thomas was knocked beneath the moving coal car and his leg was severed from his body. His father was also killed in the explosion. With the frightful tragedy went Thomas's youthful dreams of getting an education.

A friend knowing of Thomas's disappointment aided him in getting his long desired education. Along with his enterprise in school, Thomas was taught a handicraft in the art of making shoes. This art proved to be very beneficial in later years as he resorted to it many times in earning a living during critical periods.

In the fall of 1843, Thomas heard the gospel for the first time from William Davies, a missionary in England. Thomas was a devoted member of the Baptist Church, and he became disturbed by the doctrine of Mormonism. He was rather reluctant in accepting all that he heard about the Mormon religion. While walking down the street one day, a voice came to him saying, "Keep thyself for thou must yet stand for me." He was overcome by the Spirit and fell to his knees, weeping because of the lack of faith he had had in the past. He pleaded with the Lord for forgiveness. He joined the Church on July 16, 1851, being baptised by Thomas Williams.

Some useful biographical information about her family is also included. (Welsh Mormon History website - Dr Ron Dennis)

The Mormon Tabernacle Choir and its Welsh connection

Some of the Welsh church members on arrival in Salt Lake were instrumental in developing the world famous Mormon Tabernacle Choir under the initial leadership of John Parry, an early Welsh convert to the church and the first musical director. He was born in Trelawnyd, Flintshire and was at the time of his conversion a Baptist preacher.

At the October 1849 general conference Parry organised and conducted 85 Welsh converts who had formed the choir. This was just the start of British involvement with the choir for seven other British church members became the musical directors. Evan Stephens from South Wales (the longest serving director from 1890 to 1916), George Careless from London, Ebenezer Beasley from Oxford, Robert Sands of Ireland and Charles Thomas and James Smithies, both from Lancashire, were at one time all directors.

168

Joseph Ridges, a convert to the church and originally from Southampton emigrated to Australia to make his fortune in the Gold Rush. It was not to be and he joined the church there eventually emigrating to Salt Lake where he designed and built the organ specifically for the Tabernacle building which was completed in 1867. That organ was first played by another Englishman Joseph Daynes who was born in Norwich.

The names and details of all those who have ever been members of the choir or their accompanists can be found at www.moromtabernaclechoir.org and by going to the 'Historical Roster' section. Names are listed alphabetically by initial letter of the surname.

Name	Org.	From	To	Part/Assignment
Lach, Helen Lydia Gygi	MTC	1924	1937	
Lake, Patricia	MTC	1989	1995	S-16
Lamb, A.	MTC	1891		B
Lamb, DonNel	MTC	2008		A-65
Lamb, Jane	MTC	1930	1932	S
Lamb, John D.	MTC	2001	2006	B-47
Lambert, Peggy	MTC	1980	1995	A-43
Lambert, Synthia (Syndy)	MTC	1994		S-87
Lambourne, Charles	MTC	1882		B
Lambourne, Harry C.	MTC	1931	1932	T
Lambourne, William	Instrumentalist	1880		Violin

Listing of members past and present in the Mormon Tabernacle Choir
(mormontabernaclechoir.org - Intellectual Reserve Inc).

The Church in Scotland

Interestingly enough the establishment of the church in Scotland is attributed to two Scottish-Canadian immigrants. On 20 December 1839, Samuel Mulliner, a native of Midlothian and Alexander Wright, a native of Banffshire arrived in Glasgow being the first missionaries on Scottish soil. Originally arriving in Liverpool on 3 December they were delayed on their journey to Scotland because of some paperwork formalities.

The following day they proceeded to Edinburgh, where Samuel Mulliner's parents lived and where he began missionary work. Alexander Wright also had relatives in Banffshire where he concentrated his efforts. The first church members in Scotland were Alexander and Jessie Hay who became members on 14 January 1840 at Bishopston, Renfrewshire. A few days afterwards Samuel Mulliner rejoined Alexander Wright in Edinburgh and as a result of their combined efforts church membership in that area began to grow particularly in the Paisley area.

The first branch of the church was organised in Paisley. Church membership at the time in Scotland amounted to about 80 people. Following the establishment of this branch Wright and Mulliner then concentrated their efforts on Edinburgh and were joined by Parley P Pratt who was at the time a prominent church leader from America. A branch of 40 members was soon established in Edinburgh.

By April 1841 there were about 600 members of the Church in Scotland but 10 years later this number had grown to in excess of 3,000 mainly concentrated on the Edinburgh and Glasgow areas. In Edinburgh the church even publicised its meetings with the use of a broadsheet.

Because emigration was still very much encouraged many of the Scottish church members also took the opportunity to leave resulting in an almost 50% decline of members.

Most of the members from Scotland were solid working class from the industrial areas around the Clyde with many from the mining and ship building industries and from homes where religion was an important part of daily life even before joining the church. Many were strict Scottish Presbyterian. Notwithstanding this the Scottish church members were influential in the growth of the church. Richard Ballantyne established the church's Sunday School programme. David Eccles who once sold rolling pins around Glasgow was instrumental in establishing the Utah sugar industry. John Sharp, a skilled stone cutter was in charge of the stone cutting in Little Cottonwood Canyon for use on the Salt Lake Temple and he later became a railroad executive.

The Church of the Isle of Man

On 17 September 1840 John Taylor, Hiram Clark and William Mitchell arrived on the Isle of Man. They quickly saw success with a branch organised in Douglas on 25 December 1840 with 40 members. By April 1841 membership on the Island had increased to 115 although 25 of those members were about to emigrate to the USA. In 1846 a further branch was established in Peel which again had about 40-45 members. The early membership on the island appears to have peaked at about 120 around the end of 1851. Because of emigration in the period 1845-1852 membership on the island dwindled to about 50 members.

The church struggled to exist on the Island. There were no missionaries and the members who were left found it difficult to continue because of health or family reasons. However emigration slowly continued, further weakening membership and the branches were disbanded. An attempt was made in 1908 to re-establish a branch but was unsuccessful. No church existed from this point until it was re-established in the post Second World War years. Missionaries were not established on the Island until 1959 after which they had limited success with few conversions so they were withdrawn again.

In the early 1960s two female members had moved to the Isle of Man from mainland Britain and they requested that missionaries be sent back to the Island. As a result the Isle of Man branch was re-established in Douglas during August 1962. Growth continued and by 1970 the branch was established in its own purpose built chapel.

The church in Ireland

The presence of the church in Ireland happened in 1840. John Taylor was amongst the first supported by two Irish missionaries. They began to teach in Lisburn, Newry and around Belfast in Northern Ireland. Perhaps the most significant event in this predominantly Roman Catholic country was when John Taylor addressed a crowd of 600 people in Newry on 28 July 1840 which resulted in the first Irish member Thomas Tait joining the church in Lough Brickland on 31 July 1840.

The first branch of the church was organised in Hillsborough with just 20 members closely followed by another branch in the township of Crawfordsburn. Like elsewhere however most of the members of these two branches emigrated during the famine years of 1845-1847. Despite the emigration the missionary work continued in Ireland and by the end of 1847 there were about 40 members all within the Belfast and Lisburn areas.

A peculiar situation in Ireland resulted in the slow progress of missionary work. Because of the poverty within the country at the time and the impending famine those who could eke out a living were mainly tenant farmers who, if they joined the church, stood every possibility of being evicted from their homes and livelihoods by the landlords, many of whom followed the Catholic religion.

Many of the Irish who migrated because of the potato famine went firstly to Glasgow. It was reported that the Glasgow branch significantly increased in size during the famine years, so although Ireland church branches did not grow, many Irish people still joined the church but did so in Scotland. Two hundred and twenty eight Irish people were baptised members of the church in Glasgow representing about a third of the branch membership.

A similar situation existed for those Irish who went to Swansea, Newport and Cardiff in South Wales. In October 1846 it was reported by Dan Jones that nearly a thousand people had joined the church in that area and the majority (although the exact number is not known) were Irish.

The church had also established itself in Dublin by 1850 when it opened its first branch in that city. By 1852 there were one hundred and fifty two members in the Belfast area but only thirty three around Dublin. Membership in Ireland reached nearly three hundred by 1856 but the missionaries were withdrawn the following year.

From 1857 virtually half of the church members again embarked on an emigration to America leaving the remaining members scattered geographically. Throughout the whole country there were only about a hundred members left and there was little opportunity for them to undertake missionary work and increase the membership. Missionary work did not re-commence in Ireland until 1884 when the branches in both Dublin and Belfast were re-established. Of the two hundred and fourteen new members of the church in Northern Ireland between 1884 and 1899 ninety emigrated to America and a further twenty eight were ex-communicated. However because of other religious and cultural influences and indeed persecutions and disruptions to public meetings the rate of growth was far from that which occurred in other parts of Britain. In 1913 there were several drama productions in Belfast with strong anti-Mormon messages. By 1915 there were only three hundred and twenty eight members of the church in Ireland.

The church in Europe

The predominantly Protestant countries of Western Europe including Scandinavia, Switzerland, Germany, and the Netherlands played an important role in the growth of the Church providing many thousands of converts along with the United Kingdom, Canada and the USA. Asian countries also proved a source for new converts, so even if your ancestors came from far climes there is a possibility that they could have been influenced by Mormon beliefs or even converted.

The success of the church throughout Europe was, to say the least, geographically uneven. Most early converts originated in countries affected by Protestant Reformation. Conversion in countries such as France, Italy, Ireland, Austria and Hungary, which were predominantly Roman Catholic was not particularly successful in the early years and did not match the growth in the Scandinavian countries and Germany. In fact real growth in these countries did not occur until well into the 20th century. The church had virtually no access to the Orthodox Eastern European countries including the Balkans, Greece and Russian states. There were hardly any conversions of European Jews.

Converts were from various Protestant denominations and small religious sects, but virtually all of them were seeking some kind of new religion in their lives. Like the United Brethren in England, similar organisations such as the 'New Lighters' in Holland in the early 1860s converted en-masse. Most of these religious seekers had studied the Bible and were ideally looking for a church with the structure that gave apostles, prophets, and spiritual gifts which they had read about in the New Testament, this section of the Bible being their inspiration. Many were beginning to become very discouraged with the imposition of traditional religious doctrines and more particularly the behaviour of the traditional churches and their clergy.

Like those who converted in Great Britain most of the European converts came from the middle, lower middle, and working classes. Of the church members who emigrated to the United States between 1840 and 1869 a relatively small percentage (11%) were middle class artisans; the remainder falling into the working classes. Early attempts were made by missionaries to interest aristocrats and dignitaries but their work fell on deaf ears and sometimes even led to the missionaries being banished from the countries. Even Royalty was approached without success. Only during the mid twentieth century did European Latter-day Saints as a group become part of the growing middle classes as they experienced greater opportunities in further and higher education and financial success.

The European church members during the nineteenth century came from both rural and urban societies. Those who emigrated to the USA as a result of the church programme comprised of rural workers including farmers and agricultural workers who left a depressed countryside and many skilled craftsmen, artisans, industrial workers and townspeople who left the slums of industrial towns.

Three years after the Church was established in Europe, it encouraged its new members to emigrate to the USA. Before 1900 more than 91,600 did so, and thousands more followed them in the early years of the 20th century despite the church leadership actively discouraging any further emigration. Most of those who followed the early emigrants were family and extended family. Most had to scrimp and save, often for 8 -10 years to find the money needed to get from Liverpool to Salt Lake City. Church members from the Continent had to sail from Liverpool where, along with the British members, they booked passages on large emigrant ships. In later years ships also sailed from Hamburg. Many landed in New Orleans and travelled the Mississippi to Nauvoo, but in later years they landed at New York, Philadelphia, or Boston and travelled overland, sometimes by stage or train to Omaha, continuing their journey of just over 1,000 miles to Utah by covered wagon or handcart. After 1869 most continued their journey by train.

Assisted emigration from European countries

The church had by this time extended the Perpetual Emigration Fund to European members to enable families, most of whom were poor, to take up the emigration appeal. The fund continued to allow thousands of Saints to borrow the money to emigrate and then repay the fund after they were settled in the American West. European LDS emigration also peaked in the 1850s and 1860s, although a fairly constant stream, especially of Germans, continued after both world wars. Very few of these Saints or their descendants ever returned to their native lands.

The majority of European members were exceptionally good pioneers. Most held a very solid religious conviction and faith, and had a very strong work ethic, combined with practised skills inherent in their nature and upbringing. Most also worked hard to establish a new society and surroundings. By their nature they also fostered a deep respect for Church leaders recognising them as God's chosen servants. They were willing to settle where they were called to reside and developed a desire to help promote the missionary cause in their native lands. The majority were persuasive recruiters of their fellow countrymen to the new LDS settlements and many would meet incoming emigrant trains escorting incoming settlers to their new homes.

The church growth in Europe came as a result of conversions in different occupation groups from unskilled and skilled/professional people. Many members were from the labourers and skilled craftsmen but there were also businessmen, teachers, doctors, journalists, architects and musicians. Amongst the womenfolk were nurses and midwives. Europe produced its fair share of church leaders and missionaries, many of whom laboured in their native countries. In 1880, as determined by the census of that year, the total population of Utah was 143,863, and around 30 percent, were foreign-born.

As in Great Britain not all European converts to the Church emigrated to America. In many cases family circumstances meant that they would not or could not leave. Similarly many could not afford the fares or did not want to take up the facilities of the Perpetual Emigration Fund and some even lacked the faith to make such a move. Some original converts drifted away from the Church and others were affected by anti-Mormon pressures and varying degrees of persecution. Throughout Europe in the nineteenth and early twentieth centuries, many Latter-day Saints were affected by persecution and some were even jailed for their beliefs. However in the nineteenth century, the Church with its growth and influence amongst the general populations began to be taken seriously by those in power but many still regarded the Church as a non-Christian American sect. Throughout Europe there was a tradition of state and religious compatibility so much so that many political leaders were highly influenced by the clergy of the traditional Protestant and Catholic religions. Although such influence was declining it was still an important voice and added generally to the persecution of Latter-day saints.

Because of this influence some European leaders visited Utah to get a first hand view of LDS society. Most began to admire the way they conducted their daily lives and could see many good points in their community. The Church became well established in Europe and following their success in Great Britain in the 1830s and 1840s, missionaries began their work on the European mainland. They found great success in Switzerland and Hamburg, Germany, but less success was found initially in Italy and France, but even in those two nations a few converts gave rise to larger LDS communities. There was a steady growth of the Church in Switzerland and Germany, especially after German unification in 1870. A mission was established in the Netherlands in the 1860s, and over the years thousands became Latter-day Saints and emigrated to the USA.

Results were not so encouraging in the Austro-Hungarian region. In 1865 President Brigham Young sent Orson Pratt and William Riter to open that empire to missionary work. They had little success and spent time in jail for proselyting activities. Later missionaries were only successful in converting a few isolated members. Attempts were also made to try and enter Turkey which was predominantly Islamic and little progress was made before the early 20th century as was the case in Imperial Russia.

Emigration of European members gradually declined, allowing permanent congregations to emerge and grow. Conversions in the Roman Catholic countries of France, Italy and Belgium began to increase because of religious freedom and the decline of persecution. The Catholic religion was certainly loosening its ruling grip in these countries.

The rising democracy, after the defeat of Germany and its allies in the First World War, opened the door for the Church in the area. A branch of the Church was established in Vienna which served as a foundation for the Church in Austria. The effects of war meant that there was great poverty and devastation which helped the populations of the defeated countries become more receptive to the Church. Post World War One conversions in Germany were at an all-time high. By 1930 there were more church members in Germany than in any other country outside the USA. However during the Second World War all missionaries were withdrawn from Europe but members still managed to hold their meetings.

Immediately following World War Two the Church established contact again with the church congregations throughout Europe, including Britain. The welfare supplies that had been accumulating in America were made available to European members. This scheme was extended to allow others to participate. Care packages (as they were known) of relief supplies arrived from America. The church members in the former German occupied Netherlands also supplied potatoes for the packages.

Missionaries returned to Europe in 1946 and during the first decade after the war, efforts focused once again on strengthening the existing church members as well as gaining new ones.

Some other important changes within the church structure took place. Secularisation, and its associated religious freedom and the presence of many American church members who were service personnel helped to further establish the Church in European countries that previously had not been receptive to the Church because of the Roman Catholic influence particularly Italy, Spain and Portugal.

Throughout Europe the image of the Church changed. But at the same time, the Cold War made life difficult for the seven thousand church members who resided in the German Democratic Republic. Politics and Communism gave rise to new prejudices against churches generally and against people with any degree of religious conviction. The construction of the Berlin Wall isolated members even further. Some church members decided to leave the Church to appease their political leaders and avoid any further persecution and harassment. By the early 1970 chapels were being built in Western Europe helping the Church to shed its 'sect' image.

Before the 1960s, success in Europe was mainly in the predominantly Protestant countries of Western Europe. A few conversions had been made in Hungary and Czechoslovakia. During the 1960s attempts were made to establish the Church in other Eastern European countries.

Vienna became the centre of activity by the Church in Central and Eastern Europe. In the 1970s a few missionaries served in Budapest, Hungary, where the first branch of the Church was organised during the 1980s and was made up generally of the more educated and artisan Hungarians. This breakthrough was the start of church growth in a strict communist area of the world.

Records for European church members follow the same pattern as those of British church members and records of European emigrants are interspersed with records relating to other nationalities.

The Church in Australasia

The establishment of the Church and its early growth in Australasia was attributable to the English who had emigrated earlier. The Church was actually introduced into Australia by a British church convert, William James Barratt, who emigrated from England in November 1840. He was already a member of the Church before he emigrated and was encouraged to share the gospel message wherever he went. Unfortunately he drifted away from the Church, but before doing so he introduced Robert Beauchamp (also a British emigrant) who was believed to be the first Australian convert. Beauchamp subsequently became president of the Australian mission. Another British convert emigrant to Australia, Andrew Anderson, settled in New South Wales with his wife and their three children in 1841. Anderson organised the first Australian branch of the Church, in Wellington.

Missionary work commenced in Australia in October 1851. Thereafter, the Church grew slowly in Australia and it was not until the mid 1900s that chapels were built. The early days of the Church in Australia were difficult and newspapers published articles attacking the church doctrine on a regular basis. The early missionaries responded with their own articles, tracts, and by teaching the gospel in public meetings, frequently held on the Sydney racecourse. Like elsewhere many of the early converts emigrated to the USA. Many of those early converts were British who had emigrated to Australia hoping to find gold in the newly discovered Australian goldfields. Most did not realise their hopes but felt much the same about the Church as their British counterparts.

When the missionaries were recalled to Utah in 1857, the branches of the Church in Australia were ran by the members who had not yet emigrated to Utah. When the missionaries returned to Australasia their efforts focused on New Zealand and many Maoris subsequently joined the Church. As little growth was happening in Australia the Sydney Branch was discontinued in the 1880s but the Melbourne Branch remained strong. By 1896 the Sydney Branch was re-established.

One prominent member was Joseph Ridges, the designer of the original Mormon Tabernacle organ who was an Englishman born in Ealing and who emigrated to Australia where he joined the church before emigrating to Utah.

Most members of the Church in Australia lived in the larger cities and towns, but many branches also thrived in rural communities. Many Australian members travelled considerable distances to attend Church meetings. Members who lived in outback communities were totally isolated from organised branches and it was not until 1929, when recognising the need for better communication among scattered members, that the church began publishing the 'Austral Star', based upon the Millennial Star published in Britain which provided members with local and international news of the Church and messages and instructions from Church leaders.

CHAPTER SIX
Finding your Mormon Ancestor

Preliminaries

Before searching through the many different records generated by the Church and its members it is worth, as with all family history research, searching out family archive records. Try and locate other members of the extended family of your ancestor who, if still following the religion, will more than likely have gathered family history information because of the doctrines that church members follow in regard to undertaking genealogical research and the resultant religious ordinances. Besides recognised artifacts such as family bibles, letters, newspaper cuttings, civil registration documents etc. it is possible that those family members may hold copies of family group sheets used by ancestors to undertake religious ordinance work, copies of journals, diaries, personal histories, LDS church certificates relating to baptisms, blessings and other church generated records which relate to the family. Some LDS families, particularly American branches, may belong to a family organisation which will mean that you could have access to additional information held by others. Taking the time to investigate possibilities could save valuable research time if they are willing to share the information they hold. There are also various Pioneer Organisations which could hold useful information and possibly even information taken from the official records. A list of these is shown in the appendix.

An overview of records generated by the Church of Jesus Christ of Latter-Day Saints

In order to commence your research let's take a look at the many different records which can be accessed. The intricacies of using the records will be outlined later unless detailed earlier in the book. There are also several websites, some not directly associated with the Church that can prove to be a valuable resource to those involved in researching Mormon ancestry.

Records of individual LDS Church members and units have been kept since the 1830s and are perhaps the most valuable source of information. They are records compiled at local level and may contain occasional inaccurate information but nevertheless usually include names, birthplace and date, baptisms, marriages, deaths, priesthood ordinations, and other details. Also the indexed missionary records date from 1830 giving details of all full-time church missionaries. Records of priesthood groups were also kept by church units.

The Early Church Information File was compiled to identify early Church members. It is an alphabetical card index of individuals dating from 1840 to around the start of the First World War although I have found references up to 1940. The information has been extracted from LDS membership records, journals, local histories, missionary and priesthood records, immigration records, biographies, marriage records, and many others.

Many church members kept detailed diaries, daily journals, family bibles, and various personal accounts. Many have been filmed but manuscript and printed copies often exist in major libraries and in state and local historical societies rather than through the Family History Library facilities.

Histories of Church units (branches, wards, stakes and missions), describe the early history of that unit. Sometimes the names of early church members are included but these tend to be the more prominent members of a particular unit.

Every fifth year between 1920 and 1960 (except 1945) the Church took a census of its members. The pilot was actually taken in 1914. Not every member was listed in the census but where they are included shows each person in a family, whether male or female, the priesthood office held by the males, marital status, birth date, and place.

There are many printed sources containing biographical details of church members, the most important being the Latter-day Saint Biographical Encyclopedia. Many early biographical sketches are indexed in the Early Church Information File.

The Church's European mission register, ships passenger lists and departure records of the masses of emigrants, together with their journals and personal accounts, newspaper reports and other ephemera and documents, as well as details of those migrating throughout the USA are a valuable and important resource. Two important immigration indexes exist - the 'Crossing the Ocean Index' and the 'Crossing the

Plains Index'. The most complete reference for this topic is the Mormon Immigration Index, which was detailed earlier.

Of particular interest to members with British ancestry are the records of the Perpetual Emigrating Fund which cover the period 1850 - 1887 and assisted around 30,000 members to emigrate.

The 'Minnie Margetts File,' consists of indexes to selected church records, primarily relating to the USA for the period 1839-1915 but because of the date span and also the number of British emigrants will be of particular interest.

The fifty-volumes of Susan Black's 'Membership of The Church of Jesus Christ of Latter-day Saints, 1830-48', contains biographies and genealogical details for many emigrant church members. This is one of the first sources to check when seeking early Latter-day Saints.

The Church has around 8 million of its members' family group records as well as others submitted for conservation reasons. Associated with member records are the genealogies and family histories church members and other individuals have compiled.

One overlooked source of information which can prove quite valuable is the Journal History of the Church, 1830—1973 which is card indexed. This is a chronological account of events in church history extracted from periodicals, newspaper reports and many other non-genealogical sources.

As in Britain obituaries from Utah newspapers are also a useful genealogical source. There are various indexes from as early as 1848. Some recent obituaries are available on the Internet. Other church historical periodicals have also been archived. Most of the early issues have been indexed in the Early Church Information File.

Because each record is unique it may be necessary to search in more than one place for a record of an individual or family who was a member of the Church although several of the above are incorporated into various internet sites.

Church Membership records

Because research can become complex and in order that you cover every eventuality it is worthwhile making a time line of your ancestors life, particularly since the date you discovered a Mormon church connection. List all you know about your ancestor, siblings and parents and don't forget that in the early years of the church those who emigrated may well have practised plural marriage once in America and may have had more than one wife and family living alongside each other. For the early Latter-day Saints, including many British church emigrants, this was an accepted practice which has long since ceased. The Church complied with US Federal Law and stopped the practice of plural marriage from 6 October 1890. It is also important to check for church membership records of an ancestor in each locality.

During its existence the Church has made use of several types of membership records which normally cover a particular span of years. A member may be listed in more than one type of record particularly if they were members at the time of transition between different records. Initially church membership records were generated and held locally. Each branch, district or conference had its own clerk responsible for record keeping and while the majority of clerks used the standard church formats for membership records, some created their own forms. Depending upon how meticulous the clerks were will depend upon whether an index exists and how complete it is. Most indexes are in alphabetical order only by the first letter of the surname and often for the family head only, hence it may mean that any other individual included in the record, such as children or parents, were not indexed.

There were six different types of records used throughout the life of the Church.

Journal Record
The earliest membership records used between 1830 and 1877 were plain page bound books normally acquired locally. Membership clerks usually recorded standard information including: names of member, dates and place of birth, parents' names, dates of baptism and confirmation into the Mormon Church (dates of baptisms etc in any earlier denominations are not listed), who performed the ordinances, blessings of children, minutes of the meetings at which events took place, dates of marriage(s), any divorces, priesthood ordinations, details of tithes and offerings and emigration information. The amount of detail depended upon the period of record and also what the clerk actually included. There was no set format. Most of these records are not indexed so a page by page search must be undertaken.

Long Book Record Form
This printed style of record was in existence between 1877 and 1900 and came about because in 1877 many existing members were re-baptised to renew their church covenants. The long book format was initially created to record the rebaptisms and the following reconfirmations. Searching these is a lot easier as most records start with an index (although some are only indexed by first letter of the surname) and include the following information: name; birth date and place; parents' names; date of original baptism, confirmation, date of rebaptism, reconfirmation, priesthood ordinations; date the person was received into and removed from the congregation (useful in tracing

their mobility); death date; and remarks. Many contain an allocated membership number which usually remained with the member throughout his or her lifetime.

Records of membership within a CONFERENCE of the church - London Conference
(LDS Church Intellectual Reserve Inc).

Office.	Registered No.	Name.	Age	State	Residence.	Day	Mo.	Year	Town or Parish.	County.	Nation.	Day	Mo.	Year
						TIME & PLACE OF BIRTH.						TIME & PLACE		
Elder	1	John Brightman	55	M	Kempston Beds							1	3	07
Elder	2	Millie Brightman	67	M	" " " " " "							8	7	55
	3	John Nugent Swift	36	M	" " " " " "							1	3	80
	4	Susan Elizabeth Swift	36	M	" " " " " "							18	2	77
	5	Kate Elizabeth Swift	10	S	" " " " " "							10	10	89
	6	Maria Wheeler	66		Marston							9	11	08
	7	Elizabeth Rook	59	M	Heath							31	12	54
	8	William Rook	59	M	" " " " " "							10	2	90
	9	Annie Rook	19	S	" " " " " "							1	6	87
	10	Rose Rook	16	S	" " " " " "							1	6	87
	11	Louisa Clark	73		" " " " " "									06
	12	Emma Amy Simms	58		Mackhanger								11	50
	13	Matilda H. Simms			" " " " " "							14	1	83
	14	James Wells			Old Warden									67
	15	Susan Wells			" " " " " "									67
	16	Mary O'Grady		S	Bedford							18	11	83
	17	Nellie O'Grady		S	" " " "									

Saints, in   Beds and Herts District

Where.	Immersed by	Confirmed by	Day	Mo.	Year	From Whence.	Day	Mo.	Year	To Where.	Day	Mo.	Year	Day	Mo.	Year	Day	Mo.	Year	Remarks.
				E OF BAPTISM & BY WHOM CONFIRMED.		RECEIVED.				REMOVED.			EMIGRATED		CUT OFF.		DIED.			
	Jno C Perry	John Sharp	X														2	1	78	
	Theo Harding	Theo Harding																		
	Jas Brightman	J Brightman	X																	
	Theo Harding	Theo Harding																		
	Jn Redditch	I A King																		
	R H Ford	R H Ford																		
	Elder Tuckett																			
	Thos Smith									96										
	Jno Beach	Jno Beach								95										
	Elder Marsh																			
	C E Angel	J Brightman																		

Membership records recorded in the DISTRICT membership book for Bedford & District (LDS Church Intellectual Reserve Inc).

184

Luton Branch — PARTICULARS OF BIRTH.

No.	Names in full	Day	Mon.	Year	Parish	Town	County	Received by Letter, from.	Day	Mon.	Year	By Whom
1	Thomas Day	8	7	1816	Burghclere		Hants		12		1846	Thomas Squires
2	William Webster							Jun 30/53 Stampsted	20	5	1852	George Smith
3	Joseph Fletton				Hampstead		Herts		5	10	1852	John Parson
4	Ellen Bryant								5	10	1852	"
5	Eliza Bryant								5	10	1852	"
6	Hannah Day Webster	8	3	1817	Luton	New Mill End	Beds		5	10	1852	"
7	Louisa Tott	7	8	1826	Braughan		Herts		16	10	1852	"
8	Alice Cockle	4	8	1857	Luton		Beds		16	10	1852	"
9	Ann Fenn Adkins	18	5	1811	Billington		"		23	10	1852	"
10	Ann Adkins	6	2	1838	Leighton Buzzard		"		16	11	1852	"
11	Jane Tott	18	1	1838	Braughing		Herts		16	11	1852	"
12	Elizabeth Merchant Day								20	11	1852	"
13	Hannah Hamsted Fletton	21	10	1828	Hampstead				29	12	1852	"
14	Emily Shelton			1834				Watford Jan 10 - 1853				
15	Ellen Shelton							Bedford Jan 10 - 1853				
16	Sarah Woods							Birm. & Guern Jan 10 - 1853				

OF BAPTISM — PARTICULARS OF MARRIAGE. — REMARKS.

Branch	Conference	By Whom Confirmed	Day	Mon.	Year	To Whom, from, Where	Dead, Removed, or Emigrated
Luton	Bedford	Thomas Squires	1	12	1854	Elizabeth Merchant of Hertford	
"	"	John Bridges	18	10	1833	Hannah Day of New Mill End	Emigrated July 15 - 1855
"	"	John Parson	25	4	1847	Hannah Hamsted of Hampstead	
"	"	"					Emigrated Feb 15 - 1855
"	"	"					Emigrated Feb 15 - 1855
"	"	"	18	10	1838	William Webster of Grangrove	Emigrated Feb 15 - 1855
"	"	"					Removed
"	"	"					Emigrated Feb 15 - 1855
"	"	"	14	7	1834	Robert Adkins	
"	"	Thomas Day					
"	"	Job Smith					
"	"	John Parson		12	1853	Thomas Day	
"	"	Job Smith	25	4	1847	Joseph Fletton of Hampstead	
"	"	"					Emigrated March 1855
"	"	"					Removed to Bedford Oct 5 1855

Membership records maintained by a BRANCH showing marriage details and whether or not they emigrated with dates. (LDS Church Intellectual Reserve Inc).

Three-Part Record Form

This format of membership record was standard throughout the whole of the church and was used between 1900 and 1920. The books were much smaller than the Long

Books and generally started again with an index. The three parts all had a specific purpose:

Part I - Record of baptised members. This gives each member's name, date and place of birth, parents' names, date of baptism and confirmation, and who performed the ordinances, membership record numbers, and remarks which usually included arrivals and removals and information relating to death.

Part 2 - Record of Priesthood ordinances. This record related to male members of the church and records names of person ordained to the priesthood, date of ordination, which priesthood office ordained to, person who ordained the individual and reference to the membership record number enabling a cross reference to information contained in part I, and any remarks.

Part 3 - Record of children under eight years of age. Baptism in the LDS church is not necessary until a child is 8 years old. However children are blessed and given a name as infants. This record is specifically for children who have been blessed but not baptised and contains: the name of the child, date and place of birth, parents' names, date of blessing and by whom blessed, blessing number, and a reference to the transfer in part 1 upon baptism and remarks.

Example of a THREE PART membership record showing the basic information relating to individual members. - Usually indexed (LDS Church Intellectual Reserve Inc).

186

Record of Children Blessed by Elders of the Church of Jesus Christ

No.	CHILD'S NAME IN FULL		PARENTS' NAMES		DATE		
	SURNAME	GIVEN NAME	FATHER'S NAME	MOTHER'S MAIDEN NAME	Day	Month	Year
1	x Ormsby	Alice Louisa	Albert Fredk		27	8	1901
2	x Armstrong	Thomas	Thomas	Kate Hamlin	4	12	1898
3	x Armstrong	Frederick	Thomas	Kate Hamlin	7	5	1900
4	x Armstrong	Wm.	Thomas	Kate Hamlin	12	10	1902
5	x Andrew	Phyllis Elizabeth	Wm James	Lizzie Dimmiond	22	Aug	1900
6	+ Hobbs	Joseph Horace	Horace Alfred	Alice Elizabeth Barker	28	May	1904
7	x Avery	Ivy Mary	John Benzie	Minnie Pearson Allen	22	Oct	1897
8	+ Winch	Florence Maud	Morris	Ada Higbee	4	July	1904
9	Osborne	Sidney Charles	Henry Robert	Alice Jennings	29	Aug	1904
10	Armsby	Alfred Fredrick Jr.	Alfred Fredrick	Sarah Ann Smallfield	9	Apl	1904
11	Ellis	Annie Elizabeth	George	Caroline Griffith	1	Dec	1904
12	Panek	Elizabeth Matilda	Joseph	Helena Eberhart	12	Dec	1905
13	Burr	Lilian Mabel	Charles	Mary Jane Parkhouse			

of Latter-day Saints in the _____ Ward, _____ Stake of Zion.

AND PLACE OF BIRTH			BLESSED		REMARKS	Transferred to Record of Numbers to
TOWN	COUNTY or STATE	Country	Day Month Year	By Whom	Note to this column date and place received from; date and place removed to; date of baptism, death, etc.	
London	London	England	13 4 1902	Geo. 2. Morris		1351
Newbury	Berks	Eng.	1 19 6 1901	Jno. D. Hughes	Over 9 - not baptised	
Newbury	Berks	Eng.	1 13 5 1902	Jos. Newbold Jr.		
Newbury	Berks	Eng.	1 13 6 1902	Jno. D. Hughes		
Richmond	Surrey	"	1 18 Oct 1903	Frank Brown		
London		Eng.	1 19 June 1904	Richard A. Shipp	Moved to Birmingham	
Chatham	Kent	Eng.	6 July 1904	George Naylor		897
London		Eng.	1 24 July 1904	Edwin F. Tout	Baptised Nov 22-1913	1386
London		Eng.	25 Sept 1904	Frank Brown		
London	London	England	16 Oct 1904	Pres. Heber J. Grant		
London	London	England	15 Jan 1905	Richard A. Shipp		
London	London	England	8 Jan 1905	Hugh J. Cannon	Double entry 580	
London	London	England	2 Apr 1905	Pres. Heber J. Grant	Emigrated to Canada May 12	
London Edmonton	London	England	21 May 1905	Pres. Jesse W. Hobbs		

Records of Children blessed (given a name) as Infants within the Church. Part of a three-part record. (LDS Church Intellectual Reserve Inc).

Box-Type Record

Between 1920 and 1941 the Church used a box-type form with four to six grouped entries on each page. The alphabetical index in the front of each volume shows the number assigned to the box rather than a page number. For each member box there is a space for the member's name, sex, date and place of birth, parents' names, dates of blessing, baptism, and confirmation and by whom performed, dates of priesthood ordinations to which office, and by whom performed, date and cause of death, arrivals and removals into units, spouse's name, marriage date and place, and whether it was a civil or temple ceremony and any details of excommunication (date and reason) or cancellation of membership.

Card Type Record

Starting in 1941 (and still used until recently) each member's record was kept on an individual membership form. The detail on this form is the most comprehensive and includes: Name of member, date and place of birth, parents' names, citizenship, current address, dates of blessing, baptism and confirmation, details of ordinations to the priesthood (males), date of Patriarchal blessing, dates of temple ordinances, date of civil marriage, name of spouse and spouses membership status, children, removals and arrivals.

When a member left a unit, the card was returned to Church headquarters and then, upon request, sent to the member's new Church unit. These records are not available for research. If the member died, however, the card was placed in the Deceased Members File.

Live records are maintained by the member's current church unit. These records are not available to anyone other than the member to which they relate.

Members Funds Payments

The Church also kept meticulous records relative to financial transactions undertaken between members and the church authorities. The records usually maintained at Conference or District level show contributions made by each member to different funds in any one year. The funding requirements changed from time to time but the records will show the name and residence of the contributor and also the donations made to the funds existing at the time. Funds were required for tithing, emigration, assisting with a family's welfare, payment towards publications of books etc.

Whilst they may not contain a vast amount of genealogical information they show what financial commitment your ancestors would be prepared to make to the running of the Church in this country. The records cover the early years of the Church and cease in about 1875.

Member's Fund payments ledgers showing contributions of each member. (LDS Church Intellectual Reserve Inc).

Annual Genealogical Reports

The Church used annual report forms to collect genealogical information from its units between 1907 and 1983. They were kept concurrently with the membership records but do not list each member in the unit. The detail they contain varies and they only relate to members who were blessed, baptised, ordained to priesthood offices, sent or returned from missions, were excommunicated, married, divorced, or died during the year. There were two forms containing much the same information but used by different church organisations. - Form E was used by stakes (formerly

Conferences) - Form 42FP was used by missions. The 42FP included sections for information about members who emigrated to Salt Lake. Some of the information is statistical. Annual Genealogical Reports need to be searched year by year as they are not indexed. They are available on microfilm up to 1948.

Marriage Records for Church Members
Some, but not all, of the branch records of the Church in the United Kingdom contain separate entries relating to the marriage of members which are extremely useful as many of the marriages took place before they became church members and many for the period before civil registration commenced in England in 1837. The registers contain basic information including the names of both the male and female parties to the marriage, the name of the registrar and details of when, where and by whom the marriage was performed. Most of the places detail the name of the church so the original marriage record can easily be located.

Although marriages may not have taken place in the LDS church they are often recorded giving the parish where the ceremony took place. (LDS Church Intellectual Reserve Inc).

For the period 1870 to 1940 there is also a card index to marriages which took place once the church members were settled in Utah or some areas of Idaho and Wyoming. The index is compiled from the records of marriage licenses issued and is organised by counties as follows: Box Elder, Millard, Morgan, Salt Lake, Sanpete, Sevier, Summit, Utah and Weber counties in Utah State, Franklin and Lemhi counties in Idaho and Lincoln County in Wyoming. The cards are filed by the name of both the groom and the bride and contain names of both parties to the marriage, by whom married, reference to where the marriage took place, place of birth, age, parents' names including the maiden name of the mother, marital status and where the licence for the marriage was issued. This index arranged alphabetically is available on microfilm no's 820155 to 820173.

It is probable that as you search the card index you will find more than one entry of marriage for an ancestor when it is apparent that the spouse is not deceased or no record of divorce can be found. Plural marriage existed in the church during the nineteenth-century which even as early as the 1830s and 1840s led to persecution, and the public announcement of the practice on 29 August 1852 by Brigham Young, in Utah gave rise to hostility against the Church. Latter-day Saints believed that the religiously-based practice of plural marriage was protected by the U.S. Constitution but ultimately opponents used it to delay Utah statehood until 1896. US legislation against plural marriage stripped Latter-day Saints of their citizen rights and permitted the seizure of Church property before the first manifesto in 1890 announced the discontinuance of the practice.

Within the Church plural marriage was a carefully regulated and ordered system. Order, mutual agreements, regulation, and covenants were central to the practice. After the Saints left Nauvoo, plural marriage was openly practised. In Winter Quarters plural families were acknowledged and this practice continued although few new plural marriages were authorised in Utah before 1855. Generally plural marriage involved only two or three wives but there were exceptions with some having ten or more wives.

Plural marriage helped mould the Church's attitude toward divorce in Utah. Though Brigham Young disliked divorce and discouraged it he generally granted it through the ecclesiastical court system when it was sought after by a wife. He felt that a woman trapped in an unworkable relationship with no alternatives deserved a chance to improve her life but if a husband sought divorce Brigham Young counselled him not to do so.

The exact number of Latter-day Saints who participated in the practice is not known, but studies suggest this was only a very small percentage and it is thought that no more than around 15% to 20% of members were a part of the resulting plural families.

Public opposition to plural marriage led to the first law against the practice in 1862, and, by the 1880s, laws were increasingly punitive. The Church contested the validity of those laws, but the Supreme Court sustained the legislation, leading to a harsh and effective federal campaign known by the Latter-day Saints as 'the Raid.' Wives and husbands protested and many were arrested and sentenced to jail terms in Utah State and other federal prisons. This campaign severely affected the families involved, and the related attack on Church organisation and properties greatly inhibited its ability to function. Continuing plural marriage endangered both the objectives of the Church, and jeopardised statehood so the then Church President Wilford Woodruff issued the first Manifesto in October 1890, announcing an official end to new plural marriages and facilitating an eventual peaceful resolution of the conflict with the US government.

Established plural families continued to exist into the early twentieth century, often causing further political problems for the Church, and despite the manifesto new plural marriages did not entirely cease in 1890. After having lived the principle for half a century, many devout Latter-day Saints found ending plural marriage a challenge almost as complex as was its beginning in the 1840s. Some new plural marriages were contracted in the late 1890s in LDS settlements in Canada and northern Mexico. National attention in the early 1900s however forced the then church President Joseph F. Smith to issue a second manifesto in 1904 since when the practice of plural marriage ceased and the Church has not advocated or practised plural marriage since.

Deceased Members File
When a Church member dies, that person's membership record is placed in the Deceased Members File. This file is retained for ten years by the Membership Department after which the record is transferred to the Church History Department where it is available for personal research in the archive search room. It is therefore necessary to know the date of death in order that you apply to the correct department for a copy of the record.

To find information about a person who died between 1941 and 1975, you should search the following microfilms.

Deceased Members File 1941 to 1977. These films are not circulated to Family History Centres and photocopies are not allowed so a personal visit to the main library in Salt Lake City is needed or hire a professional genealogist to undertake research for you. The collection consists of:

Handwritten Cards
1941-1974 on films 884001-884392
1974-1975 on films 884393-884420
1975-1977 on films 884429-884435
Computerised Cards
1975 on film 884421
1976 on films 884422-884424
1977 on films 8844425-884428

Later records are not generally available for research but have been microfilmed.

There is an index to the deceased members' file known as the Ordinance Index which will show whether your deceased ancestor appears in the handwritten or computerised cards. This is organised by a series of batch numbers prefixed by the letter H.

There is an anomaly which researchers should be aware of: On the Ordinance Index a married woman is listed under her maiden name but on the Deceased members File she will appear under her married surname.

If the person died after 1975, the Membership Department will provide birth, marriage, baptism, priesthood ordination, endowment, and sealing information provided there is proof of death either furnished by local church leaders or by provision of a death certificate by the researcher.

Other records for deceased members

Records of Deceased Members of the Scandinavian Mission.
This is an alphabetical listing of members who died between 1852 and 1895 in Scandinavian countries excluding Finland. The information that is available is: name, date and place of birth, date and place of baptism, and date of death.

Death Records of Church Members Who Died in England, 1909-1911
This record consists of seven pages of clippings from the Millennial Star and may not be complete.

The Minnie Margetts file - The membership card index

This file contains an index of membership records of most early British branches and relates to the years 1839-1913. An index to the branches covered is included as item one on the first film of the series 415443. This index is known to be incomplete. It was compiled by Minnie Margetts who was born in Salt Lake City, Utah in 1874 of British parents Philip Margetts born 1829 in Kineton, Warwickshire and Elizabeth Bateman born 1834 in Manchester. Minnie was a volunteer with the Church Historians Office where she undertook most of the work on the index. The following Church units outside of England are also included:

International Branches: Mexico, Garcia branch; Australia, Sydney branch; Samoa, Vaiafai branch.

United States Branches: Arizona, Pima and Showlow branches;

United States Conferences: California; Georgia Harmony, Conference; Iowa; Florida, Harris Grove Conference; South Carolina Conference; Utah.

Not all of the information is included for everyone in the file but each entry should contain some or all of the following items: Name, date/place of birth, parents' names, date/place of baptism and by whom, priesthood ordinations, residence, emigration information, remarks.

Membership Card Index providing specific information about an individual (LDS Church Intellectual Reserve Inc).

When looking for women you may need to check for their maiden and married names. The Minnie Margetts Card File can be searched at the London Family History Centre.

Minnie Margetts Card File

Surnames Included on Film	Film Number
Aagard, A. - Batez, J.	415443
Bath, B. - Bryson, L.	415444
Bubb, E. - Cooper, William	415445
Cooper, William - Ekstrom	415446
Elanson, C. - Goudie, C.	415447
Gough, A. - Hess, S.	415448
Hess, T. - Johnson, Minnetta	415449
Johnson, Minnie Alice - Luker, S.	415450
Luker, T. - Moungoy, E.	415451
Mount, A. - Pfouts, S.	415452
Pfail, A. - Ryves, L.	415453
S - Startup, A.	415454
Startup, H. - Waildin, M.	415455
Wain, E. - Wood, Janet	415456
Wood, Jesse - Zytherlaan, M.	415457

Membership records finding aids

As the church units grew or diminished in size or as geographical boundaries changed, units of the Church were often amalgamated, divided or had their boundaries altered. Sometimes the unit names changed so you may have to research this information to enable you to identify the whereabouts of your ancestor's records. Some branches, particularly in the early years of the Church in Britain were so small that their records were kept with those of a nearby larger unit.

The following finding aids may help in locating the correct church unit for your ancestors once in America.

Membership of the Church of Jesus Christ of Latter-day Saints 1830 - 1848
A series of microfiche has been produced giving an alphabetical listing of all members of the church between 1830 and 1848. The information for each person includes four sections (where available), namely:

1. Vital records information such as names, dates of birth, baptism, marriage etc. together with names and details of spouses and children.
2. Church ordinance information.
3. Temple ordinance details.
4. Biographical sketches.

The information is compiled from various sources and may contain inaccuracies which need to be checked, where possible, with original sources. The listing consists of 95 fiche - catalogue number. 6031596 and is available on self selection at the London Family Centre.

```
s0    LAYTON, CHRISTOPHER              Male #      Print-Date: 4-19-90

      Reference: Nauvoo Temple Endowment Register 1845-46
                 Members of the Mormon Battalion. Easton, Susan W.
                 Roster of Mormon Battalion
                 Family Group Sheet-Self
                 Mormons and Their Neighbors. Wiggins, Marvin
                 Portrait and Biographical Record of Arizona
                   Page: 538
                 Checklist to Published Diaries and Autobiographies
                 Guide to Mormon Diaries & Autobiographies. Bitton, Davis
                 History of Arizona
                   Volume: 3   Page: 221
                 Treasures of Pioneer History. Carter, Kate. 1952
                   Volume: 4   Page: 488
                 LDS Biographical Encyclopedia. Jenson, Andrew. 1951
                   Volume: 1   Page: 363
                 Pioneers and Prominent Men of Utah. Esshom, Frank. 1913
                   Page: 44
                 Stalwarts of Mormonism. Nibley, Preston, p. 78-79
                 Utah Federal Census: Year: 1860, 1870
                 Family Group Sheet-Father
                 Autobiography of Christopher Layton, ed.
                   by John Q. Cannon,
                   Page: 1-234
                 Kaysville Cemetery Record
                 West Jordan, Utah Ward Records
                 Kaysville, Utah Ward Records
                 Thatcher, Arizona Ward Records
                 St. David, Arizona Ward Records

      s1    Birth-Data
                 Birth-Date: March 8, 1822
                 Reference: Nauvoo Temple Endowment Register 1845-46

                 Birth-Place: Thorncote, Bedfordshire, ENG
                 Reference: Nauvoo Temple Endowment Register 1845-46

                 Birth-Date-Variant: March 8, 1821
                 Reference: Family Group Sheet-Self
                           Mormons and Their Neighbors. Wiggins, Marvin
                           Family Group Sheet-Father

      s2    Parents-Data
                 Father's-Name: Layton, Samuel
                 Reference: Family Group Sheet-Self
                           Members of the Mormon Battalion. Easton, Susan W.
                           Family Group Sheet-Father

                 Mother's-Name: Wheeler, Isabella
                 Reference: Family Group Sheet-Father
                           Family Group Sheet-Self
                           Members of the Mormon Battalion. Easton, Susan W.

      s3    Marriage-Number:  1
                 Spouse's-Name: Mathews, Mary
                 Reference: Family Group Sheet-Self
                           Guide to Mormon Diaries & Autobiographies. Bitton, Davis

                 Spouse's-Name-Variant: Matthews, Mary
                 Reference: LDS Biographical Encyclopedia. Jenson, Andrew. 1951
                           Volume: 1   Page: 363
                           Family Group Sheet-Self

                 Marriage-Date: July 20, 1842
                 Reference: Family Group Sheet-Self
                           Mormons and Their Neighbors. Wiggins, Marvin
                           LDS Biographical Encyclopedia. Jenson, Andrew. 1951
                           Volume: 1   Page: 363

                 Marriage-Place: Thorncote, Bedfordshire, ENG
                 Reference: LDS Biographical Encyclopedia. Jenson, Andrew. 1951
                           Volume: 1   Page: 363
                           Family Group Sheet-Self
```

Compiled information relating to Christopher Layton within the Membership of the Church microfiche. Note some details are inaccurate and as a finding aid need to be checked. (LDS Church Intellectual Reserve Inc).

Encyclopedic History of the Church of Jesus Christ of Latter-day Saints.
This was compiled by Andrew Jensen and is available on microfilm 496776 with an index on film 928073. The publication includes brief histories of early branches and gives information about when they were formed as well as names of leaders up to 1930. It is extremely helpful in identifying the units around Salt Lake so emigrant pioneers can be easily located. It covers Utah in detail and other places in a more general way. Besides being on film it is indexed in the Early Church Information File and included in the LDS Family History Suite which is beginning to appear on-line.

LDS Place Names Gazetteer.
This gazetteer is available on film 1059499 and identifies many areas in the western United States, Mexico, and Canada where members lived as well as providing the names of the units that they attended including information about many of the disbanded units or units where names have changed. The gazetteer contains many references not found in the Encyclopedic History of the Church.

Local Unit History File 1830s -1961.
This file covers the period from the early 1830s to 1961 and is available on 20 microfiche under catalogue number 6334934. It covers the whole world but is useful in identifying 20th century church units. For each unit it lists dates when organised, disbanded, amalgamated, or divided. More specifically it is useful in detailing the name of the unit to which disbanded unit members' records were sent. This is available through local Family History Centres.

Alphabetical Index to Ward and Branch organisation.
Available on films 471843-44 this index includes dates of organisation, name changes, and other information about all church units. However a word of caution - The reference numbers shown on cards are obsolete but can still be used in relation to numbers that still appear on the membership films. You should seek the advice of the Family History Centre staff before relying on this information.

For current unit boundary information, it is best to contact local Church leaders. You can find local congregations listed on www.lds.org or www.lds.org.uk or in telephone directories under 'Church of Jesus Christ of Latter-day Saints.'

Maps of Salt Lake City, Utah, and Vicinity.
There are several maps of the Salt Lake City area dating back to the mid 1800s which will be extremely useful in locating where your emigrant ancestor resided. Such records may be available as reference sources in your local Family Search Centre or via your local library reference section. They are not available on microfilm but can be viewed as original documents at the main Family History Library in Salt Lake City.

The Reorganised LDS Church and its membership records

The Church of Jesus Christ of Latter-day Saints shares its early history with *the Reorganised Church of Jesus Christ of Latter Day Saints known since 2001 as the Community of Christ.* If you find you have 'lost' an ancestor on the journey across the plains then it is worth looking at the records of the Reorganised Church. Whilst its religious beliefs are similar there are several key doctrinal aspects which oppose or do not fit in with mainstream Mormonism. Many early Latter-day Saints, mostly of British and European origin, broke away from the mainstream Church during their journey from Nauvoo to Salt Lake City and as such will appear in the early membership records of the Reorganised Church of Jesus Christ of Latter Day Saints. Their records which are kept by the Archives of the Reorganised Church in Independence, Missouri are available for research on microfilm.

Most of the records of the Reorganised Church can be found on the Family History Library Catalogue under *MISSOURI, JACKSON, INDEPENDENCE - CHURCH RECORDS* and include the following:

• Early membership records 1890-1908 on film numbers 2027545 - 2027551.

• Minutes Card Index 1852-1871 on film numbers 1984482 - 1984483.

• Deceased members 1877-1995 on film numbers commencing 1985756 - (use the catalogue as they do not run in sequence).

• Mound Grove Independence Cemetery records 1903-1994 on film numbers 197876 - 1987678.

There is also a catalogue to all of the holdings of the Reorganised Church Archives on film numbers 1984679 - 1984685.

The Reorganised Church of Jesus Christ of Latter-day Saints was organised in April 1860 at Amboy, Illinois, under the leadership of Joseph Smith III. All of its members had until that time belonged to the Mormon Church but questioned the authority of Joseph Smith's successor, Brigham Young to the extent that some refused to continue their migration to Utah. These dissenters appealed to the prophet's son to take on the leadership of a new denomination.

The Reorganised Church evolved in the late 1840s and early 1850s from the 'succession conflict'. Before his death in 1844, Joseph Smith had supposedly (according to the dissenters) indicated various possibilities relating to his succession, one of which was the designation of his son Joseph III to succeed him as prophet-president. During the decade following Joseph Smith's assassination various dissenting factions came into existence but the main body of the Mormon Church remained at Nauvoo until 1846, when they began their trek to Salt Lake organised by Brigham Young, the then senior apostle. Brigham Young was not sustained as the President of the Mormon Church until 1847.

In 1860, Joseph Smith III, the assassinated prophet's son accepted the leadership of the Reorganised Church. During his early years in office, Smith edited the *True Latter Day Saint Herald* through which he was influential. This periodical is available on line at www.archive.org/details/saintsherald. He worked mainly to detach the Reorganised Church from plural marriage and to encourage his people to conform to monogamy, so much so that during the 1880s he was amongst those who organised the prosecution of the Mormon Church for practising polygamy.

A number of Mormons either on the trail west through Iowa or newly arrived in Salt Lake left to be re-united with Reorganised Church branches in southwest Iowa. By 1890 the center of the Church with a membership of around 25,000 had shifted from Illinois to Iowa. In the early twentieth century, the Reorganised Church established itself in Independence, Missouri.

Even today there are several congregations throughout the world including some within the British Isles.

LDS Church censuses

In order to keep track of membership growth within the Church it first took a membership census in 1914 and then every five years between 1920 and 1960 except for 1945 because of World War Two. This was worldwide not just in the USA. The 1914 to 1935 returns were amalgamated before filming, the 1940 census was filmed separately and the 1950, 1955 and 1960 censuses were again filmed together. There are also some supplementary films for cards which were sent in to church headquarters late. In total there are around 650 microfilms which cover the whole census period.

A prescribed card was completed for each census containing specific information about every family in each branch of the church. In each census some information was standard such as name, gender, age, priesthood office (for males), and marital status. Some additional information was added to census cards.

On the 1914 cards the geographical regions were marked to show where each family member was born, their address; the ward or branch, stake, or mission that a person attended; and date of the census.

In the 1920 census the maiden name of each married women, the year of birth of each person, and the Church auxiliary for each person was added.

1925 saw the inclusion of the full date of birth and the church auxiliary column was deleted.

In 1930 the census also records the place of birth. Some census cards in certain areas (presumably as a pilot) requested baptism information but this was not comprehensive.

In 1935 the census requested details of the previous church branch the family attended.

As a follow on from the previous information requested in the 1935 census the 1940 census asked for the previous residential address of the family together with the date that they moved to their current address.

No additional information was requested for the remaining census years, 1950, 1955, and 1960.

It is known that the census is incomplete as some members did not participate but if you cannot find your family on a Church census check information on the supplemental films in case the original entry was returned late, look at variant spellings of the surname and look to see if the wife is shown as the head of the household.

If your family is still not found it may be that they lived in a branch which for some reason did not participate or the census enumerator may not have been able to collect the card from the family.

In each census the records are alphabetical by head of household. The film sequence can be identified on the main library catalogue for each of the three groups of record. The films are not always in sequence but a starting point would be to search from:

- 1914-1935 census microfilm no. 25708

- 1940 census microfilm no. 367353

- 1950-1960 censuses microfilm no. 427814

Family Group records collection

This collection acts as a finding aid of 'previous research'. It comprises of about 8 million family group records created by members of the Church. The degree of accuracy is unknown but can be used to enable speedier access to the original records to check details contained in the record. There are two parts to the collection.

Archive Section
This section contains five million family group records submitted by members of the Church between 1942 and 1969. When the originals were available in the family history library some sheets were unfortunately removed by researchers so the collection is not complete. In order to prevent any later removals from the collection it was microfilmed.

The records are alphabetical by the surname of the husband, then forename and then by date of birth or baptism. 18,000 sheets were not microfilmed as part of the original collection but are available as a supplement. The whole collection is available on 1,998 microfilm reels, beginning with film no. 1273501 with the supplement beginning with film no.1750758. Use the main library catalogue to locate the film number relative to the surname you are interested in.

One point to note in relation to the archive section is an asterisk next to the name of the husband, wife, their parents, or their children which indicates that the particular individual appears on another family group record within the section. An asterisk next to the name of a child's spouse indicates another spouse is also shown usually on the back of the record.

Within the Archive Section there are other collections which relate to other countries that are organised on a similar basis. Refer to the main library catalogue for details.

Patrons Section
Between 1926 and 1979 three million records were submitted to the Patrons Section with the explicit purpose of enabling those working on same lines to share information. The way in which this collection is organised can be slightly confusing and the order does not become apparent until you actually use the records. Each collection contains some unique names and entries. Some records included a brief list of the sources from which the information shown was obtained. Some records included biographical histories for those shown on the form. In some cases there appears to be duplicate entries so it is worth checking all forms as some discrepancies in information may exist.

The 1924 Collection

The 1924 collection was filmed twice which may be slightly confusing. The first filming was in 1950 and the second in the mid 1960s and should not be confused with the 1924-1942 non alphabetical collection. The records relate to persons living from between 1700 and 1962 but there is some evidence of inclusion of persons back to the medieval period. These records are in approximate alphabetical order with similar sounding but differently spelt surnames grouped together in many cases. Some records for surnames are incomplete or missing and others are not in alphabetical order. Some of the films are slightly difficult to read but the later filming is better than the earlier filming. Use the 824 microfilms which commence with film no. 260872. These records are arranged alphabetically by husband's name or by wife's name if the husband is unknown. If there is more than one record with the same name they are chronological by earliest event date. This filming includes most of the records from the 1924-1950 beginning with microfilm no. 412088. For both series refer to the main library catalogue for identification.

The 1962 Collection

The 1962 collection exists because church members were asked to submit four generation family group sheets up to July 1979. Not every member participated and it is estimated that only about 20% of church members did so. Submissions made after July 1979 were included in Ancestral File and not the Family Group Records Collection. Those included on Ancestral File are now on-line as part of the Trees section on Family Search (see later).

The 1962 collection was also been filmed twice. The earlier filming of 1962-1977 records is arranged alphabetically and the second filming of 1962-1979 records is arranged by year of submission. The 1962 collection is available on microfilm. The first filming consists of 596 films beginning with film no. 1558711 and the second filming consists of 1,165 films beginning with film no. 428056. Again please refer to the main library catalogue for identification.

Non-alphabetical Collection

This collection should not be confused with the alphabetised, 1924- collection. Family group records were filmed in the order received so they are purely chronological and not in alphabetical or geographical order. There is some conjecture that these were the first collection of family group records received by the church. The forms were double sided so information was recorded on both the back and the front therefore they often referred to as the 'Form 2 collection' and comprises of 1030 microfilms beginning with film no. 685000.

Church centred newspapers

Besides the newspapers published by the church in the British Isles it would be beneficial to search the newspapers from the Salt Lake Valley area particularly the *Deseret News*.

(Deseret News Publishing.)

This newspaper was initially published on a weekly basis but occasionally was published more frequently and sometimes it was not printed at all. Like most newspapers it contains reports of day to day events in Salt Lake City and the surrounding area that was settled by Mormon pioneers. Some national and international news was also reported but the reports were often some time after the events took place. The value for researchers will be looking for pioneers in the following categories:

• Rosters of pioneer companies

• Letters written by leaders of the company

• Arrival dates into the Salt Lake Valley

As we have seen not all pioneer companies had a roster, so some may have arrived in Salt Lake City apparently unaccounted for. The rosters were sometimes vague in stating who had arrived such as the 'Smith Family' so if you had a child in the family that you suspect was your ancestor you will need to do undertake additional research to clarify that you have identified the correct family. The full list of Deseret News is detailed in the catalogue but the films listed below cover the main 'pioneer' period, namely Volume 1 to volume 18.

Vol. 1 (15 July 1850) - Vol. 3 (22 Dec. 1853)	26586
Vol. 4 (5 Jan. 1854) - Vol. 6 (4 Mar. 1857)	26587
Vol. 8 (11 Mar. 1857) - Vol. 9 (29 Feb. 1860)	26588
Vol. 10 (7 Mar. 1860) - Vol. 12 (24 June 1863)	26589
Vol. 13 (1 July 1863) - Vol. 15 (28 Nov. 1866)	26590
Vol. 16 (2 Jan. 1867) - Vol. 18 (Feb. 1870)	26591

The later issues on film run from 1865 on film no's 241150 to 241181.

A card index to obituaries reported in the Deseret News and other Salt Lake City newspapers between 1851 and 1963 can prove a very useful aid to research. The index is alphabetical by surname and the cards contain name of deceased, date of death, the newspaper in which the obituary appears including the date of the issue and the page number. Occasionally other information is included. The index is available on microfilm numbers commencing 26586 (Check the main library catalogue for details).

For full details relating to the card index entry you can refer to copies of the actual Deseret News. There is also a collection of clippings from Old Salt Lake newspapers running from 1875 - 1940 and includes general information about Pioneers (often mentioned by name as well as the obituaries which are indexed as above although they are not complete). These 'old newspaper clippings' are available on microfilm no. 1421993. If your ancestor was an early church member who died in Missouri, Kirtland or Nauvoo before 1868 then there is also a collection of obituaries from various church published newspapers which can be searched on film no. 413034.

The Deseret News carried both national and local news reporting on topics of interest to LDS church members. (Deseret News Publishing).

For those of your ancestry who migrated outside of Salt Lake City there are also similar indexes taken from the 'provincial newspapers' as follows:

| Ogden area 1870 -1914 | film no's 538506 - 538509 & 934251 |
| St George area 1928 - 1965 | film no's 1058731 - 1058738 |

There are also various other collections in manuscript form which are only available for research within the Family History Library at Salt Lake City and cannot be circulated to Family History Centres.

Mexican War pension records relating to the Mormon Battalion
Pensions were first granted to widows and minor children whose husbands or fathers had died in the service and to veterans who were disabled. Pensions based on 60 days of service were first granted to veterans or widows who did not re-marry in 1887. The following are the only pension records that have been microfilmed:

Pension Application Files for Members of the Mormon Battalion who served in the Mexican War, 1846-48. National Archives Microfilm reference T1196 available through the Family History Library on film no. 048129 - 048049.

Abbot, Joshua - Badham, Samuel	480129
Badham, Samuel - Bean, George W.	480130
Bean, George W. - Borrowman, John	480131
Boyd, George W. - Brown, Jesse S.	480132
Brown, John - Callahan, Thomas W.	480133
Calvert, John - Colton, Philander; Coray, William	480134
Coons, William; Cox, Amos - Dutcher, Thomas P.	480135
Dykes, George Parker - Hancock, Charles B.	480136
Hancock, George W. - Hendricks, William D.	480137
Hendrickson, James - Hunsaker, Abraham	480138
Hunsaker, Abraham - Kelley, Nicholas	480139
Kelley, William - Martin, Edward	480140
Martin, Jesse B. - Morris, Thomas	480141
Moss, David - Park, William A.	480142
Pearson, Ephraim - Richardson, Thomas	480143
Richmond, Benjamin - Shupe, James W.	480144
Simmons, William A. - Standage, Henry; Steele, Isaiah C.	480145
Stoddard, Rufus - Taggart, George W.	480146
Tanner, Myron - Wade, Edward D.	480147
Wade, Moses - Wilkin, David	480148
Willes, Ira - Zabriskie, Jerome	480149

There is an alphabetical index to the above available on film nos. 537000 - 537013 which includes the name, rank, and unit; names of dependents; date of filing and application; certificate numbers; act filed under; and state from which application was made.

Sample pages from the pension records. - Some files contain numerous records (The National Archives Washington records on microfilm at the Family History Library, Salt Lake City).

The pension applications can also be accessed on-line via the Family Search Website for which images are provided by www.footnote.com. Footnote is a subscription site but is available for free at the London Family History Centre.

In order to access the database it is essential to know at least the name of the Battalion member and preferably other terms of identification such as birth or death information.

United States, Mormon Battalion Pension Applications, 1846-1923

Description

Mexican War pension files for the 500 members of the Mormon Battalion. The files are arranged in alphabetical order by name of veteran. Index provided by Footnote.com.

Learn more »

Search Collection

First Names
Christopher

Last Name
Layton

Place

From Year

To Year

Search   Advanced search

Pension Application search page accessed from the US, Canada & Mexico section of Family Search (Family Search Intellectual Reserve Inc).

Christopher Layton
England Births and Christenings, 1538–1975

residence:	Bedford, England
parents:	Samuel Layton, Elizabeth
record title:	England Births and Christenings, 1538–1975
name:	Christopher Layton
gender:	Male
baptism/christening date:	12 Aug 1821
baptism/christening place:	NORTHILL,BEDFORD,ENGLAND
father's name:	Samuel Layton
mother's name:	Elizabeth
indexing project (batch) number:	C00342-2
system origin:	England-ODM
source film number:	826480

Search results for members of the Battalion (Family Search Intellectual Reserve Inc).

207

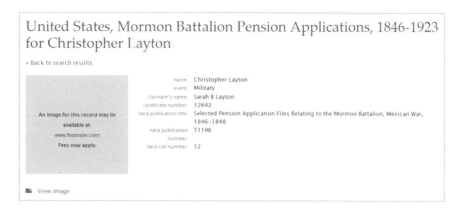

United States, Mormon Battalion Pension Applications, 1846-1923 for Christopher Layton

« Back to search results

name	Christopher Layton
event	Military
claimant's name	Sarah B Layton
certificate number	12642
nara publication title	Selected Pension Application Files Relating to the Mormon Battalion, Mexican War, 1846-1848
nara publication number	T1196
nara roll number	12

An image for this record may be available at:
www.footnote.com
Fees may apply.

View image

Expanded search results providing access to the digital images for which a fee will apply. (Family Search Intellectual Reserve Inc).

Ancestral File

The information found in the original Ancestral File is now part of the Family Search 'Trees' records. It contains lineage-linked information relating mainly to vital events, such as births, marriages, or deaths. In accordance with data protection the names of known living individuals are not available on the database.

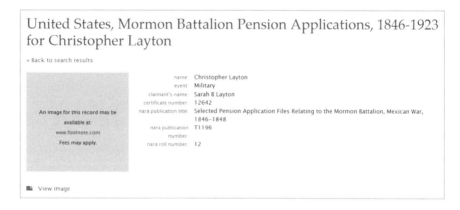

United States, Mormon Battalion Pension Applications, 1846-1923 for Christopher Layton

« Back to search results

name	Christopher Layton
event	Military
claimant's name	Sarah B Layton
certificate number	12642
nara publication title	Selected Pension Application Files Relating to the Mormon Battalion, Mexican War, 1846-1848
nara publication number	T1196
nara roll number	12

An image for this record may be available at:
www.footnote.com
Fees may apply.

View image

(Family Search Intellectual Reserve Inc)

The Ancestral File submissions often include contact information but as this is an historic (pre 1992) database this may not be current. Data submitted does not include source information so all entries for dates and places must be checked against original sources as no verification of accuracy was ever undertaken. Submissions added to the Ancestral File have now, in many cases, been merged with other data files and additions or corrections to original Ancestral File submissions are no longer possible. Each Ancestral File record has a number referred to as an AFN and where this is included in the source field indicates that some or all of the information came from the Ancestral File. The Trees section also now includes information from the Pedigree Resource File.

FamilySearch Website

Many records relating to ancestors who are members of the Mormon Church can be found on Family Search. This is particularly true of earlier members from which it is possible to locate their baptisms and marriages before they converted to the Church. Finding the record of a christening or wedding in the Anglican Church or in one of the many nonconformist denominations is vital to complete the family history of your family. As always the Family Search website acts only as a finding aid and may contain inaccuracies and should always be checked against the original records.

Membership information is currently added to the Historical records section of Family Search when a member of the Church dies. It is annotated 'LDS membership of a deceased person.' but does not include source information supporting the record.

During the 1960s, members of The Church of Jesus Christ of Latter-day Saints entered key information from the birth and marriage records of countries worldwide into a computer. These records were from the early 1500s to about 1875 as the idea was that no living person should appear.

A batch number identifies the specific collection of historical records that an extracted record came from. Most of the extracted records were published in the International Genealogical Index (IGI). Some were published in the Vital Records Index collections, both of which have been integrated into the Records' section.

To search for a specific person or family name within a batch, enter the name and enter the batch number in that field within the 'Advanced' search area.

If you need to see all of the records alphabetically organised by surname leave all fields blank apart from the batch number. You can then use the filters to narrow down a time period or place.

If you have ancestors who originally settled in Utah, it is worth searching the 'Trees' section. The Early Utah Trees contains details of around 1.7 million individuals and

568,000 marriages that are all lineage-linked. These include records from the US Census form 1850 onwards, birth, christening, marriage and death records from c 1870 to around the mid 1900s.

The Family Search website hosts all content, services, and products together accessed by using a single user password. There is a much greater use of scanned images accessed from indexes and more images will be added as indexing is completed. The search engine is responsive locating more content and thus more accurate results in response to a search request.

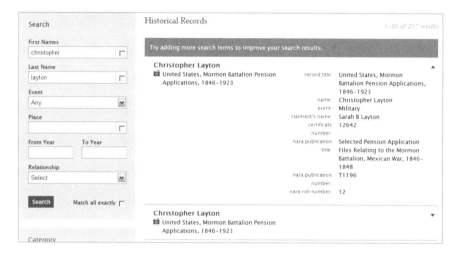

This illustration relates to Christopher Layton and his application for a Mexican War pension which is part of the 'Records' section of FamilySearch (Family Search Intellectual Reserve Inc).

Details of how to use the website and information on the changes can be accessed through the home page at www.familysearch.org.

Mormon Migration website - Brigham Young University

The Mormon Migration website **www.lib.byu.edu/mormonmigration/** includes accounts of converts who emigrated between 1840 and 1890. The autobiographies, journals and diaries relate to over 500 LDS immigrant voyages and provide a composite history of those who crossed the Atlantic and Pacific travelling by sea and overland to Salt Lake City.

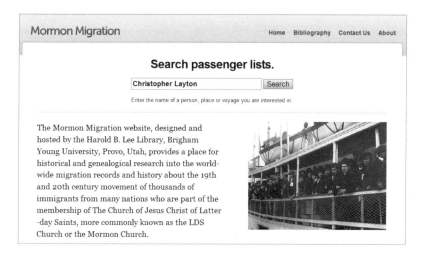

Home search page of the Mormon Migration website (provided by Brigham Young University)

The website complements the Mormon Pioneer Overland Trail Database. Not only does the Mormon Migration site provide the accounts of the church members in the early years but also the accounts of those emigrants who journeyed by rail between 1869 and 1890 thus providing the most complete emigration story. In addition, there is a link to globalmormonism.byu.edu, which provides an overview of the global movement of the LDS Church to America.

Example of search for Christopher Layton using the Mormon Migration database (Brigham Young University).

Expanded search showing details and references to Christopher Layton and his family including Samuel his father (Brigham Young University).

The Mormon Migration website includes information from the Mormon Immigration Index CD referred to earlier which documents valuable emigration information for most early LDS emigrants. It provides names, ages, origins, ports of departure and arrival, as well as the known number of Saints and their company leaders on each voyage. Major sources for the included passenger lists are the European Emigration Card Index, British Mission Emigration Register, Scandinavian Mission Emigration Register, Swiss German Mission Emigration Register, The Millennial Star and Deseret News. The European Emigration Card Index has been reproduced electronically but not so the registers. Information from the original U.S. Customs lists as far as these relate to Mormon emigrants has also been included.

LDS databases and records on ancestry

For those undertaking research into early LDS Pioneers the following records and information articles are available at www.ancestry.com some of which will provide specific information but some will enhance background information and give details of the contemporary history.

• An Enduring Legacy

• Early history of Duchesne County: preserved by the Duchesne Chapter of the Daughters of the Utah Pioneers

- From Kirtland to Salt Lake City

- History of the LDS Church, 1830-1930,

- LDS Biographical Encyclopedia

- LDS Member Name Index, 1830-45

- LDS Military Records, 1840-47

- LDS Redress Petition Listing, 1843

- Nauvoo, Illinois Tax Index, 1842

- Pioneer Immigrants to Utah Territory

- Sons of the Utah Pioneers: Biography Files (A-Z)

- Tales of a triumphant people: a history of Salt Lake County, Utah, 1847-1900

- Treasures of Pioneer History

- Utah and Idaho cemetery records

- Utah Pioneers and Prominent Men

- Utah Pioneers, 1847-50

- Utah, Our Pioneer Heritage

Other databases may well be added from time to time so it is useful to check the Research Wiki on the FamilySearch website for up to date information.

LDS databases and records available on world vital records

World Vital Records is available free at Family History Centres or via subscription from home computers.**www.worldvitalrecords.com**

The following research sources should be helpful with your research for ancestors who were early church members:

- Gravestone and Monumental Inscriptions in early Latter-day Saint burial grounds

- LDS Biographical Encyclopedia, Volume 1

- Marriages in the Nauvoo Region 1839-1845

- Members of the Ellsworth and McArthur Handcart Companies of 1856

- Members of the Mormon Battalion
- Members of the Willie and Martin Handcart Companies of 1856
- Membership of the Church 1830-1848
- Pioneers of 1847
- Property Transactions in Nauvoo, Illinois, and Surrounding Communities, 1839-1859
- Seventy Quorum Membership, 1835-1846

Summary

As you will have seen there is a wealth of information generated both within the church organisation records and in many other sources which will enable you to piece together the history and lives of your ancestors who became 'Mormons' irrespective of whether they emigrated or stayed in their native country. It may seem that there is some duplication in the content of various records and databases but as you research you will quickly realise that the majority of records stand in their own right and provide some unique information. It is therefore worthwhile searching all of the records to enable a full and detailed picture to be built up of each individual or family.

APPENDIX A
Films relating to Church
Membership Records

The following is a listing, by film number, of the records of the Church in the United Kingdom that are available on microfilm through any LDS Family History Centre.

In order to ascertain which type of membership records a film contains and also the item number (whereabouts on the film) for your place of interest you will need to refer to the main Family History Library Catalogue www.familysearch.org or the London Family History Centre catalogue **www.londonfhc.org.** The London FHC holds many (but not all) of the films relating to LDS Membership. There may be some duplication of records on more than one film. Membership records less than 75 years old are generally not available for research on microfilm.

The following definitions will help you understand the church organisation and the film content.

Branch - A branch was the local congregation. A Branch president presided over the meetings and affairs of each branch, sometimes being called to preside over more than one branch. Most branches had a minimum of 6-12 members.

Conference - A geographical area made up of several branches. Britain was divided into several conferences, each containing between 4 and 40 branches. Each conference held conference meetings twice a year where reports were received and new assignments made.

District - A district was an area assigned to a missionary companionship. There may have been several branches within one district. The names and designations of the districts often changed. In the 20th century when Missions became established the term Conference became District with a hierarchy of branch, district, and mission.

Mission - This was a level of jurisdiction presided over by a mission president and generally included several conferences. The European Mission with its headquarters in England had jurisdiction over all of Europe. Missions were sometimes divided into areas as in the British mission, which also administered the Irish and Welsh areas.

Note: Many branches ceased to exist because of the effects of emigration and others were amalgamated so the earlier date spans shown in the film synopsis often indicates the limited life of a branch.

Film Number 86975

Accrington Lancashire Branch - Record of members, 1841-1853

Aldershot Hampshire Branch - Record of members, 1906-1944

Alston Cumberland Branch - Record of members, 1857-1858

Film Number 86976

Andover Hampshire Branch - Record of members, 1851

Apperley Gloucestershire Branch - Record of members, 1840-1847

Arnold Nottinghamshire Branch - Record of members, 1849-1900

Ashburnham Sussex Branch - Record of members, 1856

Ashford Kent Branch - Record of members, 1855-1955

Ashton Under Lyne Branch - Record of members, 1837-1889

Ashton Keynes Wiltshire Branch - Record of members, 1851-1852

Askern Yorkshire Branch - Record of members, 1894-1924

Asterley Shropshire Branch - Record of members, 1847-1872

Attercliffe Yorskhire Branch - Historical record, 1849-1854

Aylesbury Buckinghamshire Branch - Record of members, 1841-1853

Film Number 86977

Badderley Edge Staffordshire - Record of members 1858-1860

Barking Essex Branch - Record of members, 1851

Barnsley Yorkshire Branch - Record of members, 1882-1948

Barrow Lancashire Branch - Record of members, 1904-1909

Barrowden Rutland Branch - Record of members, 1843-1863

Film Number 86978

Bassingbourne Cambridgeshire Branch - Record of members, 1857-1866

Bath Somerset Branch - Record of members 1844-1890

Batley Yorkshire branch - Record of members, 1892-1948

Battersea Surrey Branch - Record of members, 1847-1852

Beaminster Dorset Branch - record of members,1851-1876

Beckley Sussex Branch - Record of members, 1854-1855

Bedford Bedfordshire Branch - Record of members, 1837-1858

Film Number 86979

Bedfordshire Conference - Record of members, 1837-1858

Film Number 86980

Bedfordshire District - Record of members, 1891-1904

Bedington Northumberland Branch - Record of members, 1847-1855

Belper Derbyshire Branch - Record of members, 1847-1897

Birkenhead, Cheshire Branch - Record of members 1852-1945

Birkenshaw Yorkshire Branch - Record of members 1890-1895

Berkshire District - Record of members, 1847-1900

Bexhill Sussex Branch - Record of members, 1852-1855

Birdwell (including Wombwell) Yorkshire Branch - Record of members, 1882-1914

Film Number 86981

Birmingham Warwickshire Branch - Record of members, 1847-1908

Birmingham Conference - Record of members, 1848-1948

Film Number 86982

Birmingham Conference - Record of members, 1848-1948

Bishops Stortford Hertfordshire Branch - Record of members, 1857-1863

Blaby Leicestershire Branch - Record of members, 1843-1853

Blackburn Lancashire Branch - Record of members, 1837-1948

Blackpool Lancashire Branch - Record of members, 1899-1908

Blyth Northumberland Branch - Record of members, 1925-1931

Film Number 86983

Bolehill Derbyshire Branch - Record of members, 1849-1857

Bolney Sussex Branch - Record of members, 1854-1855

Bolsover Derbyshire Branch - Record of members, 1842-1850

Bolton Lancashire Branch - Record of members, 1838-1887

Bootle Lancashire Branch - Record of members, 1901-1912

Borrowash Derbyshire Branch - Record of members, 1848-1856

Bow London Branch - Record of members, 1851

Boxford Suffolk Branch - Record of members, 1847-1860

Film Number 86984

Bradford Yorkshire Branch - Record of members, 1842-1948

Bradford Yorkshire Conference - Record of members, 1845-1858

Braintree Essex Branch - Record of members, 1851-1857

Brandon Suffolk Branch - Record of members, 1849-1863

Brangreen Gloucestershire Branch - Record of members, 1840-1856

Branstone Staffordshire Branch - Record of members, 1842-1877

Breachwood Green Hertfordshire Branch - Record of members, 1851-1852

Breaston Derbyshire Branch - Record of members, 1848-1857

Brede Sussex Branch - Record of members, 1847-1882

Breightmet Fold Lancashire Branch - Record of members 1840-1861

Film Number 86985

Grimsby Lincolnshire Conference (including Hull and Bridlington Branches) -
Record of members, 1882-1947

Bridport Dorset Branch - Record of members, 1847-1886

Bridgewater Somerset Branch - Record of members, 1850-1855

Brighton Sussex Branch - Record of members, 1840-1947

Film Number 86986

Brighton Sussex District - Record of members, 1851-1896

Brinsley Nottinghamshire Branch - Record of members, 1839-1858

Bristol Gloucestershire Branch - Record of members, 1841-1900

Bristol Gloucestershire Conference - Records of members, 1896-1947

Film Number 86987

Bristol Gloucestershire Conference - Records of members, 1896-1947

Welsh Conference - Record of members, 1850-1922

Film Number 86988

Bristol Road Warwickshire Branch - Record of members, 1844-1857

Brixton Surrey Branch - Record of members, 1848-1850

Film Number 86989

Bromley Kent Branch (including Green Street Green, Horsham & Lenham Hill
Branches) - Record of members, 1795-1877* (Most records commence c1850 -
some pre 1830 marriage records included)

Brompton London Branch - Record of members, 1849-1852

Buckland Kent Branch - Record of members, 1849-1852

Bulwell Nottinghamshire Branch - Record of members (No year span specified)

Burnley Lancashire Branch (including Rawtenstall & Rochdale Branches) - Record of members, 1840-1948

Burslem Staffordshire Branch (including Longton and Macclesfield Branches) - Record of members, 1858-1869

Burton Derbyshire Branch - Record of members, 1842-1857

Burton On Trent Staffordshire Branch - Record of members, 1875-1901

Burton Ovary Leicestershire Branch - Record of members, 1848-1854

Bury Lancashire Branch - Record of members, 1839-1946

Film Number 86990

Calver Derbyshire Branch - Record of members, 1849-1857

Thorncote Bedfordshire Branch (including Caldecot Branch) - Record of members, 1841-1854

Calne Wiltshire Branch (including Chalford & Warminster Branches) - Record of members, 1848-1870

Calverton Nottinghamshire Branch including Belper Branch) - Record of members, 1848-1851

Canewdon Essex Branch - Record of members, 1855

Canterbury Kent Branch - Record of members, 1848-1860

Carlisle Cumberland Branch - Record of members, 1857 -1948

Newcastle upon Tyne Northumberland Conference - Record of members, 1841-1929

Carlisle Cumberland Conference - Record of members, 1843-1869

Carlisle Cumberland District - Record of members, up to 1901

Castle Eaton Wiltshire Branch - Record of members, 1841-1854

Castle Eden Durham Branch - Record of members, 1848-1855

Catford Kent Branch - Record of members, 1900-1947

Caudle Green Gloucestershire Branch - Record of members, 1841-1878

Chalford Gloucestershire Branch - Record of members, 1842-1875

Chatburn Lancashire Branch - Record of members, 1838-1854

Chatham Kent Branch - Record of members, 1851-1862

Film Number 86991

Chelmsford Essex Branch - Record of members, 1852-1857

Chelsea London Branch - Record of members, 1849-1862

Cheltenham Gloucestershire Branch Including Stroud Branch) - Record of members, 1840-1947

Cheltenham Gloucestershire Conference - Record of members, 1840-1901

Shepscombe Gloucestershire Branch - Record of members, 1843-1867

Bath Somerset Branch - Record of members, 1901

Chertsey Surrey Branch - Record of members, 1851

Chester Cheshire Branch - Record of members, 1841-1909

Chesterfield Derbyshire Branch (including Sheffield Conference and Calver Branch) - Record of members, 1841-1901

Film Number 86992

Chiddingly Sussex Branch - Record of members, 1851-1865

Chiswick London Branch - Record of members, 1908-1944

Chorley Lancashire Branch - Record of members, 1898-1910

Chosen Gloucestershire Branch - Record of members, 1851-1852

Cirencester Gloucestershire Branch - Record of members, 1842-1933

Clapham Surrey Branch - Record of members, 1850

Clay Cross Derbyshire Branch - Record of members, 1848-1869

Clayton Yorkshire Branch - Record of members, 1848-1894

Clifford Mene Gloucestershire Branch - Record of members, 1840-1856

Clitheroe Lancashire Branch - Record of members, 1838-1885

Colchester Essex Branch - Record of members, 1850-1861

Cold Ash Berkshire Branch - Record of members, 1843-1850

Colstenworth Lincolnshire Branch - Record of members, 1848-1858

Compton Abdale Gloucestershire Branch - Record of members, 1841-1893

Coventry Warwickshire Branch - Record of members, 1844-1872

Film Number 86993

Cramlington Northumberland Branch - Record of members, 1849-1860

Crescent Warwickshire Branch - Record of members, 1850-1852

Crewkerne Somerset Branch - Record of members, 1848-1879

Cross Moor Cheshire Branch - Record of members, 1842-1857

Crowland Lincolnshire Branch - Record of members, 1845-1852

Crowle Lincolnshire Branch - Record of members, 1845-1861

Croydon Surrey Branch - Record of members, 1812-1918

Film Number 86994

Dalston Cumberland Branch - Record of members, 1857-1858

Danbury Essex Branch -Record of members, 1852-1858

Darlington Durham Branch - Record of members, 1900-1929

Dartford Kent Branch - Record of members, 1828 to 1853

Deal Kent Branch (including Sandwich Branch)- Record of members, 1848-1854

Deptford Kent Branch - Record of members, 1848-1868

Deanshanger Northamptonshire Branch - Record of members, 1848-1853

Derby Derbyshire Branch - Record of members, 1843-1948

Derbyshire Conference - Record of members, 1842-1894

Devonport Devon Branch - Record of members, 1850-1881

Film Number 86995

Disley Cheshire Branch - Record of members, 1850-1894

Ditton Lancashire Branch - Record of members, 1864-1879

Doncaster Yorkshire Branch - Record of members, 1841-1947

Dover Kent Branch - Record of members, 1841-1874

Dowsby Lincolnshire Branch - Record of members, 1845-1855

Dudley Worcestershire Branch - Record of members, 1856-1910

Dudley Port Staffordshire Branch - Record of members, 1884-1945

Dunmow Essex Branch (including South Mimms, Boxford & Watford Branches) - Record of members, 1816-1873

Dunstall Staffordshire Branch - Record of members, 1842-1855

Durham Branch - Record of members, 1850-1877

Durham & Newcastle Conference - Record of members, 1817-1871

Newcastle Northumberland Conference - Record of members, 1847-1900

Stockton Durham Branch - Record of members, 1861-1900

South Church Durham Branch - Record of members, 1875-1883

Tottingham Durham Branch - Record of members, 1864-1874

Radcliff Northumberland Branch - Record of members, 1856-1869

Dursley Gloucestershire Branch - Record of members, 1842-1878

Film Number 86996

Easington Lane Durham Branch - Record of members, 1842-1855

East Coker Somerset Branch - Record of members, 1882-1891

East Dereham Norfolk Branch - Record of members, 1848-1871

Eastwood Nottinghamshire Branch - Record of members, 1847-1948

Eaton Bray Bedfordshire Branch - Record of members, 1846-1854

Edlesborough Buckinghamshire Branch - Record of members, 1849

Edmonton Middlesex Branch - Record of members, 1852-1866

Egmanton Nottinghamshire Branch - Record of members, 1849-1856

Film Number 89697

Eltham Kent Branch - Record of members, 1849-1860

Elton Cheshire Branch - Record of members, 1840-1849

Empingham Rutland Branch - Record of members, 1849-1858

Enfield Middlesex Branch - Record of members, 1863-1865

Essex Conference - Record of members, 1841-1869

Essex District - Record of members, 1890-1903

Evenwood Durham Branch - Record of members, 1853-1861

Exeter Devon Branch - Record of members, 1854

Exmouth Devon Branch - Record of members, 1851-1852

Eynesbury Huntingdonshire Branch - Record of members, 1854

Film Number 86998

Falmouth Cornwall Branch - Record of members, 1852-1864

Farcett Huntingdonshire Branch - Record of members, 1854

Farnworth Lancashire Branch - Record of members, 1851-1894

Faversham Kent Branch - Record of members, 1818 to 1892

Findon Sussex Branch (including Worthing Branch) - Record of members, 1854-1855

Finsbury Middlesex Branch (including Goswell Road Branch) - Record of members, 1842-1868

Five Houses Durham Branch - Record of members, 1852-1856

Forest of Dean Gloucestershire Branch - Record of members, 1840-1870

Brangreen Gloucestershire Branch - Record of members, 1840-1856

Froyle Hampshire Branch - Record of members, 1851

Film Number 86999

Gainsborough Lincolnshire Branch - Record of members, 1843-1947

Sheffield Yorkshire Conference - Record of members, 1843-1922

Gateshead Durham Branch - Record of members, 1878-1948

Globe Road London Branch - Record of members, 1941-1955

Gloucester Branch - Record of members, 1840-1881

Bristol Gloucestershire Conference - Record of members, 1840-1876

Gosburton Clough Staffordshire Branch (including Uttoxeter Branch) - Record of members, 1842-1901

Gosport Hampshire Branch (including Southampton & Portsmouth Branches) - Record of members, 1849-1876

Goswell Road London Branch - Record of members, 1848-1868

Film Number 87000

Grantham Lincolnshire Branch - Record of members, 1846-1873

Grassmoor Derbyshire Branch - Record of members, 1849-1857

Graveley Cambridgeshire Branch - Record of members, 1849-1852

Gravesend Kent Branch - Record of members, 1848-1958

Grays Essex Branch - Record of members, 1853-1868

Gt Harwood Lancashire Branch - Record of members, 1899-1914

Gt Staughton Huntingdonshire Branch - Record of members, 1851-1853

Gt Yarmouth Norfolk Branch - Record of members, 1935-1947

Green Street Green Kent Branch - Record of members, 1852-1877

Greenwich Kent Branch - Record of members, 1831-1859

Grimsby Lincolnshire Conference - Record of members, 1882-1947

Film Number 87001

Stoke Newington Middlesex Branch - Record of members, 1844-1858

Haggerston Middlesex Branch - Record of members, 1848-1856

Hagnaby Lock Lincolnshire Branch - Record of members, 1849-1859

Halifax Yorkshire Branch - Record of members, 1901-1930

Halshaw Moor Lancashire Branch - Record of members, 1842-1887

Hammersmith Middlesex Branch - Record of members, 1851-1918

Hampshire District - Priesthood ordinations, 1898-1902

Flamstead Hertfordshire Branch - Record of members, 1842-1853

Handforth Cheshire Branch - Record of members, 1847-1863

Birmingham Warwickshire Conference - Record of members, 1899-1945

Hanham Gloucestershire Branch - Record of members, 1940-1944

Hanley Staffordshire Branch - Record of members, 1843-1911

Worcestershire District - Record of members, 1854-1910

Hardingham Norfolk Branch - Record of members, 1849-1877

Harrowgate Yorkshire Branch - Record of members, 1892-1893

Hartlepool Durham Branch - Record of members, 1842-1904

Hartlepool District - Record of members, 1864-1908

Hartley Northumberland Branch - Record of members, 1857-1858

Brede Sussex Branch - Record of members, 1847-1882

Haswell Durham Branch - Record of members, 1852-1869

Haughton Green Lancashire Branch - Record of members, 1877-1883

Film Number 87002

Heanor Derbyshire Branch - Record of members, 1848-1878

Heaton Northumberland Branch - Record of members, 1901-1927

Hebburn Durham Branch - Record of members, 1873-1904

Hebburn Durham District - Record of members, 1864-1908

Hemel Hempstead Hertfordshire Branch - Record of members, 1842-1855

Hereford Branch - Record of members, 1847-1899

Hereford & Worcester District - Record of members, 1854-1902

Worcestershire District - Record of members, 1854-1910

Hertford Hertfordshire Branch - Record of members, 1849-1859

Hertfordshire Conference - Record of members, 1859-1875

Hexham Northumberland Branch - Record of members, 1907-1943

Heywood Lancashire Branch (including Burnley & Radcliffe Branches) - Record of members, 1840-1912

Film Number 87003

Hockham Norfolk Branch - Record of members, 1850-1866

Hockley Essex Branch - Record of members, 1853-1872

Holbeach Bank Lincolnshire Branch - Record of members, 1843-1855

Holborn Middlesex branch - Record of members, 1846-1861

Holloway Middlesex Branch - Record of members, 1847-1945

Horsham Sussex Branch - Record of members, 1844-1858

Hoxton Middlesex Branch - Record of members, 1847-1853

Hoyland Common Yorkshire Branch - Record of members, 1886-1893

Hayle Cornwall Branch - Record of members, 1851-1855

Film Number 87004

Hucknall Nottinghamshire Branch - Record of members, 1850-1948

Huddersfield Yorkshire Branch - Record of members, 1888-1915

Hull Yorkshire Branch - Record of members, 1844-1947

Hungerford Berkshire Branch - Record of members, 1843-1850

Hunsdon Hertfordshire Branch - Record of members, 1853-1854

Film Number 87005

Hyde Cheshire Branch - Record of members, 1840-1947

Hyson Green Nottinghamshire Branch - Record of members, 1848-1853

Film Number 87006

Idle Yorkshire Branch - Record of members, 1841-1860

Ingatestone Essex branch - Record of members, 1850-1852

Ipswich Suffolk Branch - Record of members, 1851-1924

Irchester Northamptonshire Branch - Record of members, 1841-1856

Isle of Dogs London Branch - Record of members, 1848-1858

Islington Middlesex Branch - Record of members, 1850-1853

Jarrow Durham Branch - Record of members, (including Hebburn & Wallsend Branches) 1849-1917

Film Number 87007

Keighley Yorkshire Branch (including Batley Branch) - Record of members, 1890-1914

Kelloe Durham Branch - Record of members, 1849-1853

Kendal Westmorland Branch - Record of members, 1840-1852

Kennington Surrey Branch - Record of members, 1847-1860

Kensall New Town Middlesex - Record of members, 1843-1850

Kensworth Hertfordshire Branch - Record of members, 1846-1871

Kent Conference - Record of members, up to 1869

Kent District - Record of members, 1869 -1903

Kersley Lancashire Branch - Record of members, early to 1876

Birmingham Conference - Record of members, 1850-1945

Kidderminster Worcestershire Branch - Record of members, 1864-1948

Kings Standing Warwickshire Branch - Record of members, 1900-1946

Kingstone Kent Branch - Record of members, 1846-1853

Knaresborough Yorkshire Branch - Record of members, 1848-1860

Film Number 87008

Leire Leicestershire Branch - Record of members, 1847-1852

Lambeth Surrey Branch (including Walworth branch) - Record of members, 1842-1886

Lancaster Lancashire Branch - Record of members, 1884-1929

Lands End Cornwall Conference - Record of members, 1849-1875

Latchington Essex Branch - Record of members, 1854-1860

Film Number 87009

Leeds Yorkshire Branch - Record of members, 1841-1948

Leeds Yorkshire District - Record of members, 1841-1928

Film Number 87010

Leicester Branch - Record of members, 1841-1901

Leicester Conference - Record of members, 1843-1894

Nottingham Conference - Record of members, 1844-1930

Leigh Lancashire Branch (including Tyldesley and Westleigh Branches) - Record of members, 1852-1887

Lenham Hill Kent Branch - Record of members, 1849-1860

Lewes Sussex Branch - Record of members, 1855-1856

Leyland Moss Lancashire Branch - Record of members, 1838-1854

Film Number 87011

Lichfield Staffordshire Branch - Record of members, 1847-1860

Limehouse London Branch - Record of members, 1849-1861

Limehouse Fields London Branch - Record of members, 1849-1858

Lincoln Lincolnshire Branch - Record of members, 1850-1894

Lincolnshire Conference - Record of members, 1843-1860

Linton Herefordshire Branch - Record of members, 1840-1854

Little Heath Staffordshire Branch - Record of members, 1857-1879

Film Number 87012

Liverpool Lancashire Branch - Record of members, 1840-1960

Liverpool Lancashire Conference - Record of members, 1872-1921

Film Number 87013

London Branch (including Theobalds Toad & Holborn Branches) - Record of members, 1841-1946

Film Number 87014 & 87015

London Conference - Record of members, 1833-1935

Film Number 87016

Longton Lancashire Branch - Record of members, 1837-1854

Longton Staffordshire Branch - Record of members, 1856-1861

Long Whatton Leicestershire Branch - Record of members, 1847-1884

Loughborough Leicestershire Branch - Record of members, 1846-1938

Lowestoft Suffolk Branch - Record of members, 1849-1948

Loxley Warwickshire Branch - Record of members, 1857-1869

Luton Bedfordshire Branch - Record of members, 1844-1947

Lye Worcestershire Branch - Record of members, 1899-1910

Lymm Cheshire Branch - Record of members, 1841-1881

Film Number 87017

Macclesfield Cheshire Branch - Record of members, 1840-1869

Maldon Essex branch - Record of members, 1850-1868

Manchester Lancashire Branch - Record of members, 1838-1946

Manchester District - Record of members, 1876-1931

Film Number 87018

Mansfield Nottinghamshire Branch - Record of members, 1848-1948

New Radford Nottinghamshire Branch - Record of members, 1848-1901

Mansfield Woodhouse Nottinghamshire Branch - Record of members, 1848-1857

Marden Kent Branch - Record of members, 1852-1856

Market Drayton Shropshire Branch - Record of members, 1840-1869

Marley Hill Durham Branch - Record of members, 1854-1855

Marylebone London Branch - Record of members, 1842-1848

Mayfield Sussex Branch - Record of members, 1856-1865

Film Number 87019

Mellor Derbyshire Branch - Record of members, 1860-1886

Merton Surrey Branch - Record of members, 1849-1850

Middlesborough Yorkshire Branch - Record of members, 1875-1948

Middleton Lancashire Branch - Record of members, 1842-1865

Middlewich Cheshire Branch - Record of members, 1840-1865

Miles Green Staffordshire Branch - Record of members, 1854-1865

Milton Kent Branch - Record of members, 1850-1868

Reading Berkshire Branch - Record of members, 1850-1876

Minster Kent Branch - Record of members, 1851-1852

Film Number 87020

Morley Yorkshire Branch - Record of members, 1873-1914

Mottram Cheshire Branch - Record of members, 1841-1857

Moulton Chapel Lincolnshire Branch - Record of members, 1845-1853

Mountsorrell Leicestershire Branch -Record of members, 1848-1852

Murton Durham Branch - Record of members, 1878-1882

Nailsworth Gloucestershire Branch - Record of members, 1844-1879

Nelson Lancashire Branch - Record of members, 1902-1944

Newark Nottinghamshire Branch - Record of members, 1848-1855

Muskham Nottinghamshire Branch - Record of members, 1848-1855

New Brinsley Nottinghamshire Branch - Record of members, 1847-1888

Newbury Berkshire Branch - Record of members, 1843-1888

Film Number 87021

Newcastle upon Tyne Northumberland Branch - Record of members, 1836-1922

Newcastle Northumberland Conference - Record of members, 1841-1929

Film Number 87022

New Mill End Bedfordshire Branch - Record of members, 1839-1849

New Mills Derbyshire Branch - Record of members, 1850-1868

New Radford Nottinghamshire Branch - Record of members, 1848-1901

Newton Lancashire branch - Record of members, 1842-1880

New Tupton Derbyshire Branch - Record of members, 1853-1855

Film Number 87023

Nonington Kent Branch - Record of members, 1846-1857

Northampton Northamptonshire Branch - Record of members, 1846-1903

Birmingham Warwickshire Conference - Record of members, 1850-1945

North Essex Branch - Record of members, 1851-1861

North London Branch - Record of members, 1859-1948

North Mimms Hertfordshire Branch - Record of members, 1852-1860

North Shields Northumberland Branch - Record of members, 1847-1860

North Walsham Norfolk Branch - Record of members, 1903-1938

Norton Gloucestershire Branch - Record of members, 1840-1850

Film Number 87024

Norwich Norfolk Branch - Record of members, 1850-1947

Norwich Norfolk Conference - Record of members, 1848-1919

Film Number 87025

Hammersmith Middlesex Branch - Record of members, 1851-1918

Nottingham Nottinghamshire Branch - Record of members, 1844-1947

Film Number 87026

Nottingham Conference - Record of members, 1844-1930

Notting Hill London Branch - Record of members, 1846-1849

Nuneaton Warwickshire Branch - Record of members, 1900-1925

Nutley Sussex branch - Record of members, 1853-1857

Film Number 87027

Ogbourne Wiltshire Branch - Record of members, 1851

Oldham Lancashire Branch - Record of members, 1840-1947

Old Kent Road Surrey Branch - Record of members, 1845-1851

Orsett Essex Branch - Record of members, 1849-1860

Orwell Cambridgeshire Branch - Record of members, c1850-1856

Otley Yorkshire Branch - Record of members, 1846-1865

Paddington London Branch - Record of members, 1850-1869

Pelton Durham Branch - Record of members, 1883-1912

Pelton Durham District - Record of members, 1883-1912

Pendlebury Lancashire Branch - Record of members, 1875-1888

Penryn Cornwall branch - Record of members, 1849-1851

Peterborough Northamptonshire Branch - Record of members, 1849-1855

Pilley Yorkshire Branch - Record of members, 1845-1878

Pinxton Derbyshire Branch (includes Portland Row Branch) - Record of members, 1849-1871

Plumbley Cheshire Branch - Record of members, 1840-1849

Plymouth Devon Branch - Record of members, 1852- 1856 and 1905 -1942

Ponts Hill Herefordshire Branch (includes Linton Branch) - Record of members, 1840-1863

Film Number 87028

Poplar London Branch - Record of members, 1841-1864

Portland Row Nottinghamshire Branch - Record of members, 1848-1871

Portsmouth Hampshire Branch - Record of members, 1844-1945

Poynton Cheshire Branch -Record of members, 1843-1854

Preston Lancashire Branch - Record of members, 1837-1948

Preston Lancashire Conference - Record of members, 1837-1868

Pulham Market Norfolk Branch - Record of members, 1861-1880

Film Number 87029

Radcliffe Lancashire Branch - Record of members, 1847-1909

Radford Nottinghamshire Branch - Record of members, 1851-1857

Ramsbury Wiltshire Branch - Record of members, 1851

Ramsgate Kent Branch - Record of members, 1850-1851

Raunds Northamptonshire Branch - Record of members, 1841-1853

Rawmarsh Yorkshire Branch - Record of members, 1931-1943

Rawtenstall Lancashire Branch (includes Heywood & Burnely Branches) - Record of members, 1855-1907

Reading Berkshire Branch - Record of members, 1850-1876

Rickmansworth Hertfordshire Branch - Record of members, 1847-1851

Ripon Yorkshire Branch - Record of members, 1908-1910

Risegate Lincolnshire Branch - Record of members, 1848-1883

Rochdale Lancashire Branch - Record of members, 1863-1948

Rochester Kent branch - Record of members, 1885-1892

Romford Essex branch - Record of members, 1852-1863

Rotherham Yorkshire Branch - Record of members, 1847-1893

Royton Lancashire Branch - Record of members, 1852-1856

Rugby Warwickshire Branch - Record of members, 1850-1935

Rumburgh Suffolk Branch - Record of members, 1851-1879

Runcorn Cheshire Branch - Record of members, 1867-1883

Film Number 87030

St Albans Hertfordshire Branch - Record of members, 1849-1947

St Helens Lancashire Branch - Record of members, 1841-1879

St Johns Common Sussex Branch - Record of members, 1850-1871

St Olaves London Branch - Record of members, 1852-1853

Sandal Yorkshire District - Record of members, 1900-1901

Sandbach Cheshire Branch - Record of members, 1857-1860

Scredington Lincolnshire Branch - Record of members, 1845-1856

Scunthorpe Lincolnshire Branch - Record of members, 1931-1948

Shearsby Leicestershire Branch - Record of members, 1848-1855

Shepscombe Gloucestershire Branch - Record of members, 1843-1867

Sheepshead Leicestershire Branch - Record of members, 1848-1891

Film Number 87031

Sheerness Kent Branch - Record of members, 1849-1875

Sheffield Yorkshire Branch - Record of members, 1843-1948

Sheffield Conference - Record of members, 1843-1922

Shepherds Bush Middlesex Branch - Record of members, 1869

Film Number 87032

Shields Northumberland District - Record of members, 1842-1902

Shildon Durham Branch (includes Pelton Branch) - Record of members, 1883-1947

Shincliff Durham Branch - Record of members, 1851-1853

Shoreham Sussex Branch - Record of members, 1851-1857

Shortwood Gloucestershire Branch - Record of members, 1849-1889

Simpson Buckinghamshire Branch - Record of members, 1849-1853

Sittingbourne Kent Branch - Record of members, 1892-1918

Skelton Yorkshire Branch - Record of members, 1900-1929

Sleaford Lincolnshire Branch - Record of members, 1850-1859

Somers Town London branch - Record of members, 1848-1878

Southampton Hampshire Branch - Record of members, 1845-1912

Southampton District - Record of members, 1849-1903

Southchurch Essex branch - Record of members, 1870-1889

Southery Norfolk Branch - Record of members, 1887

South London branch - Record of members, 1891-1948

South Mimms Middlesex Branch - Record of members, 1852-1954

South Molton Devon Branch - Record of members, 1857-1863

South Normanton Derbyshire Branch - Record of members, 1879-1894

Southport Lancashire branch - Record of members, 1911

Southsea Hampshire Branch - Record of members, 1848-1865

Film Number 87033

South Shields Durham Branch - Record of members, 1848-1948

South Street Kent Branch - Record of members, 1855-1856

Southwark Surrey branch - Record of members, 1849-1850

South Witham Lincolnshire Branch - Record of members, 1856-1864

Sparkbrook Warwickshire Branch - Record of members, 1907-1946

Spelhurst Kent Branch - Record of members, 1863-1864

Spennymoor Durham Branch - Record of members, 1880-1895

Stafford Stafforshire Branch - Record of members, 1852-1873

Staffordshire Conference - Record of members, 1840-1869

Stalybridge Cheshire Branch - Record of members, 1849-1862

Film Number 87034

Stamford Lincolnshire Branch - Record of members, 1848-1855

Standon Hertfordshire Branch - Record of members, 1854-1855

Stanion Northamptonshire Branch (includes Brigstock Branch) - Record of members, 1850-1852

Stanwick Northamptonshire Branch - Record of members, 1882-1884

Staveley Derbyshire Branch - Record of members, 1845-1872

Chesterfield Derbyshire Branch - Record of Members : 1883

Steeple-Ashton Wiltshire Branch - Record of members, 1849-1871

Calne Wiltshire Branch (includes Chalford & Warminster Branches) - Record of members : 1848-1870

Stevenage Hertfordshire Branch - Record of members, 1848-1853

Stockport Cheshire branch (includes Heaton-Norris Branch) - Record of members, 1839-1913

Stockton Durham Branch (includes Middlesborough & Darlington Branches) - Record of members, 1845-1913

Stoke Prior Worcestershire Branch - Record of members, 1842-1867

Stone Head Cheshire branch - Record of members : 1850-1868

Film Number 87035

Stratford Essex Branch - Record of members, 1858-1916

Stroud Gloucestershire Branch - Record of members, 1896-1939

Bristol Conference - Records of members, 1896-1947

Studham Hertfordshire Branch - Record of members, 1846-1856

Suffolk Branch - Record of members, 1851-1856

Somercotes Derbyshire Branch - Record of members, 1848-1858

Sunderland Durham Branch - Record of members, 1843-1904

Surfleet Seasend Lincolnshire Branch - Record of members, 1852-1857

Sussex District - Record of members, 1851-1904

Sutton in Ash Nottinghamshire Branch - Record of members, 1849-1908

Sutton-Bonnington Nottinghamshire Branch - Record of members, 1848-1854

Swanwick Derbyshire Branch - Record of members, 1848-1864

Swindon Wiltshire Branch - Record of members, 1873-1927

Swineshead Lincolnshire Branch - Record of members, 1849-1955

Swinton Lancashire Branch - Record of members, 1876-1914

Film Number 87036

Tansley Derbyshire Branch - Record of members, 1849-1852

Taunton Somerset Branch - Record of members, 1854-1878

Terling Essex Branch - Record of members, 1854-1863

Tetbury Gloucestershire Branch (includes Stroud Branch) - Record of members, 1844-1898

Tewkesbury Gloucestershire Branch - Record of members, 1840-1851

Theobalds Road, Surrey branch - Record of members, 1841-1855

Thorncote (Northill) Bedfordshire Branch (includes Caldecot Branch) - Record of members, 1841-1854

Tilston Cheshire Branch - Record of members, 1859-1860

Tipton Staffordshire Branch - Record of members, 1848-1867

Dudley Port Staffordshire Branch - Record of members, 1849-1944

Todmorden Lancashire Branch - Record of members, 1841-1854

Tottington Lancashire Branch - Record of members, 1841-1875

Tower London Branch - Record of members, 1849-1850

Trent Vale Staffordshire Branch - Record of members, 1843-1860

Trimdon Durham Branch - Record of members, 1850-1857

Trowbridge Wiltshire Branch - Record of members, 1844-1857

Truro Cornwall Branch - Record of members, 1852-1861

Tunbridge Wells Kent Branch - Record of members, 1855-1864

Tyldesley Lancashire Branch (includes Leigh and Westleigh Branches) - Record of members, 1840-1901

Film Number 87037

Uckfield Sussex branch - Record of members, 1851-1855

Upholland Lancashire Branch - Record of members, 1848-1890

Usworth Durham Branch - Record of members, 1858-1859

Wakefield Yorkshire Branch - Record of members, 1843-1915

Wallasey Cheshire Branch - Record of members, 1873-1947

Wallsend Northumberland Branch - Record of members, 1858-1859

Walsall Staffordshire Branch - Record of members, 1908-1910

Bermondsey Surrey Branch - Record of members, 1839-1856

Walworth Surrey Branch - Record of members, 1839-1857

Lambeth Surrey branch - Record of members, 1842-1886

Walworth Common Surrey Branch - Record of members, 1851-1855

Wandsworth Surrey Branch - Record of members, 1848-1868

Warminster Wiltshire Branch - Record of members, 1849-1859

Warrington Lancashire Branch - Record of members, 1881-1883

Warwick District - Record of members, 1848-1910

Watford Hertfordshire Branch - Record of members, 1841-1912

Essex Conference - Record of members, 1841-1869

Watford District - Record of members, 1899-1903

Film Number 87038

Welling Kent Branch - Record of members, 1841-1860

Wellingborough Northamptonshire Branch - Record of members, 1841-1864

West Bromwich Staffordshire Branch - Record of members, 1841-1869

West Hartlepool Durham Branch - Record of members, 1864-1948

West Lavington Wiltshire Branch - Record of members, 1845-1863

Westleigh Lancashire Branch - Record of members, 1840-1887

West London Branch - Record of members, 1886-1887

Westminster Middlesex branch - Record of members, 1848-1858

Weston Berkshire Branch - Record of members, 1844-1853

West Tarring Sussex Branch - Record of members, 1850-1854

West Walton Norfolk Branch - Record of members, 1851-1861

Whaddon & Croydon-cum-Clapton Cambridgeshire Branch - Record of members, 1857-1889

Whetstone Middlesex Branch - Record of members, 1850-1857

Whitechapel & Barking London Branches - Record of members, 1844-1889

Whitwick Leicestershire Branch - Record of members, 1844-1850

Wigan Lancashire Branch - Record of members, 1854-1948

Wilsford Wiltshire Branch - Record of members, 1851-1859

Windsor Berkshire Branch - Record of members, 1840-1860

Wingate Durham Branch - Record of members, 1848-1853

Winwick Huntingdonshire Branch - Record of members, 1852-1855

Wilton-le-Waer Durham Branch - Record of members, 1852-1860

Witton Park Durham Branch - Record of members, 1883-1884

Film Number 87039

Wolverhampton Staffordshire Branch (including Walsall Branch) - Record of members, 1840-1945

Wolverhampton District - Record of members, 1849-1922

Wooburn Buckinghamshire Branch - Record of members, 1843-1850

Wooden Box Leicestershire Branch - Record of members, 1842-1857

Woodford Bridge Essex Branch - Record of members, 1847-1852

Woodhouse Yorkshire Branch - Record of members, 1843-1929

Woodside Gloucestershire Branch - Record of members, 1840-1856

Woolwich Kent Branch - Record of members, 1841-1880

Worcester Worcestershire Branch - Record of members, 1840-1868

Worcestershire District - Record of members, 1854-1910

Worthing Sussex Branch - Record of members, 1853-1855

Wotton-under-Edge Gloucestershire Branch - Record of members, 1842-1857

Wroughton Wiltshire Branch - Record of members, 1851-1852

Wyboston Bedfordshire Branch - Record of members, 1841-1852

Wymondham Norfolk Branch - Record of members, 1848-1887

Yardley Wood Worcestershire Branch - Record of members, 1847-1865

York Yorkshire Branch - Record of members, 1903-1926

Hull Yorkshire Branch (including Grimsby & Gainsborough Branches) - Record of members, 1844-1947

Film Number 87040

British Mission - Membership records, 1846-1939

Film Number 87041

Mossley Lancashire Branch - Record of members, 1848-1874

Pulham Market Norfolk Branch - Record of members, 1861-1880

Castell Nedd Glamorgan Branch - Records of members, 1849 -1884

Middlesborough Yorkshire Branch - Record of members, 1875-1948

Film Number 87042

Bradford Yorkshire Conference - Record of members, 1845-1858

Film Number 87043

Tintwistle Cheshire Branch - Record of members, 1842-1857

Woodhouse Yorkshire Branch - Record of members, 1843-1929

Haverfordwest Pembroke Branch - Record of members, 1847-1860

Johnstone Renfrew Branch - Record of members, 1848-1864

Cape Conference, Cape Province South Africa - Record of members, 1853-1940

Film Number 87044

Middlewich Cheshire Branch -Record of members, 1840-1865

Liverpool Lancashire Branch - Record of members, 1840-1960

Manchester Lancashire Branch - Record of members, 1838-1946

Sheffield Yorkshire Conference - Record of members, 1843-1922

Long Whatton Leicestershire - Record of members, 1847-1884

Film Number 87867 - 87878

British Mission - Annual genealogical report of the British Mission, Form E, 1907-1951

Film Number 205633

Irish Conference - Record of members, 1884-1924

Manchester District - Record of members, 1876-1931

Oldham Lancashire Branch - Record of members, 1840-1947

Halifax Yorkshire Branch - Record of members, 1901-1930

Film Number 104149

Airdrie Lanarkshire Branch - Record of members, early to 1947

Aberdeen Branch - Record of members, 1841-1948

Arbroath, Angus Branch - Record of members 1845-1880

Auchenairn Lanarkshire Branch - Record of members 1848-1858

Ayr Ayrshire Branch - Record of members 1848

Baillieston Lanarkshire Branch - Record of members 1851-1853

Bathgate West Lothian Branch - Record of members early to 1868

Blackbraes Stirlingshire Branch - Record of members early to 1868

Aylth Perthshire Branch - Record of members 1849-1856

Borrowstounness West Lothian Branch - Record of members 1846-1853

Bridge of Weir Renfrew Branch 1847-1849

Burnbank Kincardine - Record of members early to 1905

Busby Renfrew Branch - Record of members 1846-1849

Balfron Stirlingshire - Record of members 1847-1855

Barrhead Renfrew - Record of members 1847-1851

Bonhill Dunbarton Branch - Record of members 1847-1855

Film Number 104150

Dunfirmline Fife Branch - Record of members early to 1889

Dysart Fife Branch - Record of members early to 1875

Calton Lanarkshire Branch - Record of members 1857-1862

Cambuslang Lanarkshire Branch - Record of members early to 1906

Campsie Stirling Branch - Record of members 1848-1854

Clackmannon Clackmannonshire Branch - Record of members early to 1877

Crossgate Fife Branch - Record of members 1885-1886

Crofthead West Lothian Branch - Record of members 1842-1868

Dalkeith Midlothian Branch - Record of members 1851-1858

Dalry Ayrshire Branch - Record of members 1846-1853

Dundee Angus Conference - Record of members 1842-1881

Cowdenbeath Fife Branch - Record of members early to 1883

Dundee Angus Branch - Record of members early to 1881

Film Number 104151

Galashiels Selkirk Branch - Record of members 1851

Galston Ayrshire Branch - Record of members 1849-1901

Falkirk Stirling Branch - Record of members 1843-1884

Freuchie Fife Branch - Record of members 1851-1854

Edinburgh Midlothian Conference early to 1868

Edinburgh Midlothian Branch - Record of members early to 1948

Girvan Ayrshire Branch - Record of members 1848-1852

Film Number 104152

Glasgow Lanarkshire Branch - Record of members 1840-1854

Glasgow Lanarkshire Conference - Record of members 1840-1887

Gorbals Lanarkshire Branch - Record of members 1857-1861

Gorebridge Midlothian Branch - Record of members 1884

Graemsay Orkney Branch - Record of members 1851-1853

Greenlaw Berwickshire Branch - Record of members 1847-1848

Greenock Renfrew Branch - Record of members 1840-1864

Film Number 104153

Harthill Lanarkshire Branch - Record of members 1844-1852

Holytown Lanarkshire Branch - Record of members 1848-1878

Hunterfield Midlothian Branch - Record of members 1844-1853

Inverness Branch - Record of members 1847-1850

Johnstone Renfrew Branch - Record of members 1848-1864

Irvine Ayrshire Branch - Record of members 1849-1883

Haywood Lanarkshire Branch - Record of members early to 1888

Film Number 104154

Kelty Fife Branch - Record of members 1880-1883

Kelvindock & Knightswood Dumbarton Branch - Record of members 1848-1856

Kilbirnie Ayrshire Branch - Record of members 1848-1854

Kilmarnock Ayrshire Branch - Record of members 1844-1909

Kilwinning Ayrshire Branch - Record of members 1857-1886

Kirkintilloch Dumbarton Branch - Record of members early to 1947

Kirkliston West Lothian Branch - Record of members 1851-1853

Lanark Lanarkshire Branch - Record of members 1844-1886

Leith Midlothian Branch - Record of members 1840-1847

Loanhead Midlothian Branch - Record of members 1844-1848

Lugar Ayrshire Branch - Record of members 1850-1852

Motherwell Lanarkshire Branch - Record of members 1869-1873

Newmains Lanarkshire Branch - Record of members 1864-1879

Oakley & Linlithgow West Lothian Branch - Record of members 1847-1850

Kirkaldy Fife Branch - Record of members 1842-1849

Loch Gelly Fife Branch - Record of members 1842-1854

New Craig Stirling Branch (includes Slamannon Branch) - Record of members
1846-1851

Maybole & Crosshill Ayrshire Branch - Record of members 1848

Film Number 104155

Parkhead Lanarkshire Branch - Record of members 1855-1882

Pathhead Fife Branch - Record of members 1881

Penston East Lothian Branch - Record of members 1851-1856

Perth Perthshire Branch - Record of members 1847-1853

Pittenweem Fife Branch - Record of members 1842-1853

Scottish Conference - Record of members early to 1929

Stewarton Ayrshire Branch - Record of members 1848-1850

Stirling Branch - Record of members 1842-1849

Portsoy Banff Branch - Record of members 1848-1853

Stobhill Midlothian Branch - Record of members early to 1867

Paisley Renfrew Branch - Record of members 1848-1912

Pollokshaws Renfrew Branch (including Busby & Thornlibank Branches - Record
of members 1848-1873

Preston Pans East Lothian Branch - Record of members 1851-1853

Rutherglen Lanarkshire Branch - Record of members 1848-1854

Film Number 104156

Tranent East Lothian Branch - Record of members early to 1868

Trongate Lanarkshire Branch - Record of members 1860-1862

West Fife & Dunfirmline Fife Branch - Record of members 1881-1887

West Wemyss Fife Branch - Record of members 1841-1847

Wishaw Lanarkshire Branch - Record of members 1870-1878

Tollcross Lanarkshire Branch - Record of members 1847-1861

Thurso Caithness Branch - Record of members early to 1866

Vale of Leven Dumbarton Branch - Record of members 1847-1879

Film Number 104166

Pontypool Monmouthshire Branch - Record of members 1848-1947

Abertillery Monmouthshire Branch - Record of members 1861-1901

Newport Monmouthshire Branch - Record of members 1848-1857

Abersychan Monmouthshire Branch - Record of members 1849-1892

Film Number 104167

Bryntroedgam Glamorgan Branch - Record of members 1847-1860

Briton-Ferry Glamorgan Branch - Record of members 1847-1853

Bryn-mawr Brecon Branch including Wainhelygen Branch - Record of members 1848-1868

Brechfa Carmarthenshire Branch - Record of members 1846-1875

Alltwen Glamorgan Branch - Record of members 1849-1859

Film Number 104168

Cardiff Glamorgan Branch - Record of members 1846-1947

Coalbrook Vale Monmouthshire Branch - Record of members 1856-1867

Cogan Glamorgan Branch - Record of members 1848-1876

Cefncoedycymer Brecon Branch - Record of members 1847-1864

Cuffern Mountain Pembrokeshire Branch - Record of members 1849-1876

Cwmcillyn Monmouthshire Branch - Record of members 1847-1856

Cwm Tillery Monmouthsire Branch (including Crumlin & Trinant Branches) - Record of members 1847-1857

Crumlin Monmouthshire Branch - Record of members 1857-1862

Llanelltud Merionethshire Branch (including Cwmbran & Treorchy Branches) - Record of members 1850-1874

Film Number 104169

Dinas Glamorgan - Record of members Branch 1848-1879

Gwernllwynbach Glamorgan Branch - Record of members 1851-1872

Festioniog Merionethshire Branch - Record of members 1846-1856

Gilwern Brecon Branch (including Llanelly Branch) - Record of members 1849-1858

Georgetown Glamorgan Branch - Record of members 1845-1847

Llanelly Carmarthenshire Branch - Record of members 1847-1882

Haverfordwest Pembrokeshire Branch - Record of members 1847-1860

Llansawel Carmarthenshire Branch - Record of members 1849-1879

Ebbw Vale Monmouthshire Branch (including Risca Branch) - Record of members 1847-1864

Llanfabon Glamorgan Branch - Record of members 1847-1869

Llanelltud Merionethshire Branch (including Cwmbran & Treorchy Branches) - Record of member s1850-1874

Llandebie Carmarthenshire Branch - Record of members 1849-1866

Llanelly Brecon Branch - Record of members 1857-1863

Film Number 104170

Georgetown Glamorgan Branch - Record of members 1845-1847

Pont-y-pridd Glamorgan Branch (including Treforest Branch) - Record of members 1877-1895

Penycae Monmouthshire Branch - Record of members 1844-1866

Machen Monmouthshire Branch - Record of members 1854-1865

Merthyr Tydfil Glamorgan Branch - Record of members 1843-1947

Nantyglo Monmouthshire Branch - Record of members 1846-1856

Pont-Llanfraith Monmouthshire Branch - Record of members 1897-1942

Film Number 104171

Pontypool Monmouthshire Branch - Record of members 1848-1947

Rhymney English Monmouthshire Branch (including Twyncarno Branch) - Record of members 1851-1887

Stepaside Pembrokeshire Branch - Record of members 1848-1857

Sutton Mountain Pembrokeshire Branch - Record of members 1853-1859

Swansea Glamorgan Branch - Record of members 1849-1870

Rhymney Monmouthshire Branch - Record of members 1850-1876

Film Number 104172

Tredegar Monmouthshire Branch - Record of members 1844-1883

Trinant Monmouthshire Branch - Record of members 1849-1853

Twyn-yr-Odyn Glamorgan Branch - Record of members1847-1901

Treboeth Glamorgan Branch - Record of members 1844-1880

Treforest Glamorgan Branch - Record of members 1851-1873

Twyncarno Monmouthshire Branch (including Rhymney English Branch) - Record of members 1851-1883

Morriston Glamorgan Branch - Record of members 1853-1868

Treorchy Glamorgan Branch - Record of members 1875-1882

Welsh Conference - Record of members 1850-1922

Ystrad Glamorgan Branch - Record of members 1885-1911

APPENDIX B
Locating a Conference -
An example using Bedfordshire

The organisation of branches and districts relating to the above films can be ascertained with reference to maps and the file cards incorporated into the Minnie Margetts file as shown below.

Bedfordshire Conference area of coverage.

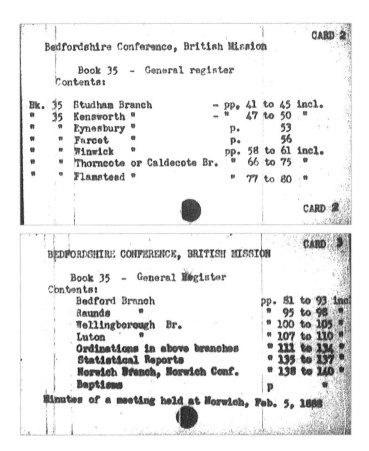

Bedfordshire Conference, British Mission

CARD 2

Book 35 - General register
Contents:

Bk.	35	Studham Branch			- pp.	41	to	45	incl.
"	35	Kensworth	"		- "	47	to	50	"
"	"	Eynesbury	"		p.			53	
"	"	Farcet	"		p.			56	
"	"	Winwick	"		pp.	58	to	61	incl.
"	"	Thorncote or Caldecote Br.			"	66	to	75	"
"	"	Flamstead	"		"	77	to	80	"

CARD 2

BEDFORDSHIRE CONFERENCE, BRITISH MISSION

CARD 3

Book 35 - General Register
Contents:

Bedford Branch   pp. 81 to 93 incl
Raunds   " 95 to 98 "
Wellingborough Br.   " 100 to 105 "
Luton   " 107 to 110 "
Ordinations in above branches   " 111 to 134 "
Statistical Reports   " 135 to 137 "
Norwich Branch, Norwich Conf.   " 138 to 140 "
Baptisms   p "
Minutes of a meeting held at Norwich, Feb. 5, 1888

The Minnie Margetts File index shows locations of registers for branches within a conference (LDS Church Intellectual Reserve Inc).

At the time the Conference consisted of the following branches:

• BEDFORDSHIRE: Studham, Kensworth, Eynesbury, Thorncote, Caldecote, Bedford, Luton, Eaton Bray, Wyboston.

• HERTFORDSHIRE: Flamstead, Hemel Hempstead, Breachwood Green, St Albans,

• NORTHAMPTONSHIRE: Irchester, Northampton, Wellingborough, Raunds,

• HUNTINGDONSHIRE: Farcet, Winwick, Gt Staughton, St Neots

• BUCKINGHAMSHIRE: Aylesbury, Simpson, Linslade.

APPENDIX C
Early Church Information File

The Early Church Information File is an alphabetical index of individuals on microfilm No's 1750655 - 1750729 and contains around 1.5 million entries from many Latter-day Saint sources. It covers sources from 1830 to the mid-1900s and includes: Latter-day Saint membership records, Ward histories, Family and local histories, journals and biographies, Priesthood and missionary records, Periodicals, cemetery records, Immigration records and some marriage records mainly covering Utah but including some from Idaho, Wyoming, Nevada, Illinois, and California. Several other well known indexes are also referred to in the Early Church Information File including Mormons and Their Neighbors and indexes to hundreds of books and microfilms.

The Early Church Information File will enable you to:

• Identify useful sources to enable you to direct your family research.

• Identify family connections.

• Find birth, baptism, marriage, death and burial information.

• Find the names of extended family members.

• Locate a specific geographic area.

• Find biographical information.

• However the Early Church Information File does not include:

• Every name appearing in all LDS sources that have otherwise been indexed.

• Every membership record that has been generated.

All sources available through the Family History Library or Family History Centres.

Using the index is recommended during the early stages of your research. Names are listed alphabetically by surname and given name. Note that names that begin with Mc or M' are listed as Mac. Abbreviated names are listed as if they were spelled out in full e.g. Saint John.

Names are often formatted in any order, but the cards are always arranged alphabetically by surname. An individual appearing in the Early Church Information File may be listed on one card or more cards depending on how much is written on the individual and how much of that material has been indexed. (see example for Christopher Layton). Although cards may appear in a variety of formats, the name is always at the top of the card and call numbers for sources listed on the cards are normally on the left or sometimes at the bottom of the card.

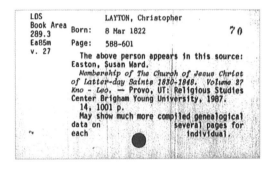

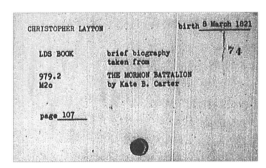

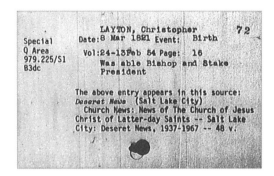

```
LDS
Film              LAYTON, Christopher
Area  Microfilm: 485333                                    67
        Item: 4

      Diary of: Bodily, R. (Journal)
          Page: 12, 13, 22, 49
        The above person appears in this source:
    Library of Congress Collection of Mormon Diaries.
        Washington, DC: filmed by the Library of
    Congress Photoduplication Service, 1950.
        1950 microfilm of Univ. of Calif., Berkeley
    transcripts made in         1936-1937 by the WPA of
    diary, journal, and  ●      life sketch manuscripts
    at various Utah              locations.
```

```
.              LAYTON, Christopher        72
Special    Date:8 Mar 1821 Event:  Birth
Q Area
979.225/S1    Vol:24-13Feb 54 Page:  16
B3dc            Was able Bishop and Stake
              President

        The above entry appears in this source:
        Deseret News  (Salt Lake City)
        Church News: News of The Church of Jesus
    Christ of Latter-day Saints -- Salt Lake
    City: Deseret News, 1937-1967 -- 48 v.
```

A selection from the various cards relating to Christopher Layton in the Early Church Information File (LDS Church Intellectual Reserve Inc)

Some sources are only accessible if you are in the Family History Library at Salt Lake City but many such sources have also been filmed so refer to the Library Catalogue. If you are at a Family History Center, request a microfilm or microfiche copy of the source. For sources not available on microform, you may be able to obtain a copy of the book electronically or through inter-library loan at a local public library.

245

APPENDIX D

The Family History Library & Family History Centres Family History Library, Salt Lake City

The Family History Library has the world's largest collection of genealogical information, including an extensive collection of books and microfilms about Church members.

The Family History Library originated in 1894, when the Church established the Genealogical Society of Utah to enable Church members to research their family history. They organised a library to distribute information about genealogical research, and to acquire genealogical records.

The library collection grew slowly at first but between 1920 and 1940 saw unprecedented growth. By 1937 the library was among the top five genealogical libraries in the USA.

In 1938 microfilming began. The first microfilm produced in the British Isles was in 1947. The Genealogical Society of Utah's (now Family Search) extensive microfilming is renowned worldwide, and its microfilm collection is now unsurpassed anywhere. Today records are digitally stored keeping pace with modern technology. Long-term storage space for the films became an issue and in 1963 the Granite Mountain Records Vault, at Little Cottonwood Canyon, about 25 miles southeast of Salt Lake City was opened.

The Granite Mountain Storage Vaults at Little Cottonwood Canyon, Utah.

As the library's record collection expanded and the number of researchers (both church members and the public) visiting the library increased, it was clear that additional space was needed. A new library facility was announced at the 1980 World Conference on Records held in Salt Lake City and was opened in 1985. The Family History Library is located at 35 North West Temple Street, Salt Lake City and is open to all.

The Family History library in Salt Lake City (author's photograph).

248

Many of the library holdings are available at all the Family History Centres worldwide although some restrictions may apply to certain books and maps. The main library catalogue on www.familysearch.org will indicate what can be obtained at the Family History Centres and what needs to be used only in the main library.

Family history centres in the British Isles as of November 2011

These centres are manned by volunteers on a part time basis and the opening hours vary from centre to centre and may be subject to change depending upon local needs. Please telephone the centre to find out opening hours and to book an appointment. The volunteers are unable to undertake extensive research on an individual basis but will be pleased to assist you whilst in the centre.

Berkshire
Reading 280 The Meadway, Tilehurst, Reading. 01189-410211

Buckinghamshire
High Wycombe 743 London Road, High Wycombe. 01494-459979

Cambridgeshire
Cambridge 670 Cherry Hinton Road, Cambridge. 01223-247010
Peterborough Cottesmore Close, off Atherstone Ave, Peterborough. 01733-263374

Cheshire
Macclesfield Victoria Road, Macclesfield. 01625-427236
Chester St Davids Park, Ewloe, Flintshire. 01244-530710

Cleveland
Billingham The Linkway, Billingham. 01642-563162

Cornwall
Helston Clodgey Lane, Helston. 01326-564503.
St. Austell Kingfisher Drive, St. Austell. 01726-69912

Co. Durham
Newton Aycliffe Shafto Way, Newton Aycliffe. 01325-313632

Cumbria
Barrow Abbey Road, Barrow in Furness. 01229-820050
Carlisle Langrigg Road, Morton Park, Carlisle. 01228-52 6767

Devon
Exeter Wonford Road, Off Barrack Road, Exeter. 01392-25 0723
Plymouth Mannamead Road, Plymouth. 01752-668666

Dorset
Poole 8 Mount Road, Parkstone, Poole. 01202-730646
Weymouth 396 Chickerell Road, Weymouth. 01305-787240

Essex
Romford 64 Butts Green Road, Hornchurch. 01708-620727

Gloucestershire
Cheltenham Thirlestaine Road, Cheltenham. 01242-523433
Forest of Dean Wynols Hill, Holcot Rd, Queensway, Coalway, Colesford. 01594-832904.
Yate Wellington Road, Yate, Bristol. 01454-323004

Hampshire
Aldershot St. Georges Road, Aldershot. 01252-321460
Portsmouth Kingston Crescent, Portsmouth. 02392-696243

Hertfordshire
Stevenage Buckthorne Avenue, Stevenage. 01438-351553
Watford Hempstead Road, Watford. 01923-251471

Isle of Wight
Newport Chestnut Close, Shide Road, Newport. 01983-532833

Kent
Canterbury Forty Acre Road, Canterbury. 01227-765431
Gillingham Twydall Lane, Gillingham. 01634-388900.
Maidstone 76B London Road, Maidstone. 01622-757811
Orpington Station Approach, Orpington. 01689-837342

Lancashire
Ashton Patterdale Road Crowhill Estate, Ashton-under-Lyne. 01613-303453
Blackpool Warren Drive, Cleveleys, Blackpool. 01253-863868
Manchester Altrincham Road, Wythenshawe. 01619-029279
Preston Temple Way, Hartwood Green, Chorley. 01257-226145

Leicestershire
Leicester Wakerley Road, Leicester. 01162-490099

Lincolnshire
Boston 1 Woodthorpe Avenue, Fishtoft, Boston. 01205- 353579
Grimsby Linwood Avenue, Waltham Road, North East Lincolnshire. 01472-828876
Lincoln Skellingthorpe Road, Lincoln. 01522-680117

London
London Regional Family Search Centre 64-68 Exhibition Road, South Kensington. 0207 589 8561

The London Regional Family History Centre (author's photographs)

Staines 41 Kingston Road, Staines. 01784-462627

Norfolk
Dereham Yaxham Road, East Dereham. 01362-851500
Kings Lynn Reffley Lane, Kings Lynn. 01553-670000
Norwich 19 Greenways, Norwich. 01603-452440
Thetford Station Road, Thetford. 01842-755472

Northamptonshire
Northampton 137 Harlestone Road, Northampton. 01604-58 7630

Nottinghamshire
Mansfield Berry Parklea, Southridge Drive, Mansfield.: 01623-662333
Nottingham Stanhome Square, West Bridgford. 01159-23 3856

Shropshire
Telford 72 Glebe Street, Wellington, Telford. 01952-257443

Somerset
Bristol 721 Wells Road, Whitchurch, Bristol. 01275-838326
Yeovil Lysander Road, Forest Hill, Yeovil. 01935-426817

Staffordshire
Lichfield Purcell Avenue, Lichfield. 01543-414843
Newcastle-under-Lyme The Brampton, Newcastle-under-Lyme. 01782-630178

Suffolk
Ipswich 42 Sidegate Lane West, Ipswich. 01473-723182
Lowestoft 165 Yarmouth Road, Lowestoft. 01502-573851

Sussex,
Crawley Old Horsham Road, Crawley. 01293-516151
Hastings 2 Ledsham Avenue, St. Leonards-on-Sea. 01424-754563.
Worthing Goring Street, Worthing. 01903-241829

Tyne & Wear
Sunderland Linden Road, Sunderland. 01915-285787

West Midlands
Coventry Riverside Close, Whitley. 02476-303316
Harborne 38-42 Lordswood Road, Harborne, Birmingham. 01214-276858
Sutton Coldfield 187 Penns Lane, Sutton Coldfield. 01213-864902
Wednesfield Linthouse Lane, Wednesfield. Wolverhampton. 01902-724097

Wiltshire
Trowbridge Brook Road, Trowbridge, 01225-777097

Worcestershire & Hereford
Redditch 321 Evesham Road, Crabbs Cross, Redditch. 01527-401543
Worcester Canada Way, Lower Wick, Worcester. 01905-42 0341

Yorkshire
Harrogate 10 Wetherby Road, Harrogate. 01423-886537
Huddersfield 12 Halifax Road, Birchencliffe, Huddersfield. 01484-454573
Hull 725 Holderness Road, Hull. 01482-701439
Leeds Vesper Road, Hawksworth, Leeds. 01132-585297
Pontefract Park Villas Drive, Pontefract. 01977-600308
Scarborough Stepheny Drive/Whitby Road, Scarborough. 01723-507239
Sheffield Wheel Lane, Grenoside, Sheffield. 01142-453124
York West Bank, Acomb, York. 01904-786784

Wales
Cardiff Heol-Y-Deri, Rhiwbina, Cardiff, South Glamorgan. 02920 625342
Chester St Davids Park, Ewloe, Flintshire. 01244-530710
Cwmbran The Highway, Croesceiliog, Cwmnbran. 01633-483856
Merthyr Tydfil Nanty Gwenith Street, George Town, Merthyr. 01685-722455
Newcastle Emlyn Cardigan Road, Newcastle Emlyn, Carmarthenshire. 01239-711472
Rhyl 171 Vale Road, Rhyl, Denbighshire. 01745-331172.
Swansea Cockett Road, Swansea. 01792-585792

Scotland
Aberdeen North Anderson Drive, Aberdeen, Grampian. 01224-69 2206
Alloa Grange Road, Westend Park Alloa. 01259-211148
Ayr Corner of Orchard Ave/ Mossgiel Road, Ayr. 01292-610632
Dumfries 36 Edinburgh Road, Albanybank, Dumfries. 01387-25 4865
Dundee Bingham Terrace, Dundee, Tayside. 01382-451247
Edinburgh 30A Colinton Road, Edinburgh, Midlothian. 01313-132762
Elgin Pansport Road, Elgin, Moray. 01343-546429
Glasgow 35 Julian Avenue, Kelvinside, Strathclyde. 01413-57 1024,
Invergordon Kilmonivaig Seafield, Portmahomack Tain, Ross. 01862-871631
Inverness 13 Ness Walk, Inverness. 01463-231220
Kirkcaldy Winifred Crescent/Forth Park, Kircaldy, Fife. 01592-64 0041
Lerwick 44 Prince Alfred Street, Lerwick, Shetland. 01595-695732
Motherwell 444-478 Orbiston Street, Motherwell, Lanark. 01698-26 6630
Paisley Glenburn Road, Paisley, Renfrew. 01418-842780
Stornoway Newton Street, Stornoway, Isle of Lewis, 01851-706709 or 0185-182 0274.

Channel Islands
St Helier Jersey Rue de la Vallee, St. Mary, Jersey, 01534-482171

Northern Ireland
Belfast 403 Holywood Road, Belfast, Co.Down. 02890-76
Coleraine 8 Sandelfields, Knocklynn Road, Coleraine, 02870-321214
Londonderry Racecourse Road, Belmont, Londonderry. 02871-35 0179

Republic of Ireland
Cork Sarsfield Road, Wilton, Cork. 00-35321-4897050
Dublin Finglas Road, Glasnevin, Dublin.
Limerick Doradoyle Road, Limerick. 00-35361-309443

Church Hisory Library

The Church History Library in Salt Lake City (authors photograph).

The Church History Library preserves all the records, relating to The Church of Jesus Christ of Latter-day Saints but does not make its collections available through Family History Centers unless the material has been microfilmed. Their staff can however respond to any research queries by e-mail at churchhistorylibrary@ldschurch.org.

The Archives of the Church History Library has manuscript material that may contain helpful genealogical information including membership records, minutes and histories of most church units worldwide and the diaries and journals of many church leaders. It also has an active publishing programme including biographies, directories, emigration books, Mormon Battalion histories and obituaries as well as the Journal of Church History.

Journal of Church History
This is a 'scrapbook' of events in Church history and the microfilm copy covers from 1830 to 1973. It includes the largest collection of pioneer company rosters 1847 to 1868, conference reports, newspaper clippings of obituaries and extracts from biographies, journals and letters, histories, biographies, and manuscript material. The journal is indexed on microfilm no's 1233503 to12233550 and 1255971 to 1255980 and will be available on-line at the new Church History website. The microfilms of the actual journal number 248 commencing at film no. 1259729. These films are not available for circulation to Family History Centres.

BIBLIOGRAPHY

Manchester Mormons. Author William Clayton, Peregrine Smith, 1974. ISBN 0879050241.

Mormonism in the British Isles 1837-1987. Authors Donald Q. Cannon and Larry C. Porter, BYU Studies 27 - Winter and Spring 1987.

The Second Century: Latter-day Saints in Great Britain, Author Derek A. Cuthbert, Cambridge University Press, 1987.

The Uncommercial Traveller Author Charles Dickens, Reprinted Edition CSP Classics 2008, ISBN.1847189229.

A Century of 'Mormonism' in Great Britain. Author Richard L Evans, Publishers Press 1984, ISBN 091609507X.

Expectations Westward: The Mormons and the Emigration of Their British Converts in the Nineteenth Century. Author Philip A M Taylor, Oliver & Boyd, 1965.

Truth Will Prevail: The Rise of The Church of Jesus Christ of Latter-day Saints in the British Isles, 1837-1987. Authors Ben Bloxham, James R. Moss; and Larry C. Porter. LDS Church 1987. ISBN 0951213008.

Mormons in Early Victorian Britain. Authors Richard L Jensen,and Malcolm R. Thorp, University of Utah Press 1990. ISBN 0874803225.

Historical Atlas of Mormonism Authors Kent S Brown, Donald Q. Cannon and Richard H. Jackson, Prentice Hall, 1994. ISBN 0130451479.

The March of the Mormon Battalion from Council Bluffs to California: Taken from the Journal of Henry Standage Author Frank Alfred Golder, The Century Co, 1928.

A Concise History of the Mormon Battalion in the Mexican War: 1846-1847
Author Daniel Tyler, 1881 reprint, Rio Grande Press 1964. ISBN 0873800117.

The Call of Zion: The Story of the First Welsh Mormon Emigration Author Ronald Dennis. Religious Studies Centre, BYU, 1987. ISBN 0884946282.

The Mormon Pioneer Companies Crossing the Plains (1847 1868) Narratives: Guide to Sources in Utah Libraries and Archives Author Melvin Bashore, Historical Department, LDS Church, 1990.

Mormons on the High Seas: Ocean Voyage Narratives to America (1840-1890): Guide to Sources in the Historical Department of the Church of Jesus Christ of Latter-day Saints and Other Utah Repositories Authors Melvin Bashore and Linda L. Haslem. Historical Department, LDS Church, 1990.

Latter-day Saint Scandinavian Migration through Hull, England 1852-1894 Authors Fred E Woods & Nicholas J Evans, BYU Studies Vol 41, no. 4, 2002.

INDEXES

Compiled by Nicholas Newington-Irving FSG
Some topics appear more than once on a page.

SUBJECT INDEX

Authors mentione din this book are listed in the
Nominal Index

**INDEX TO SOURCES AND
REPOSITORIES MENTIONED IN THIS
BOOK**

INDEX TO PLACES MENTIONED IN THIS BOOK
For Maps see the Subject Index

Sevier County, Utah 191
Skenfrith, Monmouthshire 165
Society Islands, French Polynesia 76
Southampton 58-59, 169
Southwark, Lancashire 101
Spain 176
Spanish Fork, Utah 161
Stanley Hill, Herefordshire 12
Stoke upon Trent, Staffordshire 12
Sugar Creek, Iowa 88
Summit County, Utah 191
Sutter's Mill, California 93-94
Sutter's Ranch, California 97
Swansea, Glamorgan 100, 171
Switzerland 172, 175
Sydney, New South Wales 48-50, 53, 58-60, 62, 75, 177
Tahiti, French Polynesia 49, 62, 75
Thorncote, Bedfordshire 69, 95, 97, 100, 119, 149
Thurso, Caithness-shire 11
Tooele Valley, Utah 135
Tooele, Utah 135
Toronto, Canada 21
Tredegar, Monmouthshire 165, 169
Trelawnyd, Flintshire 168
Tucson, Arizona 93, 99
Turkey 175
Upholland, Lancashire 100
Utah County, Utah 191
Utah Dixie, Utah 137
Utah State 23-24, 26-27, 43
Utah Valley, Utah 135
Vancouver, Canada 59
Vienna, Austria 175-176
Walton Hill, Worcestershire 17
Washington DC 70, 94-95, 153-154, 205-206
Washington, Utah 135
Watford, Hertfordshire 186, 244
Weber County, Utah 191
Weber Valley, Utah 135
Wellington, New Zealand 177
Wellsville, Utah 135
West Indies 45
West Jordan, Utah 135
Westbury, Wiltshire 27
Weston, Somerset 17
Westport, Missouri 125
Wigan, Lancashire 101
Windsor Castle, Berkshire 3
Winford, Norfolk 100
Winter Quarters, Nebraska 25, 101-104, 118,

120, 128, 131, 133, 191
Wolverhampton, Staffordshire 69, 96, 165

SHIPPING INDEX

Shipping Lines and Companies
Black Star Line 37
Dramatic Shipping Line 2
Great Western Steamship Company 37
Guion Line 37-38
Morris & Co 37
Wilson Line 38

Ships' Names
Abyssinia 54-55
Alacrity 50
Alaska 54-55, 57-58
Albert 51, 61
Alesto 47
Amazon 43, 50
America 47
American Congress 51
Anchoria 58-60
Antarctic 50
Argo 48
Argonaught 64
Arizona 53-58
Arkwright 51
Ashland 48
Astoria 60
Athena 50
Aurania 58
Australia 53, 55
B.S. Kimball 50-51
Belle Wood 51
Benjamin Adams 49
Bergenland (SS) 161
Berlin 48
Bridgewater 51
Britannia 45, 47
British King 56
Brooklyn 47, 128
Buena Vista 48, 166
Caravan 49
Carnatic 47
Caroline 47, 51
Cavour 51
Champion 47
Chaos 47
Charles Buck 49
Chimborazo 49
Circassia 58-59

264

NOMINAL INDEX

Please note that the nominal index refers solely to people mentioned in this book which is but a small sample of the people involved; these indexes should not be assumed to be exhaustive.

ANDERSON M. 59
ANDERSON Martha 75
ANDERSON Mary: *see* BRUCE Mary
ANDERSON May 27-28
ANDERSON N. 55
ANDERSON O. 59
ANDERSON R. 54, 60
ANDERSON Scott 27
ANDERSON W. 59
ANDERSON William (Captain) 86-87
ANDREW Lily 187
ANDREW Phyllis Elizabeth 187
ANDREW William James 187
ANDREWS Milo 73
ANDRUS M. 50
ANGUS J. 49
ANTHONY David John 167
ANTHONY Edmund 167
ANTHONY Evan Daniel 167
ANTHONY John 167
ANTHONY Mary Jane 167-168
ANTHONY Rebecca Ann 167
APPENDAHL R. 57
ARBOSEN H. 57
ARCHIBALD D. 60
ARGYLE J. 58
ARMSBY Albert Frederick 183, 187
ARMSBY Alice Louisa 187
ARMSBY Ann: *see* DAVIES Ann
ARMSBY Edward 183
ARMSBY Olive: *see* RUSSELL Olive
ARMSBY Sarah Ann: *see* SMALLPIECE Sarah
 Ann
ARMSBY Smallpiece 183
ARMSTRONG Frederick 187
ARMSTRONG Henry 187
ARMSTRONG Kate: *see* HAMLIN Kate
ARMSTRONG Thomas 187
ARNOTT J. 57
ARNSON A. 59
ARTHUR C. 48
ASHDOWN A. 59
ASHFORTH Edward 73
ASHFORTH Mary 73
ASHFORTH Sarah 73
ASHTON E. 58
ASPINALL Ann 73
ATKINS Emma 73
ATKINS William 73
ATKINSON Joshua Charles 122
ATKINSON Mary Ann 122
ATTLEY H. 55

ATTWOOD M. 51
AUBREY J. 49
AUBREY Jane 122
AUSTIN M. 60
AYRE J. 59
BADGER J. 60
BADHAM Samuel 205
BAGNALL C. 48
BAILEY Elizabeth 122
BAILEY John 122
BAILEY John Henry 122
BAKER M. 161
BAKER W. 59
BAKKER A. 58
BALLANTYNE Richard 49, 170
BALLARD A. 54
BALLARD H. 57
BALLARD Hannah Russell 122
BALLARD William 122
BALLIF S. 50
BALSER Amelia Sarah: *see* EVANS Amelia
 Sarah
BALSER John 122
BARBER G. 55
BARBER J. 54
BARCLAY Jennie 183
BARKER Alice Elizabeth 187
BARKER Josiah 65
BARLOW I. 49
BARNES Hannah 65
BARNES Sarah 122
BARRATT William James 177
BARRELL H. 56
BARRETT H. 60
BARRETT R. 59
BARTLEY Jessie 183
BARTON Albert B. 97
BARTON M. 59
BARTON Mary B.: *see* LAYTON Mary B.
BARTON P. 52
BASHORE Melvin 256
BATEMAN Elizabeth 194
BATES Joseph W. 100
BATEZ J. 195
BATH B. 195
BATT E. 59
BATT G. 53
BAUER A. 58
BAUGH F. 58
BAUSON Emily 183
BEAN George W. 205
BEASLEY Ebenezer 168

BURTON R. 52
BUTLER L. 48
BUXTON Madeleine Joan 162
CALDER D. 52
CALDWELL Charles 66
CALKIN A. 50
CALLAHAN Thomas W. 205
CALLISTER D. 56
CALVERT John 205
CAMPBELL Catherine 101
CAMPBELL R. 49
CANNON (Capt) 21
CANNON Angus 25
CANNON Ann: *see* QUAYLE Ann
CANNON David 25
CANNON Donald Q. 255
CANNON Elizabeth 25;
   see also HOAGLAND Elizabeth
CANNON George 25
CANNON George Quayle 20, 25-26, 43
CANNON Hugh J. 187
CANNON J. 55
CANNON John Q. 100
CANNON Leonora 19, 21, 25
CANNON Mary: *see* EDWARDS Mary
CANNON Mary Alice 25
CANNON Family 25
CARDEW William 190
CARE Agnes 41
CARELESS Eliza 41
CARELESS George 168
CARESWELL Alfred D. 41
CARESWELL Alice 41
CARESWELL Anna 41
CARESWELL Charles 41
CARESWELL Harriet 41
CARESWELL Joseph 41
CARLGREN Lars 41
CARLGREN Lena 41
CARLIN Ann 41
CARLIN Elizabeth 41
CARLIN James 41
CARLIN Jane 41
CARLIN John 41
CARLIN Margaret 41
CARLISLE Ann 41
CARLISLE Elizabeth 41;
   see also HOCQUAR Elizabeth
CARLISLE Georgiana 41
CARLISLE John 41
CARLISLE Joshua 41
CARLISLE Mary Emma 41

CARLISLE Samuel 41
CARLISLE Willard 41
CARLSEN Anna E. 41
CARLSEN Carl 41
CARLSEN Caroline 41
CARLSEN Else 41
CARLSEN Johan 41
CARLSEN Jorgen P. 41
CARLSON Anders 41
CARLSON Anna 41
CARLSON Anna Maria 41
CARLSON Bertha 41
CARLSON Berthi Marie 41
CARLSON Carl 41
CARLSON Carl Peter 41
CARLSON Christiana 41
CARLSON Christina C. 41
CARLSON Christine 41
CARLSON Elma 41
CARLSON Hans 41
CARLSON Ingrid 41
CARLSON Isaac 41
CARLSON Johan 41
CARLSON Johanna 41
CARLSON Kersti 41
CARLSON Maren 41
CARLSON Mari 41
CARLSON Niels 41
CARLSON Niels Christian 41
CARLSON Ole 41
CARLSON Peter 41
CARPENTER William 41
CARR George 41
CARRINGTON A. 51
CARSTENSEN P. 52
CARTER Anna 41
CARTER Eliza 41
CARTER Ellen 41
CARTER Emmanda 41
CARTER Frederick 41
CARTER George 41
CARTER James 41
CARTER Jane 41
CARTER John 41
CARTER Mary 41
CARTER Mary A. 41
CARTER Samuel 41, 48
CARTER Thomas P. 41
CARTER William H. 41
CARTLEDGE William R. 41
CARVER John 41
CARVER Sarah: *see* EAMES Sarah A.

CUTHBERT Derek A. 255
CUTHBERT John 190
DALLEY N. 56
DAVENPORT (Captain) 69
DAVIES Ann 183
DAVIS Donald E. (Captain) 93-94
DAVIS E. 56
DAVIS James 100
DAVIS W. 41
DAWSON (Mrs) 55
DAY Elizabeth Henderson 185
DAY Hannah 185
DAY Thomas 48, 185
DAYNES Joseph 169
DEANS R. 48
DENNIS Ronald (Dr) 166, 169, 256
DICKENS Charles 3, 43, 255
DIXON George A. 161
DOBSON Joseph 100
DOBSON T. 52
DONALDSON J. 54
DORLUS C. 56
DOUGLAS Ralph Briggs 100
DOUGLASS W. 52
DOVER Mary 183
DOWNS Joseph H. 161
DUNBAR D. 53
DUNNETT Jane 183
DUTCHER Thomas P. 205
DYKES (a missionary) 113
DYKES George Parker 205
EAMES Sarah A. 41
EARDLEY B. 52
EAST Mary 189
EASTER Susan 65
EASTON Susan Ward 244
EBERHARTT Helena 187
ECCLES David 170
ECCLESTONE Mary 189
EDWARDS Mary 25
EK C. 55
EKSTROM (Church member) 195
ELANSON C. 195
ELDER Joseph 107
ELDREDGE John E. 75
ELLIS Ann: *see* WAKEFIELD Ann
ELLIS Annie Elizabeth 187
ELLIS Caroline: see GRIFFITH Caroline
ELLIS George 183, 187
ELLIS William 183
ELLSWORTH Edward 106, 213
ELLSWORTH Emma Diana 97

ENSIGN M. 51, 64
ERICKSON S. 55
EVANS Amelia Sarah 122
EVANS Israel 106
EVANS J. 55
EVANS Nicholas 38
EVANS Nicholas J. 256
EVANS Richard L. 255
EVANS William 100
EYVINDSON J. 54
FAIRBANKS J. 52
FARNHAM A. 49
FARNHAM Augustus 75
FARR N. 54
FEARN J. 54
FERGUSON James 49, 100
FIELDING A. 47
FIELDING J. 47
FIELDING James (Rev) 22-23
FIELDING Joseph 2, 10, 22-23
FIELDING Rachel 22
FIFE John 100
FIFE Peter Muir 100
FIFE W. 52
FINES Susan 183
FINLAYSON J. 54
FLINT Margaret B. 97
FLITTON Joseph 185
FLYGARE N. 52-53
FORSGREN J. 48
FOTHERINGHAM W. 50
FOX Jesse W. 27
FOX Ruth: *see* MAY Ruth
FOX Family 27
FRANKS Hazel 189
FRANSDEN N. 54
FRENCH Louisa 189
FRENCH Mary A. 189
FROBISHER Hannah Day 185
FROBISHER William 185
FROST B. 49
FULLMER J. 49
GADD I. 55
GADSEN James 93
GALBRAITH Elizabeth: *see* LAYTON
    Elizabeth
GALBRAITH William 97
GARN D. 49
GATES J. 48
GIBSON W. 48, 50
GILES N. 55
GILES William 11

PRATT P. 47
PRATT Parley P. 160, 170
PREATER Susannah 26
PRESTON W. 51
PRICE Mary 97
PUGMIRE Jonathan 100
QUAYLE Ann 25
QUIGLEY J. 56
RACKWELL John 194
RAMSDEN George 38
RASMUSSEN N. 53
REEVES W. 55
RICH B. 54
RICHARDS F. 47
RICHARDS L. 47
RICHARDS Pauline 162
RICHARDS Peter F. 101
RICHARDS Samuel W. 35, 44
RICHARDS Willard 2, 10, 18-19, 160
RICHARDSON Thomas 47, 101, 205
RICHMOND Benjamin 205
RIDGES Joseph 169, 177
RISER G. 49
RITER William 175
ROBERTS B. H. 134
ROBERTS Levi 101
ROBINSON Daniel 106
ROBINSON William J. 101
ROBSON Joyce: see STORROW Joyce
RODER J. 53
ROOK Annie 184
ROOK Elizabeth 184
ROOK Rose 184
ROOK William 184
ROSKELLEY S. 54
ROSS J. 50
ROUNDY Elizabeth 97
ROWBERRY J. 53
ROWLEY George 106
ROYAL William H. 41
ROYLANCE John 101
RULLOCK T. 47
RUNOLFSEN R. 53
RUSSELL Isaac 2, 19
RUSSELL Olive 183
RYVES L. 195
SANDS Robert 168
SAVAGE C. R. 161
SCOVIL L. 47
SEAGER G. 49
SHARP John 170

SHEARMAN W. 51
SHIPLEY Joseph 101
SHIPP Richard A. 187
SHUPE James W. 205
SIM Matilda 26
SIMIES Emma Amy 184
SIMIES Matilda E. 184
SIMMONS William A. 205
SKANCHY A. 56
SMALLPIECE Sarah Ann 187
SMETHURST A. 49
SMITH (silk mill overseer) 7
SMITH Edith 186
SMITH Hyrum 85
SMITH J. 50-51, 55-56, 58
SMITH J. H. 55
SMITH Job 185
SMITH Joseph 1, 8, 17, 22, 85-86, 160, 198-
199
SMITH Joseph F. 164, 192
SMITH Leonard J. 52, 66
SMITH Lucy Maria 186
SMITH Maud Alice: see HARDING Maisie
Alice
SMITH Samuel Henry 186, 244
SMITH T. 47
SMITH W. F. 55
SMITH William 97
SMITH Family 203
SMITHIES James 168
SMOOT Abraham O. 122
SMURTHWAITE C. 54
SNOW Lorenzo 47, 69, 96
SNYDER John 2, 19, 47
SPANGBERG L. 54
SPENCER C. 50
SPENCER J. 51
SPENCER O. 48
SPRAGUE S. 51
SQUIRES Thomas 185
SQUIRES William 101
STANDAGE Henry 101, 205, 255
STARTUP A. 195
STARTUP H. 195
STEEL Jonathan 190
STEELE Catherine: see CAMPBELL Catherine
STEELE Isaiah C. 205
STEELE John 101
STEPHENS Evan 168
STEVENS A. 51
STEVENSON E. 49
STEVENSON Elizabeth 183

About the SOCIETY OF GENEALOGISTS

Founded in 1911 the Society of Genealogists (SoG) is Britain's premier family history organisation. The Society maintains a splendid genealogical library and education centre in Clerkenwell.

The Society's collections are particularly valuable for research before the start of civil registration of births marriages and deaths in 1837 but there is plenty for the beginner too. Anyone starting their family history can use the online census indexes or look for entries in birth, death and marriage online indexes in the free open community access area.

The Library contains Britain's largest collection of parish register copies, indexes and transcripts and many nonconformist registers. Most cover the period from the sixteenth century to 1837. Along with registers, the library holds local histories, copies of churchyard gravestone inscriptions, poll books, trade directories, census indexes and a wealth of information about the parishes where our ancestors lived.

Unique indexes include Boyd's Marriage Index with more than 7 million names compiled from 4300 churches between 1538-1837 and the Bernau Index with references to 4.5 million names in Chancery and other court proceedings. Also available are indexes of wills and marriage licences, and of apprentices and masters (1710-1774). Over the years the Society has rescued and made available records discarded by government departments and institutions but of great interest to family historians. These include records from the Bank of England, Trinity House and information on Teachers and Civil Servants.

Boyd's and other unique databases are published on line on **www.findmypast.com** and on the Society's own website **www.sog.org.uk**. There is free access to these and many other genealogical sites within the Library's Internet suite.

The Society is the ideal place to discover if a family history has already been researched with its huge collection of unique manuscript notes, extensive collections of past research and printed and unpublished family histories. If you expect to be carrying out family history research in the British Isles then membership is very worthwhile although non-members can use the library for a small search fee.

The Society of Genealogists is an educational charity. It holds study days, lectures, tutorials and evening classes and speakers from the Society regularly speak to groups around the country. The SoG runs workshops demonstrating computer programs of use to family historians. A diary of events and booking forms are available from the Society on 020 7553 3290 or on the website **www.sog.org.uk** .

Members enjoy free access to the Library, certain borrowing rights, free copies of the quarterly *Genealogists Magazine* and various discounts of publications, courses, postal searches along with free access to data on the members' area of our website.

More details about the Society can be found on its extensive website at **www.sog.org.uk**

For a free Membership Pack contact the Society at:

14 Charterhouse Buildings,
Goswell Road,
London EC1M 7BA.
Telephone: 020 7553 3291
Fax: 020 7250 1800

The Society is always happy to help with enquiries and the following contacts may be of assistance.

Library & shop hours:

Monday	Closed
Tuesday	10am - 6pm
Wednesday	10am - 6pm
Thursday	10am - 8pm
Friday	Closed
Saturday	10am - 6pm
Sunday	Closed

Contacts:

Membership
Tel: 020 7553 3291
Email: membership@sog.org.uk

Lectures & courses
Tel: 020 7553 3290
Email: events@sog.org.uk

Family history advice line
Tel: 020 7490 8911
See website for availability

SOCIETY OF GENEALOGISTS
The National Library & Education Centre for Family History

Other SoG titles...

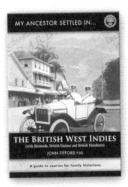

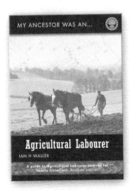
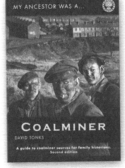

Order online at: **www.sog.org.uk** or call: 020 7702 5483.
Also available from the Society's bookshop.

14 Charterhouse Buildings, Goswell Road, London EC1M 7BA
Tel: 020 7251 8799 | Fax: 020 7250 1800 | **www.sog.org.uk**